Incorporating Your Talents

A Guide to the One-Person Corporation or How to Lead a Sheltered Life

Robert A. Esperti
Tax Attorney and Consultant
Renno L. Peterson
Tax Attorney and Consultant

McGraw-Hill Book Company

New York   St. Louis   San Francisco   Auckland   Bogotá
Hamburg   Johannesburg   London   Madrid   Mexico
Montreal   New Delhi   Panama   Paris   São Paulo
Singapore   Sydney   Tokyo   Toronto

For Andrew, Robert, and James

Library of Congress Cataloging in Publication Data

Esperti, Robert A.
  Incorporating your talents.

  Includes index.
  1. Corporation   law—United   States. 2.   Incorporation—United   States. 3.
Corporations—Taxation—Law and legislation—United States. I. Peterson, Renno
L. II. Title.
KF1414.E83 1984   346.73'066   82–14860
ISBN 0–07–019669–9   347.30666

     890 FGR/FGR 898765

ISBN 0-07-019669-9

The editors for this book were William A. Sabin and Chet Gottfried,
the designer was Dennis Sharkey, and the production
supervisor was Reiko F. Okamura. It was set in Gael
by The Kingsport Press.

Printed and bound by Fairfield Graphics.

Contents

6. Retirement Plans: Keeping Your Tax Haven at Home   65

A Little History 66   The Single Best Tax Shelters 71   The Different Kinds of Retirement Plans and How They Work 74   Defined Contribution Plans 77   Defined Benefit Plans 80   Combining a Defined Benefit Plan and a Defined Contribution Plan 81   When to Use Defined Contribution Plans 82   When to Use Defined Benefit Plans 84   Important Retirement-Planning Features 87   Borrowing from Retirement Plans 87   Vesting Plan Funds 89   Integrating Retirement Plans with Social Security 89   Voluntary Contributions 90   A Penalty for Taking Retirement Funds prior to Retirement 90

7. Running Your Retirement Plan: Translated Greek   93

Whose Retirement Plan Do You Use? 95   Who Should Invest the Funds and Do the Paperwork? 98   How to Invest Retirement Money 100   How Not to Invest Retirement Money 101   How to "Discriminate" Legally 102   The Controlled Group 104

8. The Subchapter S Corporation: The Congressional Platypus   107

The Old Law 108   The New Law 110

9. Corporate Creation: In the Beginning There Was Paper   113

Articles of Incorporation 114   By-Laws: Your Very Own Rules 115   First Minutes: Starting with a Clean Act 115   Your Employment Contract: An IRS Insurance Policy 117   Fattening Up Your Corporation 119   Cash: The Easy Way 119   Property: Another Matter 119   Debts Can Spell Real Trouble 120   Debt versus Equity 121   Accounts Receivable: A Special Problem 122

10. Problems Common to All Incorporated Talent: A Minicourse in Self-Defense   124

Whose Income Is It? 125   Incorporate Properly 125   Have Employment Contracts 126   Contract in the Corporate Name 127   Act like a Corporation 128   Avoid Income Splitting 128   The Independent Contractor Problem 129   Who Controls the Talent? 130   Right to Delegate Work Performed 131   Frequency of Services 131   Maintaining an Independent Business 132   Who Pays the Bills? 132   The Personal Holding Company Problem 134   The Unreasonable Compensation Problem 138   The Affiliated Service Group Problem 139   The Social Security Problem 141

11. Problems of Specific Talents: Going an Extra Mile   145

12. Observing Corporate Formalities: How Not to Embarrass Yourself at Your Own Dinner Party   162

13. Getting Out of Your Corporation: Breaking Up May Be Hard to Do   174

14. A Corporate Précis: The Final Curtain of the Charles Laughton Story?   189

Introduction

For many years successful people have incorporated their talents to alleviate an altogether too oppressive tax burden. Our society's economic high achievers have incorporated their talents as a defensive stratagem to thwart or, at the very least, blunt Uncle Sam's tax sword.

Most successful people incorporate because they have heard that a corporation is a panacea for their tax woes and their advisers have reinforced that feeling. They do not incorporate to experience yet another pleasure or to explore the world of high finance. It is just another saga in a never-ending tax battle. They incorporate because, in the traditional words of their advisers, "They have no choice!"

In our experience, most successful talents taking the incorporation plunge never learn to swim and view their advisers as expensive yet necessary technical lifeguards. Too many talents do not know the "whats" and "hows," let alone the "whys," of corporate existence.

On August 13, 1982, Congress further muddied the water in an already murky area by passing still another tax act. This one—the Tax Equity and Fiscal Responsibility Act of 1982 (TEFRA)—is full of changes in the tax laws that affect every corporation in the United States.

Whether you are incorporated or are taking a hard look at doing so, our task is to equip you with the right information that will enable you to make the right corporate decision. In our professional careers, we have never seen an easy-to-read book that explains the realities of corporate life geared to talented people interested in the corporation decision. We have only seen the prophets of the ultimate tax haven sell their books of corporate magic as if they were peddling cheap paper idols guaranteed to provide entry to the mysterious world of tax Valhalla.

As a result, few successful people really know how to pierce the complex world of incorporation. Our mandate is to allow you to understand:

Whether or not you should incorporate

Whether or not you should stay incorporated if you have already taken the step

The real dos and don'ts of running your own corporation

The very best bottom-line ways of reducing your tax burden

Our experience tells us that the more you know, the more comfortable and profitable you are likely to be. We would like to share our knowledge with you.

We wish to thank our many talented clients who have allowed us to practice, Jeannie Watkins and Sheri Pardini for painstakingly typing our manuscript, Arnie Guttenberg for his technical help, and Chet Gottfried for making our language a better part of the English language.

Robert A. Esperti
Renno L. Peterson

Chapter

1

The Charles Laughton Story
A Hollywood Debut

The Tax Court annals are filled with the likes of Jack Benny, Groucho Marx, Pat O'Brien, Nat King Cole, Victor Borge, and Charles Laughton, to name just a few. Other talented actors have played many a leading part in the tax law saga, but for one reason or another, they have never made their Tax Court debuts.

Let us begin with the story of one of our more creative income tax–planning pioneers—Charles Laughton.

Charles Laughton was a famous British actor whose career began in the 1920s and reached its pinnacle in the United States in the 1930s and 1940s. Laughton earned a substantial income from his American acting efforts. His American earnings were subject to the U.S. federal income tax laws, which resulted in an altogether too "high" American income tax bracket. During Laughton's heyday, the top U.S. individual income tax bracket was a whopping 75 percent.

What Laughton's real motivations might have been with regard to his tax predicament, we will never know. We can assume, however, that he did not want to pay those astronomical American taxes, that he wanted to reduce or avoid them, and that he needed the advice of others to accomplish his goals.

Laughton did find competent advisers who managed to lower his tax burden. They gave Laughton another title—"Incorporated." They must have reasoned as follows: "If incorporation has been good for United States Steel, it must surely be good for our client, Mr. Laughton."

At that time, a U.S. corporation was taxed at a maximum income tax rate of 19 percent as compared with a maximum individual income tax rate of 75 percent. The difference was massive—56 percentage points. In addition to this spread in brackets, a corporation had the ability to take advantage of a panoply of additional tax benefits that were not available to "just individual" taxpayers. The evidence was awesome and most impressive; the verdict was obvious. Charles Laughton was incorporated in his own company called "Motion Pictures & Theatrical Industries, Ltd." (We will refer to it as "Industries, Ltd.")

Incorporation was nothing new; incorporating a single talent was. Laughton and his advisers were breaking new ground and, as a result, were extra careful to follow the book and do everything just right. Laughton and his professional entourage meticulously followed all the corporate rules. A charter for the "new Laughton" was obtained, and minutes prepared. Laughton became the sole owner of his corporation.

After completing the initial legalities, Laughton signed an employment contract between Industries, Ltd., and himself. In other words, Laughton the corporation and Laughton the actor entered into a formal contractual relationship. His contract stated that he was to perform acting services for Industries, Ltd., and it alone. There would be no moonlighting by Laughton. In exchange for his exclusive services, Laughton the actor was to be paid a fixed salary in addition to his expenses. Charles Laughton signed, or should we say "double-signed," the contract for a five-year term.

Armed with its exclusive service contract, Industries, Ltd., hired Charles out to various motion picture studios. If a studio wished to avail itself of Charles Laughton's talents, the studio was required to enter into a contract between the studio and Industries, Ltd.

Industries, Ltd., would perform its contracts with the studios by telling Laughton what he was supposed to do—as if he did not already know. Charles Laughton, like millions of other employees, was now picking up his weekly paycheck. He was one more working person in a world filled with working people.

The tax result of this corporate artwork was indeed a masterpiece: Laughton, the actor, was taxed on his salary, which was substantially less than the sums Laughton, the corporation, collected from the studios. Charles Laughton's U.S. income tax liability plummeted. Industries, Ltd., used its leftover revenues to pay expenses, many, if not all, of which were on Laughton's behalf. The dollars that remained in the corporation were subject to tax at its lower income tax rate. Charles Laughton, through self-incorporation, became two separate and distinct taxpayers, both of whom were in lower income tax brackets than Charles Laughton alone prior to his incorporation.

There was more, if you can believe, to Charles Laughton's good fortune. The corporate Laughton (Industries, Ltd.) could avail itself of substantial additional benefits not available to Laughton the individual. Laughton had found a tax bonanza.

It did not take too long for the Internal Revenue Service (IRS) to hear about Charles Laughton's corporation, because it represented a new wave of emerging incorporated talent. In the eyes of the IRS, this tax dodge had to be stopped.

Armed with a bevy of tax theories, the IRS challenged Charles Laughton's corporation, along with those of a few other brave talents. The drama was now on the Tax Court stage (then known as the "Board of Tax Appeals") and had as an audience the talent of America.

The Tax Court scrutinized Charles Laughton's corporation. The court found that Industries, Ltd., acted like a corporation—all the corporate formalities had been observed—and that it looked like a corporation. It had all kinds of proper corporate contracts. As a result of these findings, the court held that Industries, Ltd., was indeed a valid corporation. Round one was over, Charles Laughton the winner.

The IRS agents were not finished with the British actor, however; they appealed to a higher court. The appellate court agreed with the Tax Court: Charles Laughton's corporation looked and acted like what it was supposed to look and act like—a bona fide corporation. The appellate court pronounced Industries, Ltd., legitimate. It also said, "Wait a minute. Tax Court, you had better give this case a second look. Maybe, just maybe, Mr. Laughton might have been too greedy."

Charles Laughton found himself back in the Tax Court. The audience waited and waited but nothing happened. Charles Laughton and the IRS settled. There was no grand finale to Laughton's drama.

Anticlimactic? Not at all. In the forty-plus years since the Charles Laughton case, no court, to our knowledge, has overturned the decision of the Tax Court. The one-person incorporated talent corporation, if it looks and acts like a corporation, is perfectly legitimate.

During the many years that have passed since the Laughton case, Congress has passed significant legislation aimed at controlling or stopping incorporated talent. The IRS has repeatedly challenged individuals who have incorporated their talents. These challenges have proved to be both successful and not so successful. The tax validity of the one-person corporation has, like so many other areas of our tax law, become murky, an area fraught with legal technicalities and significant formality.

The use of the one-person talent corporation has been hyped and sold from promises in magazine advertisements to sophisticated opinion letters signed by senior tax attorneys. Talent has incorporated and will continue to incorporate. Contemporary Laughtons are always anxious to avail themselves of income tax relief. For some time, increasing numbers of talented men and women have overcome their fears and incorporated.

Many professionals believed that incorporating talent was a tax imperative, a planning must—until August 13, 1982. On this date Congress passed the Tax Equity and Fiscal Responsibility Act (TEFRA), a massive piece of legislation that changed most of the rules. Traditional talents such as doctors, dentists, accountants, architects, lawyers, engineers, actors, artists, authors, executives, and sales professionals now face a new mandate: *Take another look!*

The TEFRA legislation, more than any other in recent memory, has changed the planning rules. Many talented people have played the corporate game; many have merely watched. Some are about to play for the first time. But the rules have been changed. TEFRA has instantly rewritten much of the rule book. Talent, whether it is already incorporated or seeking to incorporate, must understand these new rules. Many people who are looking at incorporation may want to take a second look before plunging into incorporation. Many people who are already incorporated may want to get out of (that is, liquidate) their corporations.

We hope in this volume to lay it all out; to give you the pros and cons with respect to incorporating your talent; to impart an understanding that will guide you in making the appropriate decision as to what course of action you should take.

Chapter

2

The Corporate Mystique
Removing the Corporate Veil

When thinking of corporations, many people envision moguls and Wall Street power; others believe it to be the ultimate tax dodge. Regardless of how the corporate concept is perceived, there can be no doubt that it is both strange and foreign to the everyday experience of most people. One of our goals is to remove the mystique that is seemingly indigenous to the corporate idea. We hope that a little history may facilitate your understanding.

A Brief History of Corporations

We inherited the foundations of our corporate rules from ancient ancestors. Perhaps the earliest formal recognition of a corporate entity can be found in the Code of Hammurabi, written in about 2100 B.C. The Code of Hammurabi recognized the legality of groups of individuals who had a common purpose. These "societies" were regulated by certain rules (corporate law, so to speak) that enabled their members to understand their rights as to one another.

The corporate idea also appeared within the scope of the Roman law. Rome itself was a corporation. The term "senatus populusque Romaunus—SPQR" referred to Rome as a republic, which is nothing less than a corporation.

During the Roman Empire, other corporatelike entities were formed. These included colleges, municipalities, and business societies, which were, in many cases, groups of merchants in business together. As these corporatelike groups grew not only in number but in stature and power, their existence threatened the power of the Roman Senate. Government's need to control mandated that these corporations could not be formed without imperial decree and senatorial direction. Subjecting these early corporations to regulation allowed the emperor and the Senate to not only control the power of corporations but to tax them as well.

Those early Roman corporations were recognized as separate and distinct from their individual organizers and members; the entity could survive even if its members died or simply chose to leave. Roman law gave real meaning to the corporate idea, the concept of a separate legal entity.

The Roman concept of the corporate idea was adopted by the Catholic church in its canon law because it lended itself well to an organization that intended to have perpetual existence. When the church created a bishopric, a bishop was named and property acquired. It was a straightforward and logical matter to simply "incorporate" this bishopric. The bishop became the "president" of this church corporation which now had perpetual existence. Bishops would come and bishops would go, but the entity remained forever.

Pope Innocent IV, a pope who lived in the early 1200s, may quite possibly be the father of the modern corporation. He is attributed with first acknowledging the existence of these church corporations as fictitious persons, entities apart and separate from those who created them.

In England, history witnessed the creation of the British municipal corporation, loosely patterned after the church corporation. These municipalities included cities, towns, colleges, and hospitals, all of which were recognized as separate entities with perpetual corporate existence.

The municipal corporate idea worked so well that artisans and merchants copied it and began to form their own corporations. They formed guilds and established powerful monopolies that became potent economic and political forces.

The power inherent in the guilds was not to be totally tolerated by the English monarchy. In an attempt to reduce the power of the guilds, the monarchy required royal permission before a guild could legally be formed. This permission came in the form of a charter, a formal royal decree of existence. A charter set forth the business purposes of the guild as well as certain operational rules the guild had to follow. Later, Parliament used this power to both control and tax the guilds.

Because of the revenue generated by tax on these guilds, it appeared to be in the best interest of the kingdom to protect the assets of the guilds. As a result, the concept of limited liability was created. If a guild member went bankrupt, other guild members needed the assurance that their own personal assets, as well as those of the guild, could not be taken to satisfy the debts of an individual member. Members of the guilds entered into contracts among themselves to assure this result; these agreements were upheld by the courts. The idea of limited liability became a reality and became indigenous to English, and then to American, corporate law.

The true precursors of the modern business corporation got their start with the discovery of the New World. European governments needed financial aid in order to exploit New World riches; large amounts of private capital had to be raised, and "joint-stock" companies were formed. These companies, such as the Dutch East India Company, were chartered by Parliament. Joint-stock companies represented a new coalition of business and government interests as well as increased governmental control.

The success of the joint-stock companies resulted in increased wealth, power, and, inevitably, corruption. The opportunity for a joint-stock company to create a fast buck (in the case of our British counterparts, a fast pound) and the selective nature of Parliament in granting charters encouraged the formation of a black market subculture of nonchartered corporations. Because these companies were not officially chartered, they had neither a separate legal existence nor limited liability and were not regulated by English law.

Legislation was passed to control these black market corporations as well as their legitimate counterparts. The legislation was both significant and complicated, and it resulted in an environment where transacting business in the corporate form was nearly impossible.

Our American forefathers chose not to inherit the complex English corporate laws and the lawyers that went with them. They chose to start anew. They created their own set of complicated corporate laws, which were aimed at stimulating trade.

During the constitutional conventions, there was much debate as to whether the federal government or the states should have the power to regulate corporations in order to increase trade; the states won. As a result, almost all corporations are formed and, to a great extent, regulated under state rather than federal law.

The states allowed both business and nonbusiness interests to incorporate under the states' direction and control, a system not dissimilar to the English system of allowing Parliament to issue corporate charters. This system quickly engendered graft and corruption because the states sold charters to the highest bidders. A corporate charter, more often than not, meant the official sanctioning of a monopoly. Buying a charter became a frequent and profitable endeavor.

In recognition of these and other problems, the states began passing with increasing frequency corporate statutes to control corruption. Beginning with North Carolina in 1775, almost every state passed laws which governed incorporation within their borders. These laws detailed for what purposes corporations could be formed, who could form them, and the precise legal requirements necessary to assure their continued state-sanctioned existence.

With ever-increasing interstate commerce came heightened bickering and petty jealousies between the states. The problem was, Which state had what power over which corporate business enterprise? What if a corporation chartered in one state began to transact business in another state? Which state's law would control? No one knew the answers, but regardless of the uncertainty, the states reacted quickly to these intrusions upon their territorial sovereignty. They prohibited foreign (other state) corporations from doing business within their borders. A New York corporation was, as a result, prohibited from doing business in Virginia.

These reactionary and protectionist laws quickly found their way into the chambers of the U.S. Supreme Court which soon struck them down. The general result of the Court's decisions seemed to be that as long as a corporation could manage to find a way to cross state lines in its business dealings, it could transact business between states with relative impunity.

Corporations which transacted business over state lines began shopping for the best state in which to obtain their home charter (incorporate). The laws of the state in which a corporation was formed controlled how the corporation was to be operated. For example, if one state required $10,000 of capital to incorporate and another state required only $5000, the latter became the state of incorporation. As long as a corporation could cross state lines, it could incorporate in the better (cheaper) state and still do business in the more expensive state(s). These principles are still very much with us today.

Legislatures began passing laws designed to make their state an attractive place in which to incorporate. Additional incorporated business meant additional power, influence, and tax revenues.

Over the years, however, many states have adopted corporate laws which are similar. This uniformity of state laws makes it easier to transact business and also eliminates many of the needless complexities of interstate commerce. Some states—Delaware is a perfect example—still try to encourage corporate citizenry by passing very liberal corporate laws.

Because of the Supreme Court's decisions regarding interstate commerce, it became evident that states did not have the power to exercise total control over corporations doing business within their borders. There appeared to be a void as to how interstate commerce was to be regulated, a void filled promptly by the federal government.

Under Section VIII, Clause 3, of the U.S. Constitution, Congress has the power "to regulate commerce . . . among the several states." This is called the "commerce clause" and has been used by the federal government to regulate business transactions which cross state lines. From the commerce clause has come the U.S. securities laws, labor laws, fair-trade laws, and a myriad of other federal laws.

Corporations, after a long and venerable history, are today common and acceptable business entities. They are controlled by both state and federal laws, which are complex and all-encompassing. Fortunately, federal laws rarely affect smaller corporations, especially one-person talent corporations.

There is one aspect of federal regulation which does affect all corporations regardless of their size. That, of course, is the federal income tax law.

A Historical Perspective of Corporate Income Taxation

In 1909 Congress passed an excise tax which taxed the ability of a corporation to transact business. This excise tax was really an income tax and was found to be constitutional by our Supreme Court.

Four years later, in 1913, the Sixteenth Amendment to the U.S. Constitution was passed; personal income tax had arrived.

At almost all times during the past seventy years where both an individual and corporate income tax have coexisted, the corporate rates have always been more favorable to the taxpayer. For many years, top-bracket corporate rates were as much as 56 percentage points lower than top-bracket individual rates. Corporations have also been given greater latitude in qualifying for special deductions and other tax breaks.

Since few talented people have enjoyed "overpaying" their taxes (the test being a purely subjective one, of course), they have spent considerable time and money trying to legally, and at times not so legally, reduce them. Many "legal" reduction techniques are time-tested and relatively ironclad. Other techniques involve gimmickry or new approaches that have not had the opportunity to stand the test of time.

When IRS agents question a tax reduction technique, the courts are often the forum where the ultimate question of acceptability is determined; it is in our courts where much of the tax law has been developed.

In many cases, the courts interpret our tax law contrary to the position and theories of the IRS. IRS agents can, however, keep fighting for their position on the same identical issue(s) in different courts. In essence, they can shop for a more sympathetic court in order to receive a decision favoring the IRS. In addition, the IRS can always ask Congress for legislation which will give the service the result its agents were unable to get in the judicial system. The IRS has used this congressional "lobbying" technique to great advantage.

Special-interest groups have also used the professional lobbyist to assist Congress in shaping the income tax laws. The competing interests of government and private enterprise have created one of the most dynamic and complicated income tax systems imaginable.

The use of the one-person talent corporation focuses, to a significant degree, on the conflict between the taxpayer's desire to reduce his or her tax bill and the government's desire to increase or, at the very least, maintain its revenue base. The one-person corporation heightens the strong feelings on both sides and, as a result, has been on center stage far more often than its talent would seem to deserve.

The one-person corporation is designed (remember Charles Laughton?) to be a formal legal entity under state law. It is also designed to be a viable vehicle of federal income tax savings under federal law. If both of these design goals are met, the hoped for result of considerable income tax savings should be obtained.

Let us discuss these design objectives in greater detail, observing how Congress, the IRS, and the taxpayer have tried to define the differences between legitimate incorporation and the crass use of the corporate concept to illegally avoid the payment of tax.

Chapter

3

Incorporating for Nontax Reasons
Selling Bull in a Bear Market

"Tax" is almost always touted by planning professionals as *the* reason to incorporate a talented person. Traditionally, however, there have been other reasons to incorporate. The corporation arose for far different reasons than merely saving a few dollars in tax. This chapter is a discussion of some traditional, and not so traditional, nontax reasons for incorporating.

Ego
People Enjoy Seeing Their Names in Lights

Ego can be, and often is, one of the prime reasons that people choose to incorporate. We would guess that fully 25 percent of the hundreds of corporations that we have been involved with have been the product of pure ego.

How does ego relate to incorporation? The corporate mystique is what gives an individual the aura of power, the feeling of being on the inside of big business. The corporate existence seems to tell the world that we are successful and that we have graduated to the leagues of high finance.

This perception of the corporate mystique has manifested itself in many ways. For example, when you are presented with a calling card, you probably look for the person's title. How do you react when you are presented with the calling card of someone who has no formal title, only a "mere" name? How do you react when you are presented with the calling card of a corporate president? We guess that you will initially be more attentive and respectful to the president of the corporation. This immediate sense and recognition of importance is, to many of us, a good reason to incorporate.

We have found ego motivation to be even more of an incorporation motivator when we talk to people engaged in a personal service business or profession. These types of individuals, in our experience, have the ego-need to see their name, with accompanying title, on expensive stationery. They appear to enjoy being president of their own fledgling IBM.

If other successful peers make statements that they incorporated because "their *very* expensive tax advisers told them to," the need for competing ego motivation runs rampant in the listeners' veins. "Damn the torpedoes, full speed ahead" mentality seizes them, and before they know it, they, too, are incorporated. The only problem is, afterward, they are not always quite sure why they did it.

Ego as a reason to incorporate can be fun and harmless, if you know for what other reasons you incorporated. In fact, ego can be a good reason to incorporate if you are in a business where a corporate title can open doors for you. Do not, however, get trapped in the situation where ego overcomes other planning criteria that suggest not to incorporate. Corporations are certainly easier to get into than they are to get out of!

Limited Liability

Putting the Corporation between You and Your Creditors

A corporation is a separate legal entity. Imagine it as an empty cauldron which you want to fill with ingredients in order to make a stew. Ultimately you want to sell the stew. You also want to make sure that if the stew goes bad, you cannot lose any of your personal wealth. In addition, if possible, you would like to use everyone else's ingredients, not your own.

First, you solicit ingredients based on your very good reputation. "Don't give the ingredients to me," you say, "just put them in my cauldron," and as soon as the stew is done and sold, you get part of the gravy (so to speak).

If the stew turns out to be good and sells, there is no problem. Everyone is paid off and goes away happy. But if the stew goes bad, that's another cup of tea (to mix a metaphor). The ingredients are ruined, and the people who put up their own ingredients are looking for some way to recoup their losses. "Not me," you say to these people. "My *cauldron* used your ingredients. I didn't. Sue the cauldron! That's who is responsible."

In real life, does this really happen? Under general corporate (cauldron) principles, it does. As long as everyone recognized that they were doing business with the corporation (cauldron) and not you, you are not responsible. You walk away with your assets intact.

If you follow the corporate rules, your investors or your creditors can only look to the corporation for redress. Your liability is limited to whatever ingredients that you may have put into your corporate cauldron. If you lose any of those assets, you can sue your corporate cauldron just like anyone else.

The concept of limited liability described in our cauldron story works very well for large corporations. It does not work so well in the one-person talent corporation.

Creditors and, to a certain extent, investors have figured out that corporate promoters could use the assets of others, lose them, and get away scot-free. Get away, that is, until the advent of the personal guaranty. The personal guaranty is a simple but devastating device to collar the corporate promoter. The promoter is required to guarantee that if the corporation loses its assets, the promoter will make up any losses. Good-bye limited liability; hello bankruptcy.

If you already have a corporation, you know this to be true, particularly with regard to your banker. In small corporations, the personal guaranty of the main mogul is almost always required by creditors. Those of you thinking of incorporating for the purpose of limiting your liability, welcome to reality. For the one-person talent corporation, the limited liability idea is not viable. Outside investors are usually nonexistent, and most creditors of any significance will require personal guaranties. Besides, it is our experience that talent corporations do not require outside-investor capital. Limiting one's creditor liability through the use of a talent corporation simply does not work!

There is one more type of liability that may have a bearing on the incorporation issue as it relates to limited liability. This type of liability is referred to as personal injury liability, or "tort" liability in lawyer talk. Personal injury liability occurs when someone is injured and another party is to blame. In our litigation-filled society, it is common for the injured party to sue the other party and collect damages. Today, damages can go sky-high. Areas where this type of liability can crop up include car accidents, malpractice (not a personal injury but close enough for our purposes), and product liability.

If your corporation is liable for one of these types of injuries, its assets will be subject to the claims of the suing party. If you are the corporate owner (shareholder), it would appear that you could only lose your investment in the corporation, not your personal assets. Limited liability would seem to work—or does it?

People are the cause of other people's injuries, not corporations. Who drove the car that got in that accident? Which professional malpracticed? Some individual who worked for the corporation; that's who. Odds are that the same person who owns the corporation is the culprit (a perfect probability in the one-person talent corporation). The employee is liable for the damages done as well as the corporation. Limited liability *may* be preserved if an employee other than the corporate owner causes the damage, but even this is not an ironclad legal rule.

Professionals like doctors, lawyers, and accountants would like to avoid being personally liable for their malpractice. To the best of our knowledge, there is no jurisdiction in the United States that allows this. If a professional malpractices, whether corporately or not, there is personal liability. Both the professional's personal assets and the assets of the corporation are subject to the claims of the injured party.

If there is more than one professional, the nonmalpracticing professional may have limited liability. On this and other similar issues, consult your lawyer. Each state's laws are different.

Does the corporate entity provide a foolproof way for the incorporated talent to limit his or her liability? Absolutely not. Unless your circumstances are incredibly unique, incorporation should not be undertaken to obtain limited liability.

Separating Business from Your Personal Life

When discussing incorporation, we have often told the story about the teenager who was sent to the store to buy groceries for his father. He was sent with dad's money and told to buy only groceries. He wanted to buy some personal things out of his own money. So as not to mix the money up, he put the grocery money in one pocket and his money in another pocket.

At the store he bought the groceries first. He took the money out of his . . . oops, he forgot which pocket he put what into. Being a person of decision, he picked a pocket and made the purchases. Knowing that a mistake had already been made, he threw caution to the wind and proceeded to use money out of both pockets for his purchases. At that point it seemed to be the easiest course of action. Besides, he would figure it all out when he got home.

After he got home, he was not asked to account for the money. The particulars were soon forgotten. He even threw out the receipts. Two days later, his father asked for the change. He didn't have the faintest idea how much it was or even if he had it. For many of us, this analogy hits pretty close to home. We confuse our personal and business transactions. We try to keep records, but it's just too cumbersome, and besides, we really don't have the time. It is so easy to procrastinate.

In a fit of desperation, and with our accountant's advice, we incorporate. We create our corporate entity, in part, to separate our business self from our personal self; it can make a world of difference.

When we incorporate, we have to keep separate checking, savings, and expense accounts. Because we have to keep separate books, it becomes much easier to separate our personal lives from our business lives. Too easy at times. Because our corporation seems so separate from us, its money does not appear to be our money. It becomes much easier to write a business check rather than a personal one. This phenomenon creates problems which we will discuss in a later chapter.

Incorporation can force us to change the way we account for both our income and expenses. A corporation makes it easier to separate our business and personal lives. Doing business as a corporation requires self-discipline and good accounting procedures. Incorporating does not reduce the need for good records; it increases it.

Creating an Immortal Monument

Most of us would like to live forever. Since we know that to be an impossibility, we oftentimes try to create monuments which live on after we die. Incorporation is occasionally used for this purpose.

Since corporations are separate from those who own them, the death of one of these owners does not terminate the corporate existence. The creator and sole owner of a corporation can arrange for the corporation to continue after his or her death. This ability for a corporation to survive its owner has long been considered an important attribute of a corporation.

The continuity of corporate existence, despite the status of the shareholders, is most relevant to the large corporation or to the corporation which is not service-oriented. The one-person corporation almost always relies upon the services of its owner, the single talent. The death of this key person negates the survival theory of corporate existence. The fact of the matter is that the death of the talent has the effect of ending the reason for which the corporation was created. The corporation may continue as a legal entity, but it would lose its soul and become an empty shell. It would not constitute much of a monument.

Corporate continuity may be a factor if the owner has a child who is in the same service business. It also may be relevant if there is a key employee who wants to keep the business of the corporation alive and wishes to buy it. Here, corporate immortality may be advantageous. This is a subject for a book of its own and will not be covered here.

Any professional- or service-oriented talent who is considering incorporation should not be influenced by corporate immortality. It is not usually apropos for talent.

Easy to Bring in New Owners

Stock Is Easy to Transfer

It is easy to sell, give, or transfer ownership in a corporation. Corporate ownership is evidenced by certificates of stock, which can be easily transferred. Stock exchanges, like the New York Stock Exchange or the American Stock Exchange, are ready examples of the free transferability of stock.

Bringing in new corporate owners can be accomplished without a great deal of fuss. The corporation can sell its stock out of its treasury or issue new stock, or the existing shareholders can sell their personal stock to new shareholders. The stock transfer process is merely a matter of endorsing old stock certificates and issuing new ones.

Many people have incorporated to take advantage of this ease in bringing in new owners. For example, in a family-owned business, it is quite normal for family members to transfer stock so as to allow younger members to have ownership. Incorporation has also been used to bring in key employees as owners. Bringing family members or key employees into ownership can be accomplished through gifts, purchases, or giving stock for services rendered.

How does this apply to the one-person corporation? It does not. One-person talent corporations are indigenous to that talent. They are not generally worth much, and there is seldom, if ever, a business need to transfer ownership. Ease of transferability is definitely a corporate plus, but not in the case of the incorporated talent.

Lots of Room for Lots of Different Players

One of the fun things about a corporation is the ability to bestow titles on oneself as well as on others. President, vice president, secretary, and treasurer are the corporate titles that most people are familiar with. Most states require that a corporation have corporate officers with these titles. They usually allow officers to have more than one title; president-treasurer and secretary-treasurer are examples.

All of us are familiar with the hierarchy within banks. It seems that everyone in a bank has a title. There are assistant vice presidents, vice presidents, senior vice presidents, and executive vice presidents. There is a plethora of other officers, all with a title that makes them seem like *the one important person* you wish to deal with, a technique that is not unimportant when serving the public.

Because all of us like to think of ourselves as important, and rightly so, we prefer to deal with others who are important. One of the ways that we know we are dealing with more than a mere underling is the fact that that person has a fancy corporate title. The feeling of self-worth is important. Most of us feel a lot more important if we have a title. Plain old Angus Johnson, janitor, is not nearly so impressive as Angus Johnson, Vice President in Charge of Waste Management.

Another thing that banks and other large corporations have learned is that people who are given a title tend to work for less money. To many, a title means as much as or more than a raise. Titles are easy to give because they fit perfectly within the corporate structure and cost no more than a new nameplate and stationery.

The use of the corporate structure facilitates the use of titles. Earlier in this chapter, we discussed ego as an incorporation motivator. Many people incorporate to be able to use the corporate mystique. Corporate titles are just one aspect of this mystique. If you have an organization in which titles could play an important motivational role, incorporation could be for you.

In the case of the one-person talent corporation, the opportunity to give titles in lieu of money is simply not available. There is usually only one employee—the talent!

Separating Ownership from Management

Another characteristic of the corporate form is the ability to separate ownership from management. As you remember from our history of corporations, one of the needs a corporation fulfilled was the ability to solicit large amounts of capital from a broad base of investors. Selling stock to a lot of people creates money in great quantities, thus facilitating the corporate form of doing business. The concept is used daily in our society.

The advantage of this is that an investor does not have to participate in the management of the corporation. The investor may have the right to vote on who is to manage the corporation, but probably will not take an active role in management. This is not to say that managers do not own stock in the companies they manage. It is to say that investors do not have to be managers. Under corporate principles, the functions of management and ownership are separate and distinct.

The separation of ownership and management is accomplished by using a hierarchy of duties and responsibilities that are set forth under state law. This hierarchy can be illustrated as shown in Figure 3-1. The hierarchy begins at the bottom with the owner or shareholder. The shareholder provides capital or services to the corporation and receives stock because of the capital or the services rendered to the

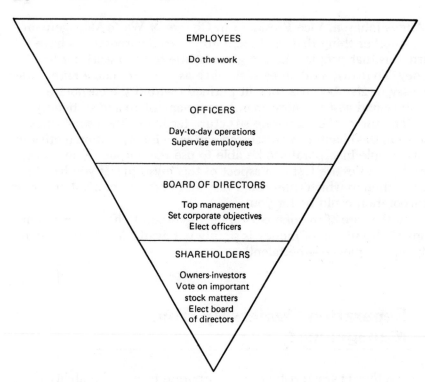

EMPLOYEES

Do the work

OFFICERS

Day-to-day operations
Supervise employees

BOARD OF DIRECTORS

Top management
Set corporate objectives
Elect officers

SHAREHOLDERS

Owners-investors
Vote on important
stock matters
Elect board
of directors

Figure 3-1 Hierarchy of a corporation.

corporation. The shareholder also has the right to acquire the assets of the corporation upon its ultimate termination. The right to the assets, however, is second to those of the corporation's creditors who have the right to be paid off. Shareholders make a return on their investment by receiving dividends or by selling their stock. Shareholders usually have the right to vote on who is to manage the corporation and whether the corporation will be dissolved or its assets sold.

The stock that shareholders receive comes in two basic varieties: common and preferred. Common stock is risk stock. Its value relates directly to the value of the corporation at any point in time. If a corporation is worth $100,000 and you own 10 percent of the stock, your stock is worth $10,000. Common stock can either be allowed to vote or may be restricted as to its voting rights.

Preferred stock generally has a face value that is a set amount. For example, $100 preferred stock means that the face value of the stock is $100. Because of the nature of preferred stock, its value does not change if the value of the corporation changes. The value of preferred stock depends on the dividend rate that is assigned to it; $100 preferred stock having a dividend rate of 15 percent means that it receives a dividend of $15 per share. If this dividend rate is favorable in the marketplace, then the value of the preferred stock may be $100 or even more. If this rate is lower than market, the value of the preferred stock may be lower than $100. This is very similar to bonds or other debt instruments.

Preferred stock is preferred as to dividends. This means that the preferred shareholders receive dividends before the common shareholders receive dividends. In addition, preferred stock is preferred upon liquidation of the corporation, so that the preferred shareholders receive funds up to the face amount of their shares before the common shareholders receive any funds.

Preferred shareholders may or may not be allowed to vote, depending upon the charter of the corporation. Voting can be restricted to a few matters or not restricted at all. The voting power of preferred stock, however, usually does not exceed that of the voting common stock.

As you can see, the shareholders of a corporation are its foundation. The shareholders provide the impetus (cash or services) to start the corporation and have the ultimate power to determine the corporation's ultimate destiny. Shareholders are, at least in corporate theory, separated from management but are responsible for determining who will manage the corporation. The shareholders select the second level of our hierarchy: the board of directors.

The board of directors constitutes the very top level of the corporation's management. The board is elected by the voting shareholders for a term which is determined either by state law or by the corporate charter or by-laws. Its function is to set the broad management objectives of the corporation and to elect the officers of the corporation.

Corporate officers constitute the third level of our corporate heirarchy. They are the managers who have the responsibility to follow the mandate of the board of directors as to day-to-day corporate operations. They are the nuts-and-bolts people who are on the line to perform. They set up the employee structure, and they are charged with hiring and firing those employees.

The employees are the last rung of the corporate hierarchy. They do the work. What more can be said?

Each level of the hierarchy theoretically has separate and distinct functions and duties. In practice, however, these distinctions get fuzzy. It is possible for one individual to be at each of the four levels. This is true in almost all one-person talent corporations.

A corporation is an entity which can separate ownership from management, and if you are raising large amounts of capital, it is a concept which works beautifully. In the case of the incorporated talent, this benefit is no benefit at all. One talent having to do everything is difficult to separate (surgery being ruled out). One-person talent corporations do not have the need to separate ownership from management.

There are many nontax reasons for incorporating. These reasons do, in many cases, seem to be logical and purposeful at the time incorporation is discussed. The lesson that should be learned from our short discussion is that many of the traditional, and not so traditional, reasons to incorporate do not apply very well to the one-person corporation.

Charles Laughtons have not generally incorporated over the years for nontax reasons. Whether they should or not depends on the needs of the specific talent.

Chapter

4

Corporate Tax Theory
As Simple as the Wheel

Because a corporation is a separate legal entity, it has its own existence and therefore its own tax liability under the Internal Revenue Code. This chapter is designed to take the very complex system of corporate taxation and reduce it to its basics. To understand this chapter is to pretty much master the mysteries of the question "Why a corporation?"

A Narrative of Tax Basics

Corporations have two basic types of income that they are taxed on. The first is known as "ordinary income." Ordinary income is that

Table 4-1. Corporate Income Tax Rates for Years Beginning 1983

Over	But Not Over	Tax Rate, %
$ –0–	$ 25,000	15
25,000	50,000	18
50,000	75,000	30
75,000	100,000	40
100,000		46

income which is derived from sales of inventory, the performance of services, interest, rent, or almost any other income source except for the sale of certain assets. Ordinary income is subject to a graduated tax rate. The tax rates for ordinary corporate income beginning in 1983 are shown in Table 4-1.

The second type of income that a corporation has is income derived from the sale of assets. Generally speaking, these assets can be a piece of equipment (like a car or a typewriter), stocks or bonds, or any other asset which the corporation does not sell on a regular basis. The tax on the gain from the sale of these assets is called an alternative tax, but for our purposes it will be called a "capital gain" tax. The tax on the gain from the sale of an asset which has been held for over one year is a maximum of 28 percent (this compares with a 20 percent maximum if an individual sold the same asset). It can be lower, but only if the corporation's income is relatively low. If the asset has been held for less than one year, the gain is generally taxed as if it was ordinary income.

For those who are aficionados of corporate taxation, you will note that we greatly simplify the corporate income tax rules for purposes of our discussion. But keep in mind that the complexities of federal income taxation of corporations are why tax lawyers and accountants exist; these complexities are outside the scope of this book.

A corporation's taxable income is calculated much like your individual taxable income. The personal income you earn is reduced by allowable deductions and the income tax is reduced by allowable credits. The same is true in a corporation; income is received, deductions taken, and the tax, reduced by any credits, is calculated. After the tax is paid, the amount left is called the retained earnings of the corporation.

While getting income into the corporation is not very difficult, at least from a tax point of view, getting it out to the shareholders and the employees, especially if they are one and the same (as is the case with incorporated talent), is extremely difficult. A corporation can distribute money in five basic ways: business expenses, payment of debts, purchase of assets, extending loans, and payment of dividends.

Business Expenses

The first way in which a corporation can distribute money is through the payment of its business expenses. These types of expenses include rent, salaries, interest, or any other expense which is necessary for the normal operation of the corporation. Payments of business expenses are considered to be deductible from taxable income, therefore reducing the amount of income which ultimately is subject to income taxation.

Almost all employee salaries, wages, and benefits, such as expense accounts, retirement plans, and health insurance, fall in the category of business expense. Salaries, wages, and some employee benefits are income taxable, for the most part, to employees when they receive them. Some employee benefits can be tax-deferred; retirement plans fall into this category. Still others can be income tax–free. These include certain medical benefits, some life insurance benefits, and ordinary and necessary business expenses expended on behalf of employees. All these categories will be more fully discussed in later chapters. In order to understand corporate tax theory, the details inherent in these categories are not important. It is important, however, to understand that all employee benefits are generally not currently taxed to the employees, while their cost is usually currently deductible to the corporation.

Payment of Debts

Paying off debt is not an expense which is tax deductible from the corporation's income. Debt is paid with the dollars that are left *after* income taxes are paid (retained earnings). The interest that is paid on debt is deductible from taxable income, however.

Corporate debt arises when the corporation borrows money. The corporation can borrow from banks or other financial institutions or it can borrow from its shareholders or employees. When the corporation does pay back its borrowings, the principal portion is *not* deducted but the interest is. The lender receives the principal amount tax-free and takes the interest into income. Sound logical? It is, but it is surprising how many businesspeople do not understand the tax treatment of debt.

Purchase of Assets

When a corporation purchases assets, it is not distributing money. It is making a substitution of dollars for an asset of equal value. The purchase of most assets, like debt, is not treated as a deduction from taxable income. Some assets, including furniture, equipment, cars, and the like, are subject to "cost recovery" (known prior to 1981 as depreciation). Cost recovery is a method under our income tax laws that allows businesses to write off (deduct) the purchase price of a business asset over a period of years. To illustrate:

> Reston Corporation purchases an automobile for the use of its president, Roy Reston, for $15,000. After checking with the accountant for the corporation, it is determined that the Internal Revenue Code allows the car to be written off over a three-year period. Thus the $15,000 can be deducted from the taxable income of the corporation over three years.

How much of the asset can be written off in each of the three years is determined by the Internal Revenue Code which sets forth rules for different types of assets. These rules determine not only how much can be written off but how long a period of time they must be written off. Cars are written off over three years, heavy trucks and some machinery five years, and real estate fifteen years.

There is a special rule that allows many types of assets to be totally expensed in the year that they are acquired rather than depreciated over a period of years. It is an elective provision of the tax law. As long as the capital asset or assets are personal property used in a business, they are subject to this special rule. Personal property used in a business is almost any asset which is not real estate.

In 1983, the amount that could be deducted instead of depreciated was $5000. In 1984 and 1985, the amount will be $7500, and for 1986 and after, it will be $10,000. That means that up to the first $5000, $7500, or $10,000 worth of these assets purchased in one year could, if you choose, be fully deducted. The rule is fraught with little snares which could trap the unwary taxpayer, and in many instances it is better tax planning to elect cost recovery (depreciation) instead of this special deduction. For example, investment tax credit is not allowed on property subject to this rule.

Some assets are not subject to the rules of cost recovery and therefore cannot be written off at all. These items include inventory, goodwill, and other assets either held for resale or considered to be so long term in duration as to not be subject to write-off. As you can well imagine, the tax laws have all kinds of rules for the treatment of assets. Luckily, the one-person talent corporation usually does not have a complicated variety of assets, which makes the job of understanding their tax implications much easier. Your corporation will most likely have assets which can be written off over a relatively short period of time.

Extending Loans

When a corporation makes a loan, it gives money in exchange for a promise of repayment. This promise to pay is made in the form of a promissory note, which the corporation holds as an asset. Because a loan substitutes one asset (cash) for another (a note), it is not a tax deductible item. Loans are a method by which a corporation lets its shareholders use corporate funds.

Payment of Dividends

The final way in which a corporation distributes its dollars is by paying a dividend. A dividend is how a corporation pays its investors (shareholders) for their investment in the corporation. This return on investment is *not* subject to an income tax deduction in the corporation. The amount paid *is* taxable, however, to the shareholder who receives it. Thus while a dividend lowers the corporate retained (aftertax) earnings, it is also taxable to the shareholders. *A dividend results in classic double taxation.*

Each of the methods by which a corporation distributes its dollars is critically important in the one-person talent corporation. In almost every case, the owner of the one-person corporation is also its sole employee. Because of this relationship, there is an inherent conflict of interest. The conflict arises because the shareholder is interested in the corporation's receiving a tax deduction for its payments to or on behalf of the shareholder-employee. The shareholder-employee is also interested in receiving, either directly or indirectly, benefits from the corporation that are either not taxable to the shareholder-employee or are taxable far in the future. Since a dividend is subject to two taxes (one at the corporate level and one at the individual level), the shareholder-employee needs substantial assurance that any payments made to or for his or her benefit are *not* going to be considered a dividend.

IRS agents, as you can imagine, are of a diametrically opposite point of view. They would like to see *all* payments made to or for the benefit of the shareholder-employee construed as dividend income; *two taxes rather than one make IRS agents smile.* Much of the IRS's position on dividend treatment centers around the proposition that the shareholder-employee is disguising a return on investment (dividend) in the form of deductible tax benefits. The service's thinking goes something like this: Since the employee is also the owner, he or she would like a return on investment but does not want to pay two taxes in getting that return; thus a significant portion of the salary and fringe benefits the shareholder-employee receives must, in reality, be dividends in disguise.

Much of this book is dedicated to the explanation of how the IRS attempts to classify corporate payments to a shareholder-employee as dividends and how you, as the shareholder-employee, can defend yourself against such a stance.

Let us take a moment to demonstrate the potentially devastating tax effect of a dividend:

Reston Corp. is in the maximum corporate tax bracket on its taxable income—46 percent. That means that for every dollar of taxable profit, $0.46 goes into Uncle Sam's coffers. Roy Reston is in the maximum tax bracket for individuals—50 percent. For every dollar that Roy is taxed on, $0.50 goes to Uncle Sam. If Reston Corp. pays a dividend to Roy or the IRS determines that a payment to Roy is a dividend, the tax results will be disastrous. A taxable dollar that goes to the corporation is reduced by $0.46 in federal income tax; only $0.54 is left. Remember, dividends are paid with aftertax dollars. The corporation then pays a dividend to Roy of the $0.54, and Roy pays tax on the $0.54 at his usual 50 percent tax bracket. Of the original dollar, only $0.27 is left. The effective tax is a whopping *73 percent.*

It is important to Roy to avoid dividends and escape a 73 percent tax. It is the task of the IRS to assure that Reston Corp. is not disguising dividends.

This example points out why understanding corporate income tax theory is extremely important whether you are incorporated or thinking of doing so. Our discussion of corporate tax theory can be simplified through understanding our "tax wheel."

The Tax Wheel

Over the years, it has become apparent to us that many people who own their own corporations or who are involved in corporations do not have a basic grasp of corporate tax theory. That is not really surprising given the fact that even sophisticated tax specialists get lost in the minutiae of the Internal Revenue Code. In our experience, many of them cannot see the money because of the dollar bills. To help our clients better understand how basic corporate taxation works, we have developed Figure 4-1, the tax wheel. It reduces corporate tax theory to a simple diagram.

Before we look at the diagram, however, let us review a few of the basics that we just discussed.

A corporation has its own tax bracket for the income it produces.

The corporation may keep the income that it has left after federal income taxes have been paid. These earnings are retained and are therefore referred to as retained earnings.

A corporation distributes its income in five basic ways:
Payment of business expenses
Payment of debt
Purchase of assets
Making loans
Payment of dividends

Generally, the only use of corporate dollars that produces an immediate and a full deduction against the income of a corporation is the payment of a business expense.

In a one-person talent corporation, the shareholder is almost always the key employee. Because of that, there is a danger that the IRS will consider payments to this shareholder-employee as dividends, which are not deductible by the corporation and are income taxable to the shareholder-employee (double taxation).

A review of these basics leads to the conclusion that the shareholder-employee in a one-person corporation would like to accomplish the following objectives through the use of a corporation:

Create tax-free income: income which goes to the corporation and which is used for or on behalf of the shareholder-employee but is not income taxable to the shareholder-employee.

Have corporate income taxed in the lowest-possible income tax bracket.

Have income which is taxable to the shareholder-employee taxed at the lowest income tax bracket.

Avoid, *at all costs*, double taxation: the payment of a dividend.

Following, in order of what we believe to be taxpayer preference, is a list of how income should be taken out of a corporation by its shareholder-employee.

Fringe benefits (a current deduction to the corporation and normally *not* currently income taxable to the shareholder-employee)

Ordinary and necessary business expenses made on behalf of the shareholder-employee; for example, travel and entertainment expense (deductible to the corporation and *not* income taxable to the shareholder-employee)

Loans to the shareholder-employee or to family members of the shareholder-employee (not deductible to the corporation but used tax-free by the recipient)

Salary (a deduction to the corporation and income taxable to the shareholder-employee)

Bonus (a deduction to the corporation and income taxable to the shareholder-employee)

Dividend (not deductible to the corporation and income taxable to the shareholder-employee)

The talent should take his or her income by following our list from top to bottom. The IRS, on the other hand, would prefer to see the talent take his or her income by following our list from bottom to top. Can you see why?

The service loves a dividend. And if incorrectly taken, *expenses, fringe benefits, loans, salaries,* and *bonuses* can all be considered dividends by IRS agents.

Can IRS agents do this? You bet they can, particularly if you do not play the corporate income tax game the proper way, a frequent consequence of not understanding corporate tax theory.

We can now tie all of this together in Figure 4-1, the tax wheel.

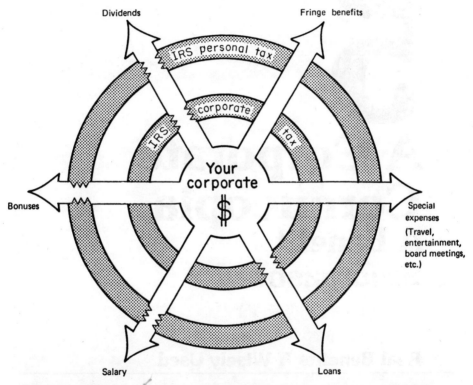

Figure 4-1 The tax wheel. Your corporate dollars have to pass two IRS hurdles before they can reach your pocket: corporate tax and personal tax. You want to avoid both hurdles by proper tax planning. The IRS is always looking to collect a tax at *both* levels.

Tax theory is all well and good if it can be put to use. And putting this theory to work is why the corporation has been called by a few overenthusiastic corporate disciples "the ultimate tax shelter." Our next chapter shows how the theory is used in practice.

Chapter

5

A Corporate Cornucopia
A Benefit Smorgasbord

Real Benefits If Wisely Used

Corporations have traditionally been associated with a broad range of tax benefits. While Congress has been steadily whittling away at these benefits, quite a few still remain. Many of the benefits that we all hear or read about, however, are overrated and can result in many more disadvantages than advantages. This chapter will familiarize you with a cornucopia of benefits and will separate those which are truly benefits from those which can mean tax-planning disaster.

A Separate Tax Year

Most of us report our income on a calendar year; income that we earn between January 1 and December 31 of each year is our taxable income for that year. Our tax returns are filed on or before the April 15th following the end of our tax year. Reporting income on this calendar-year basis is mandatory for all individuals unless special permission to the contrary is granted by the IRS.

Corporations (except for Subchapter S corporations) are free to choose any tax year, or "fiscal year" as it is commonly called, they desire. For example, a typical corporate fiscal year may begin on February 1 and end on January 31 of the next calendar year. (Corporate fiscal years normally end on the last day of a month.)

The mechanics of choosing a corporate fiscal year are quite simple. After the corporation commences business, it has twelve months in which to choose its fiscal year-end. When the officers of a new corporation want to end the corporation's first fiscal year, they file the corporation's tax return. For example, if the corporation is formed on January 1, 1983, the officers could end its first fiscal year on January 30, February 28, March 31, etc.—all the way to December 31. If the officers stopped the first fiscal year on March 31, the corporation's first year would be three months long (January 1 through March 31). Professionals call this a "short year." Thereafter, the corporation's fiscal year would be April 1 to March 31.

Having your corporation on a tax year different from your own allows for deferral of income taxes. Here is how this kind of tax deferral can work:

Jack's corporation has a fiscal year ending on January 31. His own tax year ends, of course, on December 31. During the year, Jack's investment income, plus a sale of some property, has put him into a high individual tax bracket. The salary that Jack is taking from his corporation is aggravating the situation by forcing Jack into even higher brackets. Next year, Jack believes that his income will be much lower.

Jack's tax adviser tells him to take a low salary from his corporation through December 31 of the current year. After December 31 but before January 31, the corporation can make up the remainder of Jack's salary by paying it to him during the thirty-day period in January.

The effect of this tax maneuver will be tax deferral. The income that was paid to Jack in January will be deferred until Jack's next tax year (he did not get it in his current calendar year).

This tax planning will even out Jack's income by not forcing him into higher brackets in the current year.

The corporation has suffered no ill effects as a result of Jack's planning. As long as it pays Jack's deserved salary or bonus before January 31 (see our section "Accounting for Income and Expenses"), it can take a salary deduction for its fiscal year ending January 31. The corporation does not care when it pays Jack's salary as long as it is paid and deducted during its fiscal year.

There are several pitfalls to avoid when considering the use of this tax deferral device. On IRS audit, it is not difficult for the IRS to see that you have shifted income to a subsequent personal tax year. Unless you properly document this transaction, the IRS will have the authority to shift your income *back* to the current year (good-bye tax savings).

Deferring personal taxes by timing the receipt of income through the use of a noncalendar corporate fiscal year is good business. If you choose to time your income by staggering your corporation's fiscal year with your calendar tax year, make sure all the corporate formalities are followed. Done right, this is one gimmick that can really work for you.

Accounting for Income and Expenses

To most of us, there is no mystery in determining what our taxable income is. The money we actually receive is income. Income earned but not received is no more than an expectancy. Expectancies, most of us believe, cannot be taxed until we receive them.

Expenses work much the same way. When an expense is paid, it can be deducted. Any expenses that are owed but not paid are not counted as deductions. Around December 31 of each year, when expenses matter because we want to lower our taxable income, we scurry around to find the money to pay them and usually find it by borrowing from our friendly banker. Most folks want their deductions as soon as possible.

Accounting for income when actually received and for expenses when actually paid is called the "cash method of accounting." Most Americans use the cash method when filing their personal income tax returns.

Under the accrual method of accounting, income is reported when there is a right to receive it and expenses are recorded when an obligation to pay them arises. Whether or not cash is actually received or paid is irrelevant for purposes of the accrual method of accounting.

Professional service corporations almost always choose the cash method of accounting. This method of accounting is most convenient because there is no need to record accounts receivable or accounts payable. In addition, most of us use the cash method, so it is familiar and understandable.

The main tax advantage of the cash method of accounting is one of timing. If income is only reported when it is received, it may be advantageous to collect income in one year as opposed to another. This is the same principle as was discussed in our section on fiscal years, "A Separate Tax Year." The same timing advantage also is true of expenses. If a corporation has expenses and wants to deduct them in a fiscal year, it only needs to pay them to receive the deduction.

This timing advantage can be a timing disadvantage too. If a cash-basis corporation does not have the money to pay expenses, then there is no deduction until the expenses are paid. Usually, a corporation has to earn more income to generate the cash to pay expenses. This creates a situation where taxable income is created to pay expenses, thus eliminating any tax advantage. However, cash-basis corporations can borrow money to pay expenses, thus creating a current deduction. Then income can be collected in the future with which to pay the debt. Your accountant can help you refine the use of the cash method so its tax advantages can be maximized.

There is a major exception to the cash method of accounting with regard to retirement plans. The amount contributed to a qualified retirement plan can be paid as late as the date the corporate tax return is due. Thus a deduction for a contribution to a plan can be taken in the current fiscal year of a cash-method corporation but not be paid until the tax return is due.

The accrual basis of reporting income is rarely used by personal service corporations. Some personal service corporations do not have accounts receivable and have no need for accrual reporting. Other personal service corporations have accounts receivable but do not want to pay income tax on them until they are received. It is financially difficult for them to pay taxes on income not yet received.

You are now probably wondering why *anyone* would use the accrual method of accounting. There are several reasons. The IRS requires certain businesses to use it if the business has inventory. This is not true of personal service corporations. The accrual method is sometimes used in personal service corporations to accelerate deductions. For example, some personal service corporations have outside income from investments. The sole shareholder-employee would like to take this extra income as salary. However, just as in our discussion of a fiscal year, the shareholder-employee would like to defer taking the income until another tax year. Thus the corporation "accrues" (promises to pay) a bonus to the shareholder-employee. The corporation can deduct this accrual. Since the shareholder-employee is more than likely on the cash method of accounting for personal income, the accrued salary is not recognized as income until the shareholder-employee actually receives the bonus. *Voilà!* Tax deferral.

But one must be careful. If you own more than 50 percent of the corporation (which is usually true in a one-person corporation), the bonus must be paid within seventy-five days after the fiscal year-end of the corporation to be deductible. This tax code rule seriously undermines this tax deferral technique. And just to make sure you do not let your spouse or kids own the corporation to get around this rule, the Internal Revenue Code says that if your spouse or children own stock, it is the same as if *you* own it. These rules are called "attribution of ownership."

Selecting the proper method of accounting in the incorporation process is extremely important. The methods should be thoroughly discussed with your tax advisers before one is chosen. Which accounting method is selected can have a massive effect on your taxes. It is our experience that almost all one-person talent corporations are on the cash basis of accounting for both convenience and better tax planning.

Ordinary and Necessary Business Expenses

The Internal Revenue Code allows as a deduction against income "all the ordinary and necessary expenses paid or incurred during the taxable year in carrying on any trade or business." From this phrase has come some of the most imaginative and litigated tax planning in the tax law.

You do not have to be incorporated to deduct business expenses. Anyone who is engaged in a business can deduct those expenses which are ordinary and necessary to its operation. In our experience, however, many expenses are less controversial if deducted by a corporation. To explain this phenomenon, we should again look at the nature of a corporation.

A corporation is a separate legal entity which can separate our personal lives from our business lives. The corporate mystique seems to transform expenses which may appear frivolous when taken personally to expenses which appear necessary when viewed corporately. Since a corporation is an entity which does business, its deductions must be business-related (a natural assumption from the taxpayer's point of view that is attacked from time to time by the service).

Business expenses tend to stick out like a neon sign on a personal income tax return (various forms and schedules were designed by the IRS to accomplish this). A corporate income tax return, on the other hand, is designed to eliminate these personal schedules and requires only the orderly listing of expenditures. In our experience, few corporate expenses become glaring invitations to initiate an IRS audit.

Whether an expense is necessary, ordinary, or related to a business purpose has been the subject of too many books and tax-planning courses. To list and explain all the business expenses available to the taxpayer is not a project we want to take on (others already have). We will, however, give you some general guidelines as to the deductibility of expenses:

> Business expenses are deductible if they are directly related to your business or profession.

> An employee's expenses are not personally deductible unless the employee can show that they were required by his or her employment contract or that they were incidental to the performance of the employee's duties.

> To the extent a combined business expense and personal expense is incurred, only the business portion is deductible. If your corporation pays a personal expense, it will be nondeductible to the corporation and income to you; in other words, a dividend.

> Salaries that are paid to you are deductible to your corporation to the extent those salary amounts are reasonable and are for services actually performed.

> Travel and entertainment expenses are deductible if they are used for business purposes. They must, however, bear a reasonable relationship to a business activity.

> An office in a home can be deducted if it is exclusively used on a regular basis as either the principal place of business or where business meetings take place with clients or customers.

We have found far too often that our clients have been, and continue to be, afraid to take legitimate business deductions. Their feeling seems to be that if there is a doubt as to the direct relationship of their business and the deduction envisioned, the deduction should not be taken. We patently disagree.

Any expenses which are related to your business or profession ought to be deducted. Questions of deductibility should be resolved by your taking the deduction, not by eliminating the deduction because of fear of the IRS. Upon an audit, it is unlikely that the service will allow a deduction for an expense you failed to take. But remember, only deduct expenses which are in some way related to your business.

Always make sure that your expenses are well documented. It is very important that you show the IRS the relationship between your deduction and your business. Keep a notebook which sets forth the amount of each expense, when and why it was incurred, and any people who can verify the expense. If you do not keep a notebook (and the vast majority of our clients do not), then at least make sure you mark what the expense was for on your check or credit card receipt. *Do not use cash!*

You should also make sure that the minutes of your corporation and your employment contract set forth what expenses are permissible for reimbursement, which expenses are required to be paid by you, and why the corporation expects these expenses to be incurred ("For the business, of course"—just put it in writing).

If you are thinking that business expenses can be deducted whether you are incorporated or not, you are right. A business expense is a business expense; it does not have to be a corporate business expense to be deducted.

The only point that differentiates a corporate business expense from a business expense taken on a personal income tax return is the likelihood of triggering an IRS audit may be reduced by using the corporate return.

Business expenses can and should be deducted. What you may think is a necessity of life may be—and probably is—a business expense, *if properly taken.*

Medical Reimbursement Plans

Attempting to itemize medical expenses on a personal income tax return can be a very frustrating experience. Most of our clients find that the rules for personally itemizing medical expenses are too strict; our clients seem to spend an enormous amount of time collecting and sorting receipts, only to find out that they do not qualify for the deduction.

Medical expenses, to be itemized, traditionally had to exceed 3 percent of adjusted gross income. Likewise, the cost of drugs had to exceed 1 percent of adjusted gross income to qualify. The only medical expense which seemed to be itemized on a regular basis was the premium for health insurance. The first half of this premium was deductible without any limitation, except that it could not exceed $150—not a major benefit. The remainder of the premium was then classified as a 3 percent expense.

As of 1982, these rules were changed and made even tougher. Effective January 1, 1983, a personal income tax deduction for medical expenses is permitted only to the extent that the expenses exceed 5 percent of adjusted gross income. The 1 percent limitation on drugs is eliminated, drugs are added to the 5 percent medical deductible, and only prescription drugs and insulin will qualify. The additional deduction for medical insurance premiums has been eliminated.

Even if the new higher limits are reached, the amounts of medical expenses excluded can be significant. An individual in a 50 percent tax bracket who cannot deduct medical expenses really pays double for medical costs. That individual must earn two dollars of income to pay a dollar of nondeductible medical expense; the other dollar goes to Uncle Sam.

Having your own corporation can eliminate this frustrating tax experience and make paying taxes a little more palatable. One of the significant corporate tax benefits still available is known as a "medical reimbursement plan" or "health and accident plan."

Under a medical reimbursement plan, the corporation can either reimburse an employee for all or part of the medical expenses for that employee, the employee's spouse, and other dependents or pay those expenses directly on behalf of the employee. The amounts reimbursed or paid under a qualified medical reimbursement plan are fully deductible by the corporation and are not taxable income to the employee. *The effect is to make medical expenses 100 percent tax deductible;* two dollars of income do not have to be earned to pay one dollar of medical expense—one dollar will do nicely.

Medical expenses, for purposes of a medical reimbursement plan, are defined far more broadly than they are on a personal return. Medical expenses include all costs of health and disability insurance; all drugs, whether prescription or not, including over-the-counter drugs such as aspirin, toothpaste (if it fights cavities), vitamins, and the like; and all other medical expenses, including braces for children, cosmetic surgery, and swimming pools to exercise disc-troubled backs. The basic requirement is that the expense must be related to the preservation of health or the prevention of disease. If the item is related to one of these, it will qualify. This plan should excite you. We still get excited, and we have been working with such plans for years.

Medical reimbursement plans were dealt a hearty blow under the Tax Revenue Act of 1978. Prior to that law, medical reimbursement plans could be used for certain employees to the exclusion of others. As a result, higher-paid employees or shareholder-employees were usually included, while all other employees were not. Under the Tax Revenue Act of 1978, employees must be covered across the board without discrimination among them.

One of the pleasant features of a one-person talent corporation is that it usually has only one employee; if there are additional employees, they are usually family members. As a result, one can throw caution to the wind and utilize a nondiscriminatory medical reimbursement plan. Clearly, the cost of providing benefits for nonfamily employees is simply not relevant.

Depending upon the age, family size, and health of the talent and the talent's dependents, a medical reimbursement plan can provide good to outstanding bottom-line tax benefits. Remember, $5000 of nondeductible personal medical and health-related bills may cost a taxpayer in the 50 percent bracket $10,000. They cost an incorporated talent with a medical reimbursement plan $5000.

For a medical reimbursement plan to operate successfully, corporate formalities must be observed. These can be summarized as follows:

Your medical reimbursement plan should be in writing.

Your plan should be approved in the minutes of the corporation.

Your plan should set forth all the requirements that an employee must meet in order to be eligible for the plan.

Your plan should include what expenses are covered and how and when payments are to be made.

Your plan should require eligible employees to submit receipts, canceled checks, or other evidence of medical expenses.

Your plan should not reimburse an employee for expenses that are covered and otherwise paid by insurance.

Appendix C is an example of a medical reimbursement plan. Your advisers may have their own, but ours will give you an idea what they look like and how they work.

Adopting a properly written medical reimbursement plan in your corporation can provide you and your dependents with tax-free health care. There is no doubt that these plans work. The key is knowing how to use them. Remember, if your expense is related to the preservation of health or the prevention of disease, it is probably 100 percent deductible. When in doubt as to any potentially qualifying expenditure, see your accountant or tax attorney.

Group Term Life Insurance

Another tax benefit provided to employees of regular (non-Subchapter S) corporations is group term life insurance.

Group term life insurance premiums are paid and deducted by the corporation. The corporate employee on whose life the insurance is purchased can name the beneficiaries of the policy and does not incur income as a result of the corporation's payments.

The obvious tax advantage is that the premiums paid by the corporation are deductible to the corporation and are *not* taxable income to the employee. Like almost all life insurance, the proceeds received by the beneficiary upon death of the employee are income tax–free, but they may be subject to death taxes. There are limitations, however, to this life insurance bonanza.

The maximum amount of life insurance purchased for an employee that will qualify for tax-free treatment is $50,000. Premiums for amounts of life insurance greater than $50,000 are considered taxable income to the employee. The life insurance can only be term insurance; it can never accumulate a cash fund like permanent insurance. In addition, the group life insurance plan must cover all employees unless the benefit has certain restrictions as to eligibility for age or other factors.

What does this mean to the shareholder-employee of the one-person corporation? Having a group plan when you are the corporation's only employee is difficult. The IRS frowned on this for a long time, but it is now possible, taxwise, to cover yourself as the sole employee of your corporation. The trick is finding a life insurance company who will provide the insurance, particularly at group rates. You see, to qualify as a group plan according to the Internal Revenue Code rules, no physical examinations can be given. Only a medical questionnaire can be used. Insurance companies are not too willing to insure any single life without a physical examination. It would appear to us that a group of one may find it difficult to find a willing insurance carrier.

There are other rules that must be followed to qualify for a group of one. The talent who wishes to avail himself or herself of this benefit should see his or her insurance adviser.

Putting Your Family on the Payroll

If one has a corporation, one has the ability to "hire" family members as employees. The two most commonly avowed reasons for hiring family members are income-splitting and qualifying loved ones for social security.

The theory of splitting income among family members is that many times, family members are in a lower tax bracket than the shareholder-employee. If the income generated at the corporate level can be diverted to other family members, it will then be taxed in their lower tax brackets. This technique does not work between spouses if they are filing a joint return for the obvious reason that both their incomes are reported on the same return. However, in our experience, many otherwise sharp tax planners seem to forget this fact and try to income-split between spouses. This obviously does not have much chance of working.

Why would a shareholder-employee want to divert income to family members? Here is a typical example:

Martha Sampson is a singer who has incorporated her talent. Martha and her husband, Ray, are in the 50 percent income tax bracket. They have two children, Anne and Tom. Both Anne and Tom are in college and are supported by Martha and Ray's income. For almost every dollar that is earned by Martha and Ray, 50 percent goes to pay federal income taxes. The remaining 50 percent is left for expenses, including the payment of their children's college expenses.

Martha decides to put both Anne and Tom on her corporate payroll. By doing so, income that would normally be taxed at 50 percent if Martha had taken it will now be taxed at the children's lower brackets. Assuming that Anne and Tom are in a 15 percent income tax bracket, $0.35 is now saved on each dollar earned. The children have an additional $0.35 per dollar earned to meet their expenses.

Income splitting sounds good, but it does not always work. Upon IRS audit, Anne's and Tom's functions in the corporation will be scrutinized by the service to determine whether or not they are true employees. Some of the questions that Martha will have to answer are, "What do the kids actually do? How many hours do they work? What is the business purpose for putting them on the payroll?"

If these questions are not answered satisfactorily, the IRS will disallow the corporate income tax deduction for their salaries, in whole or in part, and will consider these amounts as dividends to Martha. To make matters even worse, the IRS may construe the dividends as gifts to the kids, and another tax may be due!

Putting family members on the payroll for income-splitting purposes only works when there is practical justification for their being there. In our example, if either Anne or Tom had skills that could actually be used by their mother's corporation, her decision to put them on the payroll would be justifiable and darn good tax planning. Overpaying for these skills or not having the work actually performed rarely generates the hoped for tax result if an IRS agent comes knocking on your door. Actual work must be done at realistic pay levels for income splitting to be a viable tax-planning alternative.

Social security benefits are sometimes used as a justification for putting family members on the corporate payroll. In 1983, the first $35,700 of most working Americans' salaries was subject to a 13.4 percent social security tax. In the case of corporate employees, half of this was paid by the employee, half by the corporation. This amount is going to go up in future years. Many people put family members on the corporate payroll in the mistaken belief that less social security taxes would be due. This is simply not true. Employees of most corporations are subject to the same social security rules regardless of their family ties.

The only exception dealing with family members is when family members are employed in a family partnership or a sole proprietorship. No social security is payable for sons or daughters of the owners of these types of business entities if the sons or daughters are under the age of 21. The parents must still pay a form of social security tax called "self-employment tax," but the rate in 1983 is only 9.35 percent of wages earned. This amount is scheduled to increase dramatically in 1984 and after, however.

From a social security perspective, there is only one reason that one may wish to hire a family member as an employee of the talent corporation: so that the family member can actually pay in to the system and, thereby, qualify for social security benefits on his or her death, disability, or retirement.

If you wish to put family members on your corporation's payroll, remember·

They must actually expend worklike efforts on the corporation's behalf.

Their corporate remuneration must be reasonable in relation to the work they are being paid for.

You should be prepared to prove to an IRS agent that both are in fact being done.

Writing Off Your Home as Corporate Headquarters

Everyone needs an office—or two—especially if both of them can be written off and one happens to be in the den in front of the fireplace with all the amenities of home. Taxpayers have believed this for years. They have even gone to the extreme of writing off all the expenses of a room which was used for clipping bond coupons. Yes, everyone needs an office at home.

As is true with all really good tax angles, the use of the home office has been the target for thorough IRS and congressional examination. The result has been to bring the "abuse" of a home office to a screeching halt. No longer can a taxpayer set up a typewriter and desk in his or her den and automatically qualify the den as an income tax haven. New rules make it very difficult for most taxpayers to garner tax benefits for working at home.

To qualify a home office for a personal tax deduction under the new rules, the following conditions must be met.

The office must be used exclusively for business purposes.

There can be no personal use of the office.

The office cannot be used just to transact business occasionally. If you do not do most of your work at home, do not attempt to write off a portion of your home.

While the rules appear stringent at a first glance, they are really only designed to eliminate the tax cheaters, the tax entrepreneurs who will try anything for a few dollars of tax write-off. Legitimate use of an office in your home is perfectly all right.

Many of our clients are interested in what types of expenses they can deduct when writing off the home office and how the amount of their write-off is determined. The answer to both these questions involves a basic understanding of the difference between expenses and cost recovery (depreciation).

Office supplies like pens, paper, typewriter ribbons, and other consumable items are deductible when they are purchased. These are ordinary and necessary to carrying on a business. Sound familiar? There are other things that are ordinary and necessary for carrying on a business in an office. Heat, light, and power can also be deducted. If you do not have a separate meter for your office, the amount used in your business pursuits has to be calculated. The most common method of calculating the amount used is to compare the number of square feet in your office to the total square feet in your house. You can then calculate the percentage of your home devoted to your office. This percentage is then multiplied by your monthly utility bills to determine how much can be written off. For example:

Suds Clifton, a championship bowler, has an office at home. Suds has made some good money over the years on the tour, and in addition to a lot of promotional work, Suds has his hand in a few outside businesses.

All of Suds's business is conducted in a room in his home, which used to be a bedroom. Its area is 150 square feet. His home has a total area of 3000 square feet, so Suds writes off 5 percent of his monthly utility bills.

Another monthly bill which can amount to a lot of money, at least in our homes, is the phone bill. If you do not have a separate phone line in your office (a separate business phone is totally deductible if it is used 100 percent for business), you can write off a portion of your monthly telephone bill. All business long-distance calls are fully deductible. A percentage of the basic bill can be written off depending on the amount of time you use the phone for business purposes. Using the telephone 50 percent of the time for business means a write-off of one-half the basic monthly charge.

While all these types of business expenses are consumed on a daily basis, some expenses are incurred for assets which have a life of more than a year. Assets which are personal property usually are written off over a period of years (cost recovery), except if a special election is made to expense them. Real estate is not subject to the special deduction rule and is almost always written off over fifteen years, which is the length of time that most real estate can be written off under Internal Revenue Code rules.

The same is true of the actual room (real estate) you are using.

Suds's house cost $100,000. Since 5 percent of the house is used for his office, $5000 of the cost of the house can be written off by Suds. This $5000 must be written off over a fifteen-year period.

In order to determine your home office deductions, you only need gather your expense information and determine the applicable business percentage use. As long as the appropriate rules for using your home as an office are met, you should be able to successfully take the write-off.

We have a suggestion for those of you who are wondering how your one-person corporation can deduct the costs of using an office in your home: Lease a portion of your home to your corporation. The following example will illustrate the suggestion.

Suds decides to incorporate his talent after reading an excellent book on the subject. All his office supplies are paid by his corporation, and the corporation deducts them. Suds bills his corporation on a monthly basis for utilities the corporation uses (the square-foot percentage approach will be used).

The corporation receives another monthly bill from Suds: It is for use and occupancy of the office space (rent). Suds determined the rental amount by finding out what office space of the same quality is renting for in town. The amount determined is $10 a square foot per year. The monthly rent is $125 (150 square feet times $10 divided by 12). This amount is deductible to the corporation because the corporation and Suds have entered into a formal written lease evidencing the contractual relationship between Suds, the landlord, and Suds, the corporation. The rent is income to Suds and must be reported on his personal income tax return.

Suds also gets a tax break. Since he is the owner of the office space, he is now in the rental business. He is entitled to write off the space used by the corporation on his personal tax return. This write-off is taken over a fifteen-year period on the cost of the office ($5000).

The fact that Suds is a landlord will probably make the corporation's office expense deduction easier to justify on audit. This rather circuitous tax shelter seems, at least in our experience, to create less of a fuss with an IRS agent than the traditional method of taking the write-off personally. This is especially true when the corporate formalities are meticulously observed and the rent and other expenses are fair.

There is nothing wrong with having an office in your home. Like all legitimate tax deductions, an office in your home is not frowned upon by the IRS if there are sound business reasons for having the office and it is used exclusively for your business on a continuing basis.

Borrowing Money from Your Corporation

The ability to borrow money from your own corporation can be a very effective method to reduce income taxes. Borrowing from your corporation does, however, necessitate following relatively strict rules. If a corporation is used as a bank, banking rules must be followed.

An example of the tax savings potential of borrowing can be illustrated in the following case:

Karen Anderson is in a 50 percent individual income tax bracket. Her main source of income is from her corporation, which is in a 30 percent income tax bracket.

Karen would like to take additional money from her corporation to invest in the stock market. If Karen takes out additional salary, it will be subject to a 50 percent income tax. To make a $5000 investment, she will need to take out $10,000 in salary. She would be much better off if she took the $10,000 as a loan from the corporation.

Corporate loans are made with aftertax earnings; the corporation can invest its aftertax dollars in loans rather than in the stock market or in a savings account. The same $10,000 which would generate only $5000 to Karen as salary will generate $7000 as a loan. The corporation pays only $3000 in tax, not $5000. Karen has $2000 more to invest

This example demonstrates the basic premise on which corporate loans to shareholder-employees are predicated.

The IRS frowns upon taxpayers using their corporations as private lending institutions. If IRS agents discover a loan transaction during an audit, they will take extra time to make very sure that all the proper loan rules have been followed. Improperly made loans are treated as dividends; in the service's eyes, they are nothing more than a device to distribute corporate earnings.

The best way to follow sound banking rules is to pretend that your corporation is making a loan to a business associate rather than yourself. Normally, when a loan is made to someone other than ourselves, we tend to make sure that all the I's are dotted and T's are crossed. This is exactly what must be done to successfully borrow from your corporation.

All loan transactions should first be approved in the minutes of the board of directors. This formality will give the corporate officers the appropriate authority to make the loan. All the loan terms should be approved by the board. These would include the amount of the loan, the interest rate, the length of the loan, its pay-back terms, and the required security, if any. The loan should be made only upon the signing of a promissory note which has identical terms to those approved in the corporate minutes. When the paperwork is complete, the loan can be made.

Many of our states have specific laws with regard to loans made by a corporation to officers, directors, or employees of the lending corporation. You should always have your advisers review any loan transactions between yourself and your corporation. If your borrowing violates your state's laws, the transaction may be invalidated, giving Uncle Sam the opportunity to collect an extra tax; *dividends do pay double tax.*

Proper paperwork is only half the battle in making sure that the loan is not a dividend upon an IRS audit. There is one other key element that *must* be followed. There must be an ongoing attempt to pay off the loan. If payment dates are ignored or if the loan is not reduced over a period of time, there is a better than even chance of dividend treatment. The loan transaction has to be treated as real loan transactions would be treated, not just as a method of avoiding income tax; real loans are paid back.

Many people are curious as to the interest rate that a corporation must charge when making a loan to a shareholder, director, officer, or employee. Unless state law requires an interest rate, there is currently no requirement under federal income tax laws for *any* interest rate to be charged. Yes, you can take an interest-free loan from your corporation. Just make sure that all the other loan formalities are followed. IRS agents may still try to attack the transaction, but to date they have been highly unsuccessful in convincing most courts that there is some inherent income and resulting tax generated by using an interest-free loan. This factor greatly increases the attractiveness of using one's corporation as a lending institution. If your corporation is in a lower income tax bracket than you are, it would make good tax sense to borrow from it, bearing in mind that corporate loans·

Can be an effective way to lower income taxes

Can increase the aftertax dollars of shareholder-employees

Must be evidenced by a written promissory note

Need not charge interest

Must follow all the banking rules

Turning Board Meetings into Vacations

Expenses incurred by members of the board of directors when attending a board meeting can be paid by the corporation. The expenses are tax deductible to the corporation and are not considered to be taxable income to the board members. This leaves a lot of room for creativity, especially in the one-person talent corporation. The IRS is well-versed in policing this area.

> Jack and Zelda, a married couple, and their daughter Mary are the directors of Jack's corporation. Jack is a very successful lawyer, practicing alone through his one-person corporation. Mary is in college at the University of Hawaii, and as you can imagine, Jack and Zelda like to visit her as much as possible. The trips are expensive and are not even tax deductible.
>
> To reduce the cost of these trips, Jack decides to call them directors meetings. Jack will then have the corporation pay for all the expenses of the trips as legitimate business expenses. As a little bonus, he will even have the corporation pay directors fees so that the three directors can have a little extra pocket money for those unexpected Hawaiian necessities (ten different grades of suntan lotion).

Not a bad idea—until Jack is audited, of course. You see, certain criteria must be met to take deductions for these directors meetings. The expenses must be incurred primarily for the board meeting. Personal time, such as lying on a beach or touring, should not occupy much of the workday. As a rule of thumb, 80 percent of the business day should be spent on business-related activities. If not, all or some of the expenses will be disallowed. Those expenses which are disallowed will be treated as income to the recipients, creating a dividend.

Directors' expenses, especially in the one-person talent corporation, are one of the first, if not the first, areas the service examines on audit Why? Because this area has been abused for years by too many taxpayers. Almost all of us, at one time or another, have done a little exaggerating on our travel expenses. It appears to be basic human nature to want to use the corporate dollar rather than our own. The IRS figured this one out years ago.

Only try to deduct your vacation as a board meeting if you are truly going to conduct real board business. Have meetings and, most importantly, keep minutes. Minutes are great evidence of the fact that business was transacted. Keep a record of all business activities: who you talked to, where you went, and why the activity was business-related. A contemporaneous record made during your trip is almost conclusive proof to the IRS that you were indeed doing business. Make sure all the directors are involved; having one director do everything does not help the other directors' expense deductions. Their expenses can be disallowed if they did not engage in serious business.

The key to deducting vacationlike directors meetings is to not vacation too much. There must be some substantial business reasons for the meeting, and you must be able to prove what they were. Taking a little care can allow you to deduct expenses, but remember that the IRS agents will be looking for proof

Driving a Company Car

One of the questions we are most frequently asked by our clients deals with the company car. Should the corporation own the car, or should the shareholder-employee own it? The answer, more often than not, is that the corporation should own the car.

There are a couple of reasons for this answer. The first deals with the relative tax brackets of the shareholder-employee and the corporation. It is often better for the corporation to buy assets at its tax bracket. In most cases, the shareholder-employee is in the 50 percent bracket. That means buying an asset costs twice as much; a car that has a purchase price of $20,000 really costs $40,000. Because the corporation is almost always in a lower tax bracket, the total amount of dollars it expends for that same car will be less.

A second reason for the corporation owning the car is purely practical. When any employee uses his or her car in a business and wants to deduct the business use of the car, a separate income tax form is filed. It is this type of form that many times seems to trigger an audit by the IRS. Even if this form does not trigger an audit and some other factor does, the automobile expenses will surely be closely examined

Automobile expenses, because they are so akin to personal expenses, are a subject near and dear to the hearts of IRS agents. Many otherwise honest taxpayers seem to cheat (at least a little) on their car expenses, and the IRS knows it. They have long taken the position that only that portion of an automobile's expense which is directly attributed to a business purpose may be deducted.

When a business car is used exclusively by one employee (our talent), there is going to be some personal use of that car. The expense of commuting from home to an office is considered to be a personal expense. Since most of us do travel from home to office, we do have personal expenses. The IRS catches our clients on this point time and time again. The solution is to admit there is some personal use with respect to the company car. The corporation should charge a monthly fee to the shareholder-employee for personal use. By doing this, you concede a minor amount of money to win a deduction; the service will have their pound of personal expense flesh and will probably look elsewhere. The same principle is true for those who own their cars personally and charge the corporation for business use. A percentage of the use will be considered as personal.

Company cars are a legitimate cost of doing business and are, in our opinion, a good idea. They will be picked up if you are audited, however, so be prepared to give a little to get a lot.

The $5000 Death Benefit

Many how-to-do-it books written to sell to the nonprofessional market advertise this benefit as if it were a major reason to incorporate. In our opinion, it is a minor benefit. We only cover it because so many others have advertised it in their literature.

The $5000 death benefit is simply a quirk in the tax law which allows a corporation to pay $5000 to the stated beneficiary of a deceased employee tax-free. The corporation receives a deduction for this amount, and the beneficiary does not pay income tax on it.

A Seldom-Used Stock Deduction

One of the benefits of incorporating a smaller business is referred to as "1244 stock." This benefit is heralded as a major one by most do-it-yourself books. It may be for some corporations, but it plays a very small part in the one-person talent corporation.

When you buy a stock in the market, it is considered to be a capital asset. That means when you sell the stock at a later date, you will have either a capital gain or a capital loss. A capital gain generates a maximum income tax of 20 percent in most circumstances. Taking a capital loss is not an ideal situation because you are limited in taking the loss. If you have capital losses in excess of capital gains, the most you can take in any one year is $3000. As a result of this rule, a large loss can take many years to totally deduct. Because of other rules, you may not even be able to use the loss; it just disappears.

Section 1244 of the Internal Revenue Code was designed to avoid limiting the amount which can be deducted upon taking a small business corporation stock loss. In a small business corporation, the sale of the stock at a gain still generates capital gain tax. However, a sale at a loss or upon that stock's becoming worthless does not generate a capital loss. Section 1244 allows the taxpayer to deduct the loss without the capital loss restrictions up to $100,000 in any one year if a joint tax return is filed, $50,000 if a single return. The loss is only restricted to the basis of the stock. Basis is generally the cost or investment in an asset.

Rarely does Section 1244 stock come into play for incorporated talent. Their initial investment is usually very low, limiting the loss that can be taken. Section 1244 stock plays a small role in the one-person talent corporation. Luckily, it is an automatic benefit; it does not have to be planned for or written up.

Alleged Benefits That Do Not Always Work

Splitting Income between Two Brackets

Because a corporation is a separate legal entity, it is taxed at its own income tax brackets. Table 4-1 in our prior chapter shows how the federal government taxes corporate income.

Corporate and individual income tax rates are difficult to compare. Individuals are taxed at different rates depending on whether or not they are married, filing jointly or individually, as a single person, or as the head of a household. Individuals also have different "exemptions," "zero-bracket amounts," and, after 1985, the availability of "tax indexing." These concepts are outside the scope of this book

justified as reasonable for the real business needs of the corporation. The tax is 27½ percent on the first $100,000 of unreasonably accumulated earnings and 38½ percent on unreasonably accumulated earnings after the first $100,000. These taxes are on top of the regular federal corporate income taxes that have already been paid on these same amounts.

What amount of retained earnings constitutes "reasonable" accumulations of earnings? This issue-oriented question has been the subject of hundreds of court cases. Suffice it to say that retained earnings over the $150,000 statutory "gimme" for service (talent) corporations are going to get their talents in a great deal of tax-related trouble. Reaching $150,000 over a period of years is not very difficult, especially if your investments turn out to be lucrative and inflation continues to stay with the economy.

Another problem that an investment-oriented talent corporation can run into is that of the personal holding company. (We discuss this at length in Chapter 10, "Problems Common to All Incorporated Talent.") If the talent corporation's investments generate income, all the income of the corporation may be taxed at the 50 percent bracket whether or not it is taken out of the corporation. This result does not help the talent's tax planning one bit. It does, however, generate interesting tax problems for his or her advisers.

While there are other problems associated with using a talent corporation as an investment vehicle, there is one other overriding problem that must be considered. Even if none of the problems we have mentioned crop up, there is probably going to be a time when the talent would like to take some of the accumulated riches out of his or her corporation. When that day comes, so comes the day of reckoning. A second tax is going to have to be paid.

Taking the accumulated earnings out of a corporation almost always generates a second tax; the only issue is what type of tax will have to be paid. Usually, the shareholder-employee wants to use corporate earnings for personal uses. If so, they could be paid out as salary. There is a deduction to the corporation (if it can be justified—see the section "The Unreasonable Compensation Problem," in Chapter 10), and the shareholder-employee takes that amount into income at his or her current bracket. If this is the case, it seems like a waste of time to have accumulated the earnings in the first place. It may have been better to have initially distributed the earnings as salary.

Another method of distributing corporate earnings is by making a dividend payment. No sane taxpayer would do this unless there was an IRS-motivated reason to face up to Uncle Sam's demand for double taxation. This method is a last resort that lies somewhere between Armageddon and the Rockefeller Plateau, Antarctica, on a winter's day.

Still another way of distributing corporate dollars is by use of the shareholder loan, which has some problems of its own, as we have seen. You might be interested in knowing that the IRS treats shareholder loans as further evidence of accumulated earnings. Feel the walls closing in on your idea of making your talent corporation an investment entity? You should, because you are playing with the IRS's deck, and it is stacked against you.

As a last resort, a talent can always liquidate his or her corporation in order to get at those corporate earnings. Chapter 13 is devoted to liquidations and the taxes which have to be paid when doing so. Suffice it to say that many talents might wish that they had not been so dead set on accumulating earnings for what they thought were good tax-planning reasons.

Accumulating earnings in your corporation is not all bad. Realistically, it will occur over time anyway. Every time that your corporation buys an asset, like a car or a word processor, corporate aftertax dollars are used. Most talents will want to keep a cash cushion in their corporation for operating purposes, and this "cushion" will probably be subject to the lower corporate income tax brackets. Just like everything else, accumulating earnings is not bad when used with moderation and foresight. It is only when we get a little greedy that our hands get caught in Uncle Sam's cookie jar. If you have incorporated mainly to take advantage of lower corporate tax brackets, you have made a mistake.

On the other hand, if you incorporated, in part, to utilize your corporation's tax brackets to reasonably acquire business-related assets, you may have made a wise decision. The $150,000 accumulated earnings allowed by Uncle Sam is significant, even though it is $100,000 less than the ceiling allowed for nonservice corporations.

Leasing Assets to Your Corporation

Instead of accumulating assets in their corporations, many shareholder-employees prefer to personally purchase assets to be used in the corporation and then lease those same assets back to the corporation.

When you buy an asset like a computer or a chair or most other assets that will be used in your business, several tax rules come into play. The purchase of these assets is not immediately deductible. If you are in the 50 percent tax bracket and you decide to buy a $20,000 computer, you must earn $40,000 to net the $20,000 to purchase the computer. You may, however, take a credit against your tax in the year you first use the computer in your business. This is called an investment tax credit, which is a tax break to encourage businesses to purchase capital assets. The amount of the credit is as high as 10 percent of the purchase price, but may be lower depending on the type of asset purchased. The computer, for example, will qualify for a 6 percent investment tax credit, or $1200. This credit would lower the purchaser's actual income tax by $1200.

A second tax break given to purchasers of certain assets is called cost recovery (depreciation). Cost recovery allows the price of the asset to be written off (deducted) against income over a period of years. The computer, in our example, could be written off over a three-year period. While the amount written off is adjusted for the investment tax credit taken, the result is that the purchase price turns out to be deductible over a period of time.

Cost recovery and investment tax credits apply to almost all assets purchased and used in a business enterprise. Shareholder-employees sometimes like to be able to take advantage of these tax breaks. The reason given is that these shareholder-employees are in a higher tax bracket than their corporation and the shareholder-employee needs the use of the tax breaks worse than the corporation. The solution is to have the shareholder-employee buy the asset and lease it to the corporation. In that way, the shareholder-employee gets the investment tax credit and the cost recovery deduction, while the corporation gets the use of the asset. Sound good? So does the pot of gold at the end of the rainbow Whether they both exist is another matter.

The most glaring weakness of this leasing gimmick involves tax brackets which, of course, are fundamental to the use of this leasing gimmick. The corporation is likely to be in a lower tax bracket than its shareholder-employee. While the shareholder-employee (in the 50 percent bracket in most cases) would have to earn $40,000 to buy the $20,000 computer in our example, a corporation in the lowest corporate tax bracket (15 percent) would only have to earn $23,530 ($3530 of tax and $20,000 to buy the computer). The front-end dollar savings would be $16,470—almost enough to buy a second computer.

Our example is simplistic because there is more to the actual calculation. You should, however, get the picture. Regardless of the investment tax credit and cost recovery, the economics, in our opinion, inevitably point to the use of the corporate dollar. Incidentally, this is one of the few examples where leaving income in the corporation is justified.

Another frequently sold virtue of leasing equipment to your corporation is your resulting ability to take "tax-free" income out of the corporation. This tax-free income is the rent you charge the corporation to use your equipment. The rent is tax deductible to the corporation. You must take the rent into your personal income. Here comes the tax-free part: Since you are writing off the purchase price, the write-off is sheltering the income you receive.

What many of us overlook, however, is the fact that the computer cost $40,000 before taxes. This means that it is going to take quite a while for you to get your investment back, and remember, you can only write off approximately $20,000 as cost recovery and $1200 as investment tax credit. The difference between the cost recovery and investment tax credit and the $40,000 will be taxable to you at 50 percent. Care to check how long it will take for you to break even? Methuselah should live so long.

Another nail in the leasing stratagem coffin deals with the use of the investment tax credit by the shareholder-employee. Internal Revenue Code rules are *very* restrictive about shareholder-employees leasing their assets to their corporations and taking investment tax credit. In almost every case where talent wants to lease assets to their own corporation, the investment tax credit will not be able to be taken by the shareholder-employee. The net lease provisions of the Internal Revenue Code effectively deny this tax benefit.

If that's not enough, you are required to have an "arm's length" transaction. The lease must be fair as to terms and rates. If not, watch out. You may have dividend problems.

Buying assets personally and leasing them back to your own corporation is not usually a good idea. It does sound sexy or, if you prefer, just exciting. It is touted by many not-so-expert advisers. The facts are, however, to the contrary. Buying assets to lease to your corporation is usually poor economics, at least for the incorporated talent.

Selling Assets to Your Corporation

Many creative shareholder-employees of the past have found another way in which to save taxes: the sale of assets to their corporations. In some cases the shareholder-employee had an asset which had gone up in value but was depreciated down to nothing. There was no longer the ability to write it off. The shareholder-employee would sell the asset to his or her corporation, pay a capital gain tax, and have the corporation begin depreciating the asset at its new value. This stratagem was also used in reverse. Congress acted quickly to diffuse this loophole. No longer is a capital gain allowed when related parties buy and sell assets which are subject to depreciation or cost recovery.

The same is true for assets which have gone down in value. To lock in a loss for tax purposes, shareholder-employees were known to sell the asset to their corporations or vice versa. Control would be retained over the asset, but an immediate tax loss would be generated. This, too, did not appeal to Congress's sense of fair play and is no longer allowed.

Because there was a concern by Congress that it could not specifically cover all the variations produced by the fertile minds of taxpayers to avoid taxes in transactions between shareholders, their corporations, and other related business enterprises, a catchall provision was added to the Internal Revenue Code. It states that the IRS has the ability to reallocate income and expenses among related tax-paying entities. The bottom line is that if you or your advisers come up with a "better" way to create losses or gains between related taxpayers, be careful. Uncle Sam may have your loophole covered (or should we say, uncovered?).

Owning Real Estate in Your Corporation

A corollary of putting your personal investments in your corporation is buying or contributing real estate to your corporation. It has almost been a crusade of ours to halt totally the practice of putting real estate in a one-person corporation. Such a practice, in our opinion, can best be described as a tax-planning masochism.

It is easy to put or purchase real estate in a corporation. Sometimes it is contributed when the corporation is first formed; other times it is purchased by the corporation. The most commonly used rationale for putting real estate in a one-person corporation is that the lower corporate tax bracket can be used to pay for it. Normally, real estate is subject to a mortgage. Payments of mortgage principal are not deductible. Therefore, if a corporation is in a 15 percent tax bracket and an individual is in a 50 percent tax bracket, it would appear to make sense to use corporate aftertax dollars instead of personal aftertax dollars to pay off the real estate debt. This realization has hit too many naive but earnest do-it-yourself tax planners.

When the tax brackets look so attractive, why does the tax effect turn out to be bad? There are several reasons.

Real estate consists of two basic elements: land and buildings. The buildings are subject to cost recovery (depreciation). Depending upon when the building was acquired, this cost recovery represents a write-off of the cost of the building over a certain number of years. Generally, a building purchased after 1980, for example, could be written off over a fifteen-year period.

The write-off on buildings is one of the better tax shelters available today. Because a building can be written off over a relatively short period of time, the yearly write-off can be quite high. This means that the write-off can shelter income from taxation. A building that costs $300,000 can generate a write-off of at least $20,000 per year ($300,000 divided by 15). This write-off can shelter income of the same amount each year. The owner of that building can have $20,000 of income which is not subject to tax. This $20,000 can be used to help pay off the building. The result is the use of tax-free (sheltered) dollars to pay off debt. This factor makes the use of aftertax dollars in a corporation far less attractive simply because the corporation cannot use the write-off to the extent that the talent can. It's in a lower tax bracket, remember?

The interest on the debt is deductible. The result of its deductibility is the same whether written off corporately or personally. If written off personally, however, the deduction will be against income taxed at 50 percent.

Even if the use of corporate dollars vis-à-vis personal dollars can be justified, there are still other problems. Taxable income from real estate is passive income and can be subject to the personal holding company penalty tax. This is discussed in detail in a later chapter, but for now suffice it to say that the penalty tax is 50 percent. That should provide enough incentive for talent to resist the temptation of having their corporations own real estate.

Having one's corporation own speculative real estate or real estate which is not related to one's talent or profession can generate another tax problem. Having this type of investment in your corporation may manifest an unreasonable accumulation of earnings. Just like all those personal investments made with corporate dollars, real estate in a talent corporation automatically draws IRS attention. If there is no business purpose for your corporation owning real estate other than speculation, investment, or the blatant use of lower tax dollars, watch out. You may have tax problems.

All the reasons discussed above are minor compared with one other tax factor often overlooked by lay people and some not so professional planners. Let us assume that your corporation does not have personal holding company problems or accumulated earning problems and that it does not look like you are engaging in flagrant income splitting. What else can go wrong?

The typical scenario goes like what happened to one of our clients a few years back.

Sam was a very successful neurosurgeon who was incorporated. He was advised to buy some real estate in his talent corporation. The advice was based on Sam's strong desire to leave property to his two children upon his death. He did not want them to fight (they did not get along very well) or to sell the property immediately on his death. Sam was told that a corporation could preserve the property for his kids and stop any fighting between them. It looked like the perfect way to go.

Sam became more and more successful, as did his children. The children did not need a large inheritance, and besides, Sam wanted to retire in a few years. Sam and his wife were going to take off and see the world and did not plan to leave a significant inheritance to their kids. They intended to spend their money.

The real estate in Sam's corporation had increased in value. From a $50,000 initial cost, it had grown to a $250,000 bonanza. Sam's corporation had also acquired a lot of other assets over the years which made Sam's one-person corporation quite valuable. The corporation also had lots of accounts receivable from wealthy but slow-paying clients.

Sam came to us as a referral from an accountant. It seems that Sam had been made a $300,000 cash offer for the real estate. That was more than the property was worth, but the buyer had money and maybe some inside information. Sam wanted to sell at the lowest-possible tax cost and put the money in his and his wife's war chest (Sam's favorite term for spending money).

We had the unpleasant task of breaking the bad news to Sam. If the property was sold, there would be a tax at the corporate level of about 28 percent of the gain. Since the gain was $250,000 ($300,000 price less $50,000 cost), the tax was going to be in the neighborhood of $70,000. Sam gasped. He thought the capital gain rate was 20, not 28 percent. We told him that this was not so in a corporation. This oversight meant that an additional $20,000 had to be paid in taxes.

Even with a 28 percent tax, Sam thought he was going to have a lot of money. Wrong again. Sam wanted to take the money out of the corporation and put it in his personal war chest. We told him he could, but he would pay a second tax to get the property out of the corporation. The minimum tax he would have to pay was 20 percent (another capital gain tax), and the probable tax would approximate 50 percent.

We did the best we could, but Sam ended up paying a lot of tax. We saved him from paying two taxes on the real estate, but to do so, we had to liquidate his corporation. This approach generated additional tax on the other assets in his corporation.

Whoever gave Sam the advice to put real estate in his corporation gave Sam bad advice. If you put real estate in your one-person corporation, the odds are very high that you will pay two taxes upon the sale of the real estate. At the very least, you will have to liquidate your corporation to escape one of the taxes. In Chapter 13, we discuss liquidations and their tax implications. When you read it, you will see that getting out of a corporation may not be very pleasant, at least from a tax point of view.

What would have happened if Sam decided to sell the real estate but not to liquidate? Nothing very good. Sam would have had an immediate accumulated earnings problem. An IRS audit would have most likely produced some sort of accumulated earnings penalty tax. If the IRS agents did not audit, there still would be potential personal holding company problems. Sam would not only have had to pay an extra capital gain tax but Sam would also have incurred a lot of legal and accounting fees.

The worst aspect of the nonliquidation approach is that Sam would only be postponing that second tax. Upon Sam's retirement, he needs the money out of the property. When that day arrives, so will Sam's day of reckoning. A second tax will be levied.

Sam's only hope of avoiding two income taxes was to die. Our estate tax laws allow a tax break for people dying with corporately owned real estate. An explanation of this break is outside the scope of this book, but even with it, death is too high a price to pay for proper tax planning.

We have not exhausted our repertoire of tax reasons not to have real estate in a one-person corporation. Sam's horror story is not unique. We have, and continue to see, too many Sams in our practice. Do not put real estate in your talent corporation! If one of your advisers suggests it to you, run, rather than walk, to another adviser and get a second opinion. Corporately owned real estate generally proves to be a terminal tax illness.

Putting Your Talent Where It Does Not Belong

In the last few years there has been a commercial on television for oil filters. The first scene is in a garage where a mechanic is standing in front of a car which is having a new engine installed. The mechanic turns to the audience and tells them that had the owner of the car purchased the right kind of oil filter for $4, then the engine repair of $400 could have been avoided. "Pay me now—or pay me later," says the mechanic with a condescending look. Forget that he just made a killing on the cost of the oil filter. He cried, we would guess, all the way to the bank.

The same is true in the area of incorporation or business and tax planning in general. What may look quite simple to a novice can be extraordinarily complex. Tax planning is for pros. Do your advisers a favor, do all the work yourself, and then when it goes wrong, you can pay them double, triple, or more to fix what you messed up. And odds are—you will mess up!

Every time you step on an airplane and read the in-flight magazine, you see advertisements for books on incorporation. For only $49.95 you can incorporate yourself and do all the tax planning that a corporation requires. For only another $50 you can get a book on how to sustain the corporation and avoid all of those "unnecessary legal and accounting fees." This is pure hokum. A sound building requires a solid foundation. Those initial corporate documents are the foundation upon which your business will rise. Should one do their own heart surgery? "Welcome to do-it-yourself medical school" advertisements will, no doubt, surface one of these days.

Beware of forms and beware of those who tell you to use forms. While you will certainly understand most of these forms (we have bought most of them—we believed the ads), you probably will not be qualified to change them to fit your particular needs. Find experienced advisers who can explain what you need to do and who will do what needs to be done in a professional and responsible manner.

It will probably be a waste of your time and talent to practice law or accounting on yourself. This is even true for lawyers and accountants. The old saying that "an attorney who has himself for a client has a fool for a client" has certainly proved true in our experience. Someone else will work on your behalf because they are being paid. They will take the responsibility of getting the job done and will stand accountable for their work product.

Saving a few dollars on the front end by being a do-it-yourselfer is likely to cost you a bundle. "You can pay me now or pay me later . . . ha, ha" applies to more than oil filters.

The attraction of the one-person corporation is something that seems to be ingrained in the psyche of many tax-conscious, talented people. There is a host of corporate literature which is filled with the glories of the corporation as the absolutely best answer to everyone's tax problems. Unfortunately, many authors and hucksters alike have hyped the corporation to such an extent that many of its viable attributes have been unduly distorted. After an unsuspecting individual incorporates, there is often a day of reckoning where reality replaces false hopes. Many times this occurs when that individual takes time to talk to a tax professional. These are the good cases, because many of the mistakes due to erroneous information can be cured before trouble develops. To be cured by an IRS audit is tantamount to asking for hemlock to treat a headache. The rude awakening of an IRS audit can be very expensive in terms of dollars and time. Use of nonworkable tax gimmicks is a good way to get in trouble fast. Do not believe all of the hype, know the basics, and retain the best of advisers.

Chapter

6

Retirement Plans
Keeping Your Tax Haven at Home

Before TEFRA, the main tax reason that talent incorporated was to take advantage of qualified corporate retirement plans (offered all corporations except those choosing Subchapter S Status). TEFRA changed the rules of the retirement plan game. Today, almost all businesses enjoy the same retirement benefits regardless of whether or not they are incorporated. Congress gave noncorporate entities more retirement benefits and corporate entities less than they already had. This chapter gives you a little history of retirement plans, explains how they work from a tax perspective, and compares retirement plans before TEFRA to those that are available today.

A Little History

What They Are, How They Come About, and Why Congress Favors Them

A qualified retirement plan is a strict legal arrangement which provides retirement, disability, and death benefits and which qualifies for special tax benefits under the Internal Revenue Code. All qualified retirement plans have four distinct tax benefits:

> Contributions made to a qualified plan are income tax deductible.
>
> Any income earned on assets in a retirement plan is not subject to current income tax; it accumulates income tax–free.
>
> The assets in a qualified plan and any income earned on them are only taxed when they are taken out of the plan.
>
> The first $100,000 of proceeds from qualified plans can avoid the federal estate tax.

Qualified retirement plans are very technical legal documents that few people can stand to read, let alone understand. Despite all the legal mumbo jumbo in these plans and congressional efforts to make them understandable, it seems that their true character has been obscured from all but a few specialists who try, without much success, to explain them to nonexperts. Once you understand the theory behind them, however, they should not seem so difficult.

A qualified retirement plan is an employer's attempt to give a retirement benefit to certain employees. But the benefit is tempered with what many have called "golden handcuffs." The employer does not want to give these benefits outright because once given, employees can leave, taking their retirement benefits with them. In most cases, employers want to cover only certain classes of employees, such as shareholder-employees or management personnel. In the case of the incorporated talent, the obvious goal is to cover that talent.

The employer also wants to receive a current tax deduction for those amounts which are put into the retirement plan. This is where the term "qualified" plays such an important role. Under traditional tax law, a deduction can only be taken by a business if someone else takes that same amount into income. Since the recipient of a retirement benefit does not receive the amount of the benefit when it is paid into a retirement plan, the recipient does not want to take the amount into income. On the other hand, the employer definitely wants a current deduction for the dollars put into the plan.

The Internal Revenue Code solves this deduction dilemma by setting forth complex rules which, when followed, qualify the plan. This qualification gives the employer a current income tax deduction and delays the time when the employee must report his or her taxable income. As always seems to be the case under our tax laws, the rules to qualify these plans (for what seem to be pretty straightforward and reasonable tax benefits) have gotten somewhat out of hand. To better understand how these complexities have evolved—and why—let us look at their history.

Almost since the inception of the federal income tax, corporations have provided retirement plans to their employees. The problems of providing these early retirement benefits were much the same as we discussed above. The company wanted to deduct the amounts it paid against its taxable income. It wanted to benefit, in most cases, only some of its employees, usually those who were shareholders or were higher up in the echelons of management. Corporations wanted to assure themselves that no employee would actually receive a benefit before retirement. They wanted to delay taxation on the benefits to the employees until those benefits were actually paid.

Prior to 1921, there were no rules governing any of the tax benefits or detriments of retirement plans. The absence of formal retirement rules created a tax planner's dream, and professional advisers implemented every conceivable form of retirement plan. Payments to these plans were made under the auspices of the "ordinary and necessary business expense" provision of the first Internal Revenue Code and were therefore considered tax deductible. Employees, more often than not, never bothered to take these benefits into income on the basis that you ought not pay taxes on something until it is in hand.

There were real abuses in the use of these retirement plans. Corporations would put a tremendous amount of money in these plans with the intent of never paying a benefit, except to a few key managers who were coincidentally the shareholders of the corporation. The plans were, in many cases, flagrant attempts at tax evasion.

The Revenue Act of 1921 was the first in what has turned out to be a long line of tax acts covering retirement benefits. This act was aimed at eliminating some of the abuse and confusion surrounding retirement plans. It provided for the tax-free accumulation of retirement funds and attempted to delineate when employees were to be taxed on their retirement benefits.

Congress made another stab at defining the retirement plan rules in 1928. This was its first attempt to specify what retirement amounts could be deducted. It also more clearly explained how a plan had to be set up, including the establishment of a separate employees' trust.

The 1928 law did not begin to eliminate the abuses of retirement plans. Employees were still, in the main, not receiving what their plans promised. The amounts employers were deducting were still subject to some question, and discrimination in favor of shareholders and executive employees was still prevalent.

In 1942, the first pension legislation of any scope was passed. The 1942 law was really Congress's first major attempt at reforming the retirement laws. Most of the pension concepts we use today are remnants of the 1942 law. The whole tenor of the 1942 act was to eliminate the use of a retirement plan as a tax shelter and to reconstitute retirement plans as legitimate employee benefits. More definite limits as to the amounts employers could deduct, as well as requirements as to which employees had to be covered, were included in the law. It was truly a congressional attempt to more equitably apply retirement plans to the American worker.

Rightly or wrongly, the loopholes left in the aftermath of the 1942 law were not insignificant. While corporations lost some of the benefits they were previously enjoying, they still retained wide latitude for using their retirement plans for tax shelter and tax avoidance.

Up to this point we have referred to corporations when we have discussed the retirement plan as a tax shelter. What about partnerships and sole proprietorships? That is another story in and of itself. Ever since the income tax laws were passed, retirement benefits, as well as most fringe benefits, have been designed to provide for employees. Partners and sole proprietors have never been considered employees; they work for themselves. Because they are not employees, they were not allowed to participate in traditional retirement plans. The nonowner employees of partnerships and sole proprietorships could be in a plan, but not owners. In order for business owners to be included in a retirement plan, they had to be doing business as a corporation.

This exclusion of partners and sole proprietors continued despite significant outcries and intense lobbying efforts until 1962. In 1962, the Self-Employed Individuals Tax Retirement Act was passed. This law, also known as "HR-10," allowed limited retirement plans for self-employed citizens. These Keogh plans (named after the congressman who cosponsored the bill) allowed a contribution of up to $2500 per year for self-employed individuals. This amount was a far cry from the limits allowed for corporate plans and was lower than the original bill Congressman Keogh proposed; his bill would have allowed a $10,000 contribution. This lowering of benefits led detractors to refer to the bill as passed as HR-2½. Not only was the contribution not very high, but in addition, the administrative limitations placed on these plans were far greater than those on their corporate counterparts

Similar contribution limitations were also extended to the shareholder-employees of Subchapter S corporations. While Subchapter S corporation plans had somewhat more flexibility than true Keogh plans, the shareholder-employee of a Subchapter S corporation was still not on par with the shareholder-employee of a regular corporation.

In 1974, the first major reform of all the pension laws since the 1942 act was passed. The Employee Retirement Income Security Act of 1974 (ERISA) was legislation aimed at curbing the continuing abuses under the retirement plan laws. ERISA extended coverage of qualified plans to more Americans and, more importantly, attempted to assure plan members that their expected retirement benefits would be there for them at retirement.

The immediate effect of ERISA was the termination of a great number of qualified plans. Many employers felt that the provisions of ERISA increased the administrative expense of their plans to such a degree that their use became economically prohibitive. Thankfully, this was a short-term effect. As a result of ERISA, in our opinion, many Americans received their promised retirement benefits and the abuses of their administration by employers and labor unions alike were sharply and decisively curtailed.

ERISA increased Keogh plan contributions to $7500 per year. It also put a new lid on the dollars that could be put into qualified corporate plans. The maximum amount allowed for most plans was $25,000, but this amount was to be adjusted each year based on the consumer price index. Keogh plans and plans for Subchapter S shareholder-employees were *not* given the benefit of this indexed inflation protection.

Individual retirement accounts (IRAs) were another product of ERISA. These accounts, for the first time, allowed all Americans not covered by a qualified plan to have their own retirement plan, complete with income tax deductibility. The maximum contribution was $1500 per person or $1750 if a nonworking spouse was covered.

ERISA was indeed a major piece of legislation. Many professionals quickly predicted that it would either be the end of private retirement plans or, at the very least, the last piece of legislation that would be passed affecting their use. They were dead wrong on both counts.

Changes affecting qualified retirement plans have been coming at a rate unsurpassed in our income tax history. One of the major changes occurred in 1981, when Congress passed the Economic Recovery Tax Act (ERTA). ERTA increased the allowable contributions to Keogh plans and to Subchapter S plans to a maximum of $15,000 per person. This 100 percent increase in the contribution maximum was far less than the maximum for corporate plans. The maximum for a corporate employee was $45,375, after the inflation adjustment was taken into account. The increase was, however, indicative of the congressional mood—equality for all—or at least sort of equality for all. ERTA even increased the maximum IRA contribution to $2000, a change that was not dramatic but was helpful to many Americans hurt by inflation. In addition, IRAs were extended to all citizens, whether or not they were covered by another plan.

On August 13, 1982, one year to the day after the passage of ERTA, Congress passed the Tax Equity and Fiscal Responsibility Act (TEFRA). TEFRA, like ERTA, was awesome. Once again, Congress had managed to change most of the rules. Seasoned professional tax advisers began to consider seriously the merits of early retirement: their own. Enough was enough. Congress had redone, in the space of a couple of years, what it had taken decades to previously create; tax minds, ours included, were short-circuiting.

TEFRA made three major legislative thrusts into changing the nation's retirement plan procedures:

Highly paid talented individuals (just highly paid as far as Congress was concerned) would have to take reduced retirement benefits.

Corporate retirement plan rules and programs became available to partners and sole proprietors. The exclusivity of the corporate employee in the world of retirement was at an end.

The ability of retirement plan participants to use their retirement funds prior to actual retirement was sharply curtailed.

TEFRA has intensified the argument with regard to the validity of our social security system. Many professionals believe that our social security system, as historically structured, is doomed to failure and collapse; that TEFRA is but the first of much legislation to come which will broaden the private pension sector; that it is but a matter of time until private business will have to provide mandatory private retirement benefits for all their employees.

There can be absolutely no doubt that Congress has looked upon retirement plans as the prodigal child. Qualified deferred compensation plans have, in the main, been congressional darlings for years. Unfortunately, however, Congress has become a stern parent with regard to its more talented children (or should we say, an envious parent?). It has shown a new penchant for substantially reducing the benefits of our more successful citizens. This penchant may or may not affect the incorporating motives of successful talent.

In this chapter we discuss how retirement plans work, how they can be differentiated from one another, and how they can be used to produce the desired tax result. We compare the arguments, pro and con, to their use (both on a pre- and post-TEFRA basis). If you do not understand retirement plans, you will not understand why corporations *were* considered the ultimate tax shelter prior to TEFRA. If you are incorporated in a one-person talent corporation, this chapter will help you decide whether to continue in your corporate activity, and if you are not incorporated, it will show you how the new law will affect your decision of whether to incorporate or not.

The Single Best Tax Shelter

"So what's the big deal about retirement plans? What do they do, except tie up my money until I retire?" These questions and many more like them are asked by our clients all too frequently. Too frequently, because if better understood, people would realize that retirement plans just may be *the best* tax shelter that money can buy.

A tax shelter is any *investment* which either eliminates income tax or, at least, defers that tax to a later time when, it is hoped, the income will be taxed in a lower bracket. We emphasize the word "investment" because it is our experience that most so-called shelters have little, if any, possibility of generating an economic profit, let alone the likelihood of returning the original investment back to our client. Sure, there are exceptions, but if your experiences are like ours, the good shelters are few and far between. Many so-called tax shelters involve substantial risk: the risk of losing more than one's original investment and/or the risk that the tax deduction is disallowed, because the tax theory just does not pan out. When compared to these other tax shelters, the qualified retirement plan is, more often than not, much more attractive.

The qualified retirement plan offers four distinct advantages (we referred to them earlier in this chapter) to the successful talent. The first is income tax deductibility, a concept that is critical to every tax shelter.

A contribution made to a qualified plan, whether it is a corporate, partnership, or individual plan, is a tax deduction against the income of the entity or person making the contribution. For example:

Price Corporation, a one-person corporation, with Paul Price as its sole owner and shareholder, has income subject to taxation of $130,000. The federal income tax due is $39,550. If the corporation contributes $30,000 to a qualified retirement plan, the tax is reduced to $25,750. The tax saving is $13,800. That is $13,800 that goes into the pocket of the only employee, Paul Price, not into the hands of the federal government.

Irene Adkins is an individual who owns a sole proprietorship. Her taxable income is $200,000, of which at least $30,000 will be taxed in the 50 percent federal income tax bracket, generating a tax of $15,000. If Irene contributes $30,000 to a qualified retirement plan, she will reduce her tax burden by $15,000 and put $30,000 away for her retirement.

The second tax benefit of a qualified plan is tax-free accumulation of the funds in the plan. This is an incredible tax benefit. In our opinion, it destroys the assumption of many professionals that retirement plans only defer rather than avoid tax. We make this statement based on our example in Table 6-1. This table shows what can happen when a taxpayer in a 50 percent federal income tax bracket decides to use a retirement plan in lieu of a personal savings account. It compares the growth of $10,000 placed in each, where the interest earned is 10 percent. Keep in mind that the $10,000 investment *is not* tax deductible when put into a savings account but is deductible if put into a qualified retirement plan. Also, remember that the money in the qualified plan accumulates income tax–free.

At the end of twenty years, the dollar difference between the two approaches is stunning, and that may be an understatement. There is more than three times as much cash available in the retirement plan than in the conventional savings account. The tax-free accumulation of tax deductible funds in the retirement plan makes a tremendous difference.

The third tax benefit that is afforded by a qualified retirement plan is the delay in taxation of the amounts in the plan. In Table 6-1, the taxes on the savings account were paid each year both on the contribution and on the interest earned. Because those taxes were paid each year, there was less in the savings account to accumulate. This amount did not accumulate as fast because the taxes halved the rate of return from 10 percent before taxation to 5 percent after taxation. Thus at the end of twenty years, there was far less in the savings account.

The funds in the qualified retirement plan are subject to income taxation. This income taxation occurs in the future and does not have the effect of reducing the growth rate of the fund on a current basis.

Table 6-1. Comparison of a Savings Account to a Qualified Plan, as to an Individual in the 50% Tax Bracket, with $10,000 Invested at 10% Interest over 20 Years

Year	Savings Account*	Qualified Plan†	
1	$ 5,000	$ 10,000	Contribution
	250	1,000	Interest
	$ 5,250	$ 11,000	Total for year
2	$ 5,000	$ 10,000	Contribution
	10,250	21,000	Total funds
	513	2,100	Interest
	$ 10,763	$ 23,100	Total
5	$ 5,000	$ 10,000	Contribution
	27,629	61,051	Total funds
	1,381	6,105	Interest
	$ 29,010	$ 67,156	Total
10	$ 5,000	$ 10,000	Contribution
	62,891	159,374	Total funds
	3,145	15,937	Interest
	$ 66,036	$175,311	Total
15	$ 5,000	$ 10,000	Contribution
	107,895	317,725	Total funds
	5,395	31,772	Interest
	$113,290	$349,497	Total
20	$ 5,000	$ 10,000	Contribution
	165,333	572,749	Total funds
	8,267	57,275	Interest
	$173,600	$630,024	Total

* These are *aftertax* amounts in this column.
† These are *before-tax* amounts in this column.

The end result is that the retirement plan grows, or compounds, as our banker friends say, at a much faster rate.

The real test of whether or not a retirement plan works is whether it provides more aftertax dollars to the investor talent. How much is in each fund after both are adjusted for federal income taxes? If we assume that the retirement funds are in a 50 percent federal income tax bracket (this is the maximum personal income tax bracket, as we write this) at the end of twenty years, there is still a fund of $315,012 (50 percent of $630,024). The savings account has only $173,600—a difference of $141,412!

Many professionals will tell you that the difference is because of the principles of tax deferral. We tell you that the extra $141,412 is tax-free, pure and simple. There is, under our example, $141,412 available by using a qualified retirement plan: That is a tax-free savings in our book.

The fourth tax benefit indigenous to qualified plans deals with the federal estate tax. Under the law before TEFRA, the full amount of the proceeds of a qualified plan received by a beneficiary upon the death of a plan participant could be preserved totally free of the federal estate tax. TEFRA devastated this tax benefit. Now, only the first $100,000 can be exempt from the federal estate tax and then only under restricted circumstances. While for many Americans this is still a tax benefit, it does represent an erosion in the favored status of qualified retirement plans.

The tax advantages of qualified retirement plans are, as you can see, fairly massive. To review, these advantages are:

Income tax deductible

Income tax–free accumulation

Deferral of tax, which creates tax-free income

A possible $100,000 exemption from federal estate tax

To understand fully how the tax benefits created by qualified retirement plans apply to the one-person talent corporation, it is important that you have a grasp of how these plans work and are distinguished from one another.

The Different Kinds of Retirement Plans and How They Work

One of the primary reasons successful talent incorporated over the years was in order to take advantage of the income tax savings that resulted from using corporate retirement plans. The decision as to whether or not to incorporate a particular talent usually boiled down to a single issue in the offices of most advisers: Was the talent better off for income tax purposes with or without specific retirement plans? Most advisers would calculate a talent's tax liability with and then without corporate retirement plan deductions; if the difference was substantial enough, the talent would bite his or her lip and say, "I'd better incorporate."

Once again Congress has both muddied and fouled the tax

waters. Because of TEFRA, most of the rules that professional advisers traditionally relied on when making their incorporation recommendation have changed. Now, more than ever, the successful talent should understand the basics of retirement planning prior to making the incorporation decision. The days of making simple tax calculations are over.

In order to assist you in understanding retirement plans, we will do the following:

> *Explain the differences between various retirement plans apropos for talent.*
>
> *Describe what they could and could not do for talent over the years.*
>
> *Highlight the changes brought about by the new law.*

In attempting to meet our goals, we will simplify extremely technical and complex concepts. As we lay out the basics, resist the temptation to skip ahead; please stay with us, your understanding will be much the better for it.

All retirement plans operate within the same basic framework:

The employer puts away funds for the eventual use of the employee.

The employer takes a current income tax deduction equal to the value of those funds.

The employee does not pay immediate income tax on the employer's contribution or on the income those funds generate.

The employer cannot use the funds once they are contributed, and they will not be subject to the claims of the employer's creditors.

The employee, with some notable exceptions, cannot use the funds for his or her benefit until retirement.

The funds are not subject to the claims of the employee's creditors and cannot be assigned or pledged by the employee.

The funds must be safely invested and managed for the employee. Basic fund transactions must be reported annually to the Internal Revenue Service.

In order for the above principles to work, the employer must arrive at a formula or method that will enable it to determine the amount that will be contributed for the employee. Retirement plans can be differentiated, from one another, based on the contribution method that is selected by the employer.

One of two fundamental approaches has been generally used in configuring a talent's retirement plan. The first is designed to enable the employer to fund the employee's retirement plan based on a percentage of the employee's compensation. This percentage is in addition to the employee's regular compensation. It is defined by the employer and is therefore referred to as a "defined contribution plan"; the employer makes *defined contributions*. The second allows the employer to select the benefit the employee will receive when he or she actually retires. Since it allows the employer to define the employee's retirement benefit, it is called a "defined benefit retirement plan."

The differences generated by these two approaches are massive. Each method is used to accomplish different tax-planning objectives. In order to assist you in visualizing the basic difference between them, let us look at the following examples:

Herb Cook is the shareholder-employee of his own corporation. Herb's salary is $100,000 a year. The decision is made to put 10 percent of Herb's compensation into his retirement plan. Herb's corporation contributes $10,000 to the retirement fund. (If Herb's salary was $150,000, $15,000 would be put into the fund.)

The initial $10,000 contribution will grow in value through investment. Neither it nor its investment growth will be taxed while in the retirement fund.

Herb will not be able to predict how much that $10,000 will earn over the years, nor will he be able to predict what the value of future contributions will be. His compensation might go up, or then again, it might go down. Both Herb and his advisers do know that on Herb's retirement, Herb will have funds in his plan (assuming they have not been lost or reduced through poor investment), plus the earnings from those funds. They do not know what the amount of the fund will be on that day.

The amount of the employer's contribution has been defined (10 percent of Herb's compensation), not the precise dollar amount of the retirement benefit that Herb will receive.

Let us differentiate the above example with the following:

Sarah Smith is a friend of Herb's and is a successful author. Her compensation is also $100,000 a year. Both Sarah and her advisers want to design a retirement plan for Sarah that will provide her with 50 percent of her salary to be paid to her annually after her retirement.

Sarah and her advisers know the benefit they want her to have. They do not know how much money has to be put away over time to provide that benefit.

They must seek the services of an actuary (specialized mathematician) who will calculate on an annual basis exactly how much money has to be put away in order for Sarah to meet her objectives.

The amount of Sarah's retirement *benefit* has been defined (50 percent of her annual compensation), rather than just the employer's current contribution.

Our examples of Herb and Sarah should enable you to conceptualize the difference between a defined contribution and a defined benefit retirement plan. Given this foundation, let us take a closer look at each.

Defined Contribution Plans

There are two basic types of defined contribution plans that have frequently been used by incorporated talent. These are called profit sharing plans and money purchase pension plans. The major difference between the two hinges on the concept of flexibility, as it applies to the annual contribution made to the plan by the employer.

Profit Sharing Plans. As their name implies, profit sharing plans allow an employer to share its profits with its employees. Typically, an employer makes a contribution for the employee based on a percentage of the employee's compensation (just like in the case of Herb Cook). The percentage is determined by the employer on an annual basis. In a high-profit year, the employer might decide to make a 15 percent contribution (the legal maximum). In a mediocre year, the employer might elect to make a lesser contribution. In fact, the employer might elect not to make any contribution.

Profit sharing plans are flexible because the amount of the employer's contribution can vary from year to year. Even if the employer makes a healthy profit, there is no mandate that a contribution be made to the plan. Nor does a bad year necessarily mean that a healthy contribution will not be made. The fact is that profit sharing plans enable the employer to decide what annual percentage it will contribute to the plan; that percentage can be as high as 15 percent or as low as zero. They provide much comfort for the employer, not necessarily for the employees. In the case of the one-person talent, the comfort obviously goes both ways.

Under the pre-TEFRA law a talent that had a profit sharing plan could contribute the lesser of 15 percent of compensation or $45,475. Today that same talent is limited to the lesser of 15 percent of compensation or $30,000. Beginning in 1986, the $30,000 can be adjusted for increases in the cost of living.

Money Purchase Pension Plans.   Money purchase pension plans work just like profit sharing plans. The employer puts a percentage of the employee's compensation into the plan on an annual basis. There is, however, one notable and crucial difference between the two; the employer has little flexibility with regard to the amount of the contribution it makes to the retirement fund.

If an employer selects a money purchase pension plan, it must pick a percentage it will contribute on behalf of the employee. Once that percentage is selected, it cannot be reduced. It can be increased, but once it is, the new amount cannot be decreased in later years. The employer's inability to reduce the percentage amount from year to year is the flaw in these types of plans.

One might wonder why any employer would ever select a money purchase pension plan, in lieu of a profit sharing plan. The answer is that a higher percentage of the employee's compensation can be put away for the employee on an annual basis by use of a money purchase pension plan. Under the pre-TEFRA law a talent that had a money purchase pension plan could contribute the lesser of 25 percent of compensation or $45,475. Today that same talent is limited to the lesser of 25 percent of compensation or $30,000 (adjusted for increases in the cost of living beginning in 1986).

Traditionally, money purchase pension plans have enabled employers to make contributions on behalf of their employees which exceed profit sharing limits by as much as 60 percent (25 percent of compensation versus 15 percent). The old adage "if a little is good, more is better" would certainly fit this type of plan. This is especially true when comparing it to its profit sharing counterpart. The following example should clarify this difference.

Ted Miller is an architect who works for his own corporation. Ted is paid $100,000 a year and has a 25 percent money purchase pension plan. Ted's corporation must therefore put away an additional $25,000 for Ted in his retirement plan.

Two years after Ted's corporation instituted its plan, good went to bad. Ted had a disastrous year and his corporation lost money. As a result, Ted did not wish to make the $25,000 contribution to his plan required on his $100,000 salary (his corporation just did not have the money).

Ted's advisers had some bad news for Ted: His corporation would either make the $25,000 contribution, ask the IRS for formal permission to waive the contribution because of business hardship, pay a penalty if the contribution is not made or is late, or even potentially invalidate his entire plan.

Ted now wonders if the extra contribution benefit of his money purchase plan was worth it. If he had elected to use a profit sharing plan, he would not have to make a contribution.

Money purchase pension plans allow the employer to put away more, but they also exact a price in return. Once you start with a money purchase pension plan, it is hard to stop.

A Combination of Plans. A third type of defined contribution retirement plan simply combines the other two. Let us assume that a talent wanted to obtain the larger benefits of a money purchase pension plan but also wanted the flexibility of a profit sharing plan. With these goals in mind, a combination plan could be designed so that both plans would be used. The money purchase pension would be fixed at 10 percent of compensation, the profit sharing plan at a maximum of 15 percent of compensation. This would allow a total of 25 percent to be contributed in a good year and 10 percent in a bad year. This combination of plans has given many an incorporated talent a partial opportunity to have the best of both.

When using a combination of plans, the maximum that can currently be contributed under the new law for the talent is $30,000 or 25 percent of the talent's annual compensation, whichever is less. Using both plans does not increase the allowable contribution; it just provides more flexibility.

Under the combination approach, Ted's situation would be dramatically different:

Ted's corporation could still make a $25,000 contribution in each of the first two years (25 percent of Ted's salary).

In the disastrous third year, Ted's corporation would only have to make a 10 percent contribution, rather than a 25 percent contribution. Ted's corporation could decide that it would not make a profit sharing contribution.

Because Ted chose the combination route, he was able to reduce his funding liability by $15,000, a 60 percent reduction.

The alternative of a combination of plans can maximize contributions in good years and minimize contributions in bad years. This approach is more flexible than a single money purchase pension plan and less flexible than a single profit sharing plan.

Defined Benefit Plans

A defined benefit pension plan enables an employer to define the retirement benefit that an employee will receive. All defined benefit plans have the same general parameters, but every plan is different depending on the configuration sought by the employer.

This type of retirement plan is rarely understood by nonexpert professionals, due to the fact that so many technical terms are used to explain it. This is regrettable and need not be the case.

Please remember that an employer using this approach simply chooses to define the benefit its employees will ultimately receive. This benefit is usually defined in terms of a percentage of compensation (50 percent of the highest three years' wages, for example) or as a designated dollar amount.

In selecting this approach, the employer is defining the benefit it wishes to contribute, not the precise amount of the contribution. Its contributions will be determined by the calculations of actuaries.

There is *no* direct limitation on the amount of contribution that the employer can make. The legal limitations are rather on the benefit the employee may receive.

The pre-TEFRA rule was that the benefit could not be higher than the average of the employee's top three consecutive years of compensation. In addition, the benefit could not exceed $75,000 per year, adjusted for inflation; the inflation-adjusted dollar amount before TEFRA was passed was $136,425. Just think, talent could retire on an income of $136,425 a year. Today this no longer remains the case.

The dollar amount has been reduced to $90,000, a reduction of $46,425. The $90,000 will, however, be adjusted for inflation beginning in 1986.

The employer must select a "benefit formula" when using a defined benefit pension plan. The formula will describe the benefit the employee is supposed to receive on retirement. Most formulas take into account the age of the employee, the age at which the employee plans to retire, and the amount of the employee's salary. Defined benefit pension plans absolutely require the services of an actuary. Once the actuary is given this information, he or she mathematically calculates how much money needs to be currently contributed in order to provide the desired benefit on the employee's retirement.

Actuaries must obviously use many assumptions in plying their trade. These generally include anticipated increases or decreases in the employee's salary, investment yields, revised dates of retirement, inflation, and other factors. The actuary constantly changes the assumptions from year to year as the reality of experience is monitored. Actuaries tend defined benefit pension plans like shepherds tend flocks; the actuary is seldom far away and is constantly coordinating the direction in which the flock is moving.

Combining a Defined Benefit Plan and a Defined Contribution Plan

Prior to TEFRA, there was an advantage for one-person corporations to combine a defined benefit plan with a money purchase pension plan. This combination could greatly increase the total contribution (deduction) allowable to the talent. Under TEFRA, this advantage has been eliminated for one-person corporations. While the plans can still be combined, there is no longer an ability to increase the contribution. For those who have the two-plan system, we would advise eliminating the money purchase plan. Since the increased contribution can no longer be used, there is little reason to face the expense of having two plans when one can do the job.

Combining a defined benefit plan and a profit sharing plan is not particularly a good idea. Because of our pension laws both before and after TEFRA, this combination can actually reduce the amount of contribution that could be taken if a defined contribution plan was used alone. The only advantage of using the combined defined benefit plan and profit sharing plan is to inject a little flexibility into planning. Rarely is this a good enough reason to limit the size of the deduction in a defined benefit plan.

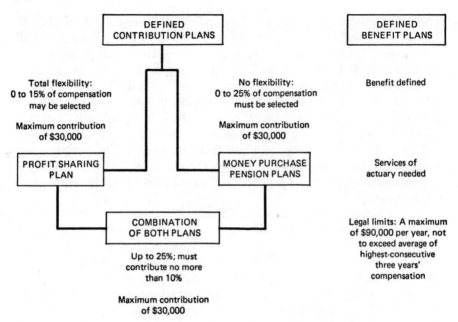

Figure 6-1 Basic retirement plan formats used by successful talent.

Figure 6-1 should put these different retirement plan alternatives in perspective for you.

Now that you have a background in the types of retirement plans used by successful talent, let us take a closer look at each of them. It is important that you understand the basic rules of these plans. We strongly believe, as a result of too many bad experiences, that successful talents can undergo undue levels of tension, anxiety, and even economic hardship because they *do not* understand the basics of their retirement planning. Retirement plans, like a loaded gun, can kill the person using them if not properly used.

When to Use Defined Contribution Plans

Defined contribution plan rules limit the amounts that can be contributed to the employee's plan each year. The maximum amount that could be contributed to all defined contribution plans for an employee prior to the new law was $25,000, adjusted for inflation. Because of the inflation adjustment, $45,475 could be contributed in 1982, almost double the preinflation amount.

Congress reduced the amount that can be put into profit sharing or money purchase pension plans. The new maximum under TEFRA is $30,000, a reduction of $15,475 from the prior law. This is very disappointing. It represents, in our opinion, an attack on the ability of higher-paid citizens to put away funds commensurate with their income for their eventual retirement.

The $30,000 maximum contribution rule also applies to a combination of plans. Thus regardless of the type of defined contribution plan selected, the maximum a talent can put away is $30,000.

In our opinion, Congress took away too much from talented people. It did, however, throw talent a small bone; beginning in 1986 the $30,000 will again be adjusted for inflation.

Following is a review of the defined contribution plan rules, before and after TEFRA:

There are two types of defined contribution retirement plans: profit sharing plans and money purchase pension plans. Both remain today.

A profit sharing plan had a limitation of 15 percent of an employee's compensation, not to exceed $45,475. The percentage remains the same, but the maximum amount has been reduced to $30,000.

A profit sharing plan remains flexible; the contribution can be changed each year at the corporation's discretion.

A money purchase pension plan still has a percentage limitation of 25 percent of an employee's compensation. Under the old law, the contribution could not exceed $45,475. Today the dollar limitation is $30,000.

A money purchase pension plan remains inflexible. The percentage that an employer selects cannot be reduced in subsequent years without a lot of red tape.

A profit sharing plan and a money purchase pension plan can still be combined. The maximum that can be contributed for both plans remains at 25 percent of an employee's compensation.

Under the old law, the contribution could not exceed $45,475 Today the dollar amount cannot exceed $30,000.

Successful talents making at least $200,000 per year should choose a profit sharing plan over a money purchase pension plan, in order to maximize their contribution ($30,000) and retain maximum flexibility.

Successful talents making less than $200,000 per year should either select a money purchase pension plan or a combination of plans to maximize their contribution. Either alternative can generate a 25 percent contribution. The advantage of selecting just a money purchase pension plan would be that only one plan is used. The cost of a single plan in terms of legal, accounting, and administrative fees is less than using a combination of plans. The disadvantage would be that a single money purchase pension plan is less flexible than a combination of plans. In our opinion, the combination of plans is the superior approach for the talent earning less than $200,000, because of flexibility.

If a successful talent wants to put away more than $30,000 a year and is not concerned about maximum flexibility, he or she should consider using a defined benefit plan.

When to Use Defined Benefit Plans

Defined benefit pension plans allow professional advisers to be extremely creative when attempting to generate sizable income tax deductions and retirement benefits for the talent corporation. The reason is because there is no limitation on the amount that an employer can contribute and deduct when making the contribution. The only limitation is on the benefit the employee will receive on retirement.

TEFRA dealt a significant blow to the economic future of successful talent who were already using qualified retirement plans. This is particularly true in the case of those talents who were making maximum contributions to their defined benefit plans. The reduction in the amount of the retirement benefit from $136,425 to $90,000 has hurt. The $90,000 retirement is attractive, but $46,425 less attractive than it could have looked, absent a congressional zeal to take away from the fortunate. The defined benefit plan still represents a wonderful way to put away large sums of tax-free dollars.

Following is a review of the basics of defined benefit retirement plans:

There is generally no limit on the amount of the employer's contribution. This can provide extremely sizable current income tax deductions to the talent's company.

They are used to provide a specific retirement benefit that is usually expressed as a percentage of compensation.

Prior to TEFRA, the benefit limitation was the average of the three highest consecutive years of compensation, not to exceed $136,425. Today the dollar limitation is $90,000, which will be adjusted for inflation commencing in 1986.

Older individuals should strongly consider using a defined benefit plan because this type of plan allows them to make up for lost ground. Larger contributions can be made over the remaining preretirement years in order to fund the retirement benefit properly. This would be impossible to do with any kind of defined contribution plan.

The following example should assist you in understanding this point:

Jessica Johnson, 55 years of age, is a successful artist. Her paintings and sculptures have finally caught the public's fancy. For the last two years she has been making over $100,000 per year and has paid too much to Uncle Sam.

If we assume that she will probably retire at age 65 (at least for purposes of collecting her pension plan proceeds), there would only be ten years over which she could contribute enough dollars to amass a retirement fund that would pay her $90,000 a year for the rest of her life.

Contrast Jessica's situation with that of Isadora Imes, a brilliant 24-year-old scriptwriter:

Isadora Imes is earning $250,000 writing scripts for popular television series. If she elected to use a defined benefit retirement plan, she would have forty-one years over which to contribute enough money to retire on $90,000 a year.

Isadora should probably look to using a defined contribution plan to build her retirement fund and reduce her income tax. If she uses a defined benefit plan, her annual contributions will be small because she has so many years to build her retirement fund.

Defined benefit pension plans, in our experience, work beautifully for anyone over 45 years of age who can afford to place a very high

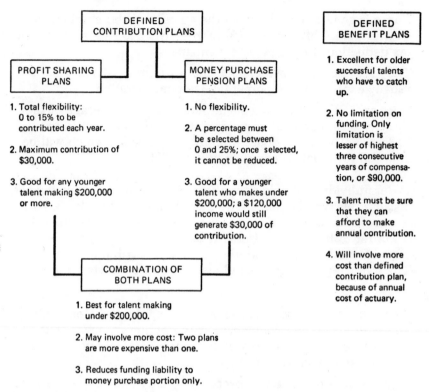

Figure 6-2 Application of basic retirement plan formats for successful talent.

percentage of income into a retirement plan. In fact, anyone 40 years of age and older should have professionals "run the numbers" to see whether a defined benefit plan will produce better tax and economic results than a defined contribution plan.

The ability of a successful talent to make the required defined benefit contributions is a critical issue that must be addressed prior to implementing such a plan. We have represented some incredibly successful talents who demanded that we reduce their income tax liability. When we did and they were "soaking away" tens of thousands of tax-free dollars in their plans, they soon found out that the disposable income they had left was not enough to support their lifestyle. Believe it or not, one can do too much income tax planning.

Figure 6-2 should put all these rules in perspective.

Important Retirement-Planning Features

Of the many rules that apply to retirement plans, we have selected a few which, because of their significance to the successful talent, should be highlighted. These include borrowing from retirement plans, vesting plan funds, integrating retirement plans with social security, voluntary contributions, and the penalty for taking your retirement funds before you retire.

Borrowing from Retirement Plans

Prior to the passage of TEFRA, most of our clients who incorporated their talents borrowed significant sums from their retirement plans. If they properly borrowed from their retirement plans, they could generate additional tax benefits and utilize the borrowed proceeds for other investment opportunities. Prior to TEFRA, the borrowing game was generally played as follows:

The talent's corporation would contribute money to the talent's plan (income tax deduction number one).

The talent would borrow the money from the plan and pay the plan interest (income tax deduction number two).

The talent would invest the money in a good investment and pay the plan back from the profit on that investment. When the talent paid the plan interest and principal, the plan did not have to pay any income tax.

In essence, under the old borrowing rules, talent would, in reality, borrow their own money, pay themselves interest, and deduct the interest. The retirement funds were used with tremendous tax benefits. Borrowing one's retirement funds was good business until 1983.

As a result of TEFRA, there are now strict parameters on borrowing from one's retirement plan. The maximum that can be borrowed is one-half of one's vested account, not to exceed $50,000. There is, however, an exception to this rule. Up to $10,000 can be borrowed even if $10,000 exceeds one-half of the account. *All* loans must be paid back within five years unless the loan proceeds are used to acquire or improve a residence for the participant or the participant's immediate family members.

If a plan participant uses the funds to acquire, construct, or substantially rehabilitate the principal residence of the participant or a family member (brothers, sisters, spouse, descendants, or ancestors), the loan does not have to be paid back within five years.

This exception creates an excellent opportunity for the talent to use his or her retirement plan as an additional tax savings device. For example:

> Digger Spade, an incorporated geologist, wants to purchase a new home. Digger's corporation has a profit sharing plan that currently has $75,000 invested in bank certificates of deposit. Digger has $100,000 of personal savings and wants to purchase a $150,000 home.
>
> Since Digger can only put $100,000 down on his new home, he will have to obtain a $50,000 mortgage. His local bank will loan him the money for twenty years at 15 percent interest. If Digger borrows the money from his bank, it will earn the interest on the loan in addition to getting the $50,000 repaid. Digger will receive an income tax deduction for the interest payments.
>
> Digger's tax attorney advises him to borrow the money from his corporation's profit sharing plan, which Digger did. He gave his profit sharing plan a twenty-year mortgage at 15 percent interest. As a result, Digger saved money.
>
> The interest payments that Digger will make to his plan are not income taxable to the plan, and Digger can still deduct them on his personal return. In effect, Digger will be paying himself interest, which he will deduct, in one pocket, while receiving it tax-free in his other pocket. Digger is obviously pleased with his tax counsel; paying oneself is always good business, but getting a tax savings in addition is even better business.

This exception in the loan repayment rules should be utilized, if at all possible, by all incorporated talents. It represents an excellent opportunity to legally self-deal and save tax at the same time.

The new TEFRA borrowing rules make it clear that any talent should make absolutely sure that he or she can maintain their lifestyle without the use of retirement plan contributions. Congress, by changing the rules, has made it more than clear that the sums placed in these plans are to remain in them until retirement.

Table 6-2.   Vesting Schedules Under TEFRA

Years of Employment	Percent Vested
1	0
2	20
3	40
4	60
5	80
6	100

Vesting Plan Funds

Vesting means that the funds contributed by an employer to a plan do not immediately belong to the employee but will belong to that employee over a specified period of time. The idea behind vesting is to make sure that an employee stays with the employer for a period of time according to a specified formula.

Vesting is not important in the pure one-person talent enterprise. If the talent is the only employee, the talent's plan may as well vest the plan contributions immediately. If, however, the talent has other employees, vesting can become very important.

Prior to TEFRA, vesting schedules were seldom shorter than ten years when incorporated talent had other employees. As a result of the new TEFRA rules, a vesting schedule cannot be longer than that shown in Table 6-2.

Table 6-2 simply means that if an employee leaves the company in the fourth year and there is $10,000 of contributions and income earned on contributions, the employee would be entitled to $6000 (60 percent of $10,000).

If you have other employees, your retirement plan vesting schedule can be shorter than the one we have described; it cannot be longer. All sums left in the plan by employees who leave the company go to the benefit of the remaining participants (hopefully just you).

Integrating Retirement Plans with Social Security

A talent should never integrate his or her plan with social security unless other employees participate in the talent's retirement plan. Integration is a technical device that reduces the employer's contribution for lower-compensated employees. This technique assumes that social security benefits will be available to a retiring employee and allows an employer to include a percentage of the anticipated social security benefit to offset a portion of the employer's contribution.

The result of integrating one's retirement plan with social security is to give higher-paid employees a higher percentage of the contributed funds. If you have additional employees, this technique should be discussed with your advisers.

Voluntary Contributions

If a successful talent elects to utilize a retirement plan, contributions of additional sums can be made in addition to the sums contributed by the business entity. The sums voluntarily contributed cannot be deducted by the talent. However, the income generated by voluntary contributions will not be taxed until it is ultimately taken out of the plan by the talent. The limitation on voluntary contributions both before and after TEFRA is 10 percent of the employee's annual compensation.

If a successful talent has excess cash to invest, serious consideration should be given to investing it in a retirement plan as a voluntary contribution. If this is done, income could be generated income tax–free. A talent with excess investment cash in a 50 percent personal income tax bracket would double his or her investment return by utilizing this approach.

Voluntary contributions made to a retirement plan can always be taken out of the plan income tax–free. The earnings also can be taken out at any time, but tax will have to be paid on them.

A Penalty for Taking Retirement Funds prior to Retirement

Prior to TEFRA, incorporated talent could terminate retirement plans without paying a penalty tax. The result was that the participants of the plan had to pay income tax on the funds they received in the year they received them.

TEFRA changed this result. If a talent receives retirement funds prior to retirement and before he or she attains 59½ years of age, a penalty tax is assessed. The penalty tax is 10 percent of the amounts received and must be paid in addition to the normal income tax. Congress created the penalty tax in order to encourage the public to leave their funds in their retirement plans.

Table 6-3.   Pre-TEFRA Comparison of Corporate and Keogh Retirement Plans

Maximum Benefits Allowed	Corporate Retirement Plan	Keogh Plan
Amount per person allowed to be contributed in plan: defined contribution plan	25% of compensation, not to exceed $25,000 as adjusted for cost of living (1982 limit was $45,475)	15% of compensation, not to exceed $15,000; no cost of living adjustment.
Amount of benefit per person allowed: defined benefit plan	100% of compensation, not to exceed $75,000 per year, adjusted for cost of living (1982 limit was $136,425)	Compensation and age limitations reduced amount of benefit: It was always lower than corporate-defined benefit maximum. No cost of living adjustment.
Vesting	Maximum of 15 years, but 11 years was normal; waiting period counts for vesting	No vesting; 100% vesting after waiting period.
Waiting period	1 year	3 years.
Minimum age	25	None.
Integration with social security: defined contribution plan	A 7% advantage to higher-paid employees	Could be done but effect was negligible.
Integration with social security: defined benefit plan	Advantage to higher-paid employees much greater than defined contribution plan	Could rarely be done and effect was negligible.
Trustee	Anyone corporation chooses; broad investment opportunities within "prudent" guidelines	Bank or other corporate trustee, which limited types of investments.
Borrowing	Could borrow whole account, whether vested or not, if security was given	None.
Distributions	Could be distributed prior to retirement, disability, or death with no penalty	10% penalty for distributions prior to age 59½ except for disability and death.
Voluntary contributions	Maximum of 10% of compensation	Limited to $2500 per year per employee.

You should consider the impact of the new penalty tax prior to making a retirement plan commitment. We know many talents who created their retirement plans solely for short-term objectives. They were mainly interested in the current tax savings generated by such a plan and were fairly cavalier about the impact of their retirement plans on their future economics. They felt that if they needed the money, they would simply terminate their plans and pay the normal income tax, hopefully in a year when they were in lower brackets.

Because of the new penalty tax, short-term use of retirement planning can be expensive. A 10 percent penalty on top of the normal income tax should dissuade most talents from prematurely terminating their retirement plans.

Up until 1983, the rules for corporate retirement plans and Keogh plans were totally different. Table 6-3 compares just how different the rules were.

As a result of TEFRA, the rules are precisely the same for all business entities whether they are incorporated or not! Some of the rules became effective with TEFRA, others have been timed to take effect later. Generally, after 1983 the rules are the same.

The discriminating reader will have noticed we used noncorporate labels vis-à-vis corporate labels. You do not have to incorporate to take advantage of any of the retirement plans discussed here.

Please do not drop the book, gasp, and take our names in vain! There are other reasons to incorporate. There are also other reasons not to incorporate. Contrary to the opinions of many professionals, it would appear that talent should and will continue to incorporate. The essence of why you should or should not incorporate is not now solely for retirement plans. There are other reasons that must be considered.

Regardless of your incorporation decision, if you elect to use one or more of the retirement plans we have discussed, you will have to seek professional advice, pay professional fees, and assiduously follow all the retirement plan rules. If you have a basic grasp of the material in this chapter, you will be far ahead of most, if not all, of your professional peers when it comes to reducing income taxes and building your retirement nest egg.

Please remember that you do not have an employer other than yourself who will provide for you when your creative well runs dry. How often we have heard brilliant talents exclaim, "Social security is a travesty! If I just had the opportunity to invest my own funds, I wouldn't have to worry about my later years!" Our response, although we acknowledged the truth of their statements, has been: "You can. *Let us tell you about . . .*"

Chapter

7

Running Your Retirement Plan
Translated Greek

Let's face it: Retirement plans, whether corporate or Keogh, are lots of pages of legalese that no rational, non-tax specialist can understand. Invariably, these plans are written like a Greek tragedy, except nobody bothered to translate it into English. Most people do not understand the plot and do not even know who the players are. If you decide to implement a retirement plan and wish to be assured that it will work, the following translation may prove to be indispensable.

At the outset, it is important to understand the basic elements of a retirement plan. Many of you have heard the term "trust" associated with retirement plans. The term retirement plan is synonymous with the term retirement plan and trust. Retirement plan is the more accepted shorthand version.

The "plan" part of a retirement plan and trust refers to that portion of the document which sets out the administrative aspects. Here you learn the type of plan (defined benefit, profit sharing, money purchase, Keogh), who can be in the plan, the vesting schedule, age requirements, and the myriad of other technical rules required by the Internal Revenue Code.

The "trust" portion refers to the administration and investment of the assets actually in the retirement plan and trust. It also names who can invest the assets and lists the rules as to how those assets can be invested. The plan and trust are usually part of one very long document and are collectively referred to as the retirement plan.

There are three players found in retirement plans:

Employer (sometimes called sponsor)

Plan administrator

Trustee

Each has a different function to perform. Often, one person is cast in two or all three of the roles.

The employer, or sponsor, is the business which sets up the plan. It, in our opinion, is the single most important player because it (or at least its owner) selects the type of plan that is desired. It also names the other two players: the plan administrator and the trustee.

The sponsor is totally responsible for the plan and the assets in it. The bottom line is that the sponsor is ultimately liable to the IRS and the plan participants for mistakes of law or judgment. This may sound like a very strong statement (which it is), but it is the truth. When you reflect on the interaction between the players, you will acknowledge our point.

The second player is called the plan administrator. Usually, the plan administrator is also the employer or the trustee (the next category of administrator). Plan administrators are generally responsible for running the plan (not the trust). Filing IRS forms and tax returns and keeping track of members of the plan, vesting, and other qualification rules are all functions of the plan administrator. The plan administrator is also the go-between for the employer and the trustee.

The trustee is the third player. Trustees administer the trust; they are in charge of investing the retirement plan funds. The duties of the trustee are defined in the plan and trust document. These duties include the types of investments that may be made and the required accounting.

All three players, or administrators, as they are properly called, are held to the highest level of responsibility. They are considered to be experts by law, and if any mistake is made which an expert normally would not make, the administrators will pay for that mistake out of their own pockets.

Oftentimes, the shareholder-employee or owner-employee will act as all three administrators at once. Liability? No doubt about it. That is why it is important to understand, at least in general terms, the process of creating and maintaining a plan.

The initial question is whether a plan should be set up. You must ultimately decide whether you are interested in the tax and retirement benefits offered by the use of a qualified retirement plan. If it seems like a viable concept, your next step is to confer with your tax advisers. A tax lawyer and tax accountant are preferable. Let them air their views as to whether they think you should have a plan, what type of plan it should be, and some of the basic parameters of the proposed plan. They should also address the following areas:

How a retirement plan is drafted—whose plan will be used and why.

Who will invest the funds and do the paperwork.

How the funds should be invested.

How the funds should *not* be invested.

How you can keep a majority of the funds for your benefit (assuming you have other employees) and not for the disproportionate benefit of your employees.

The sections that follow address these issues so that you can be forearmed with some of the normal considerations surrounding these aspects of a retirement plan.

Whose Retirement Plan Do You Use?

The Bank's, the Insurance Company's, or Your Own?

Once the decision has been made to establish a qualified plan, and the general parameters of the plan have been discussed and tentatively agreed upon, it is time to decide where the plan and trust are going to come from. Somebody has to either provide a form that you can use or draft a plan just for you. The former is called a "prototype" plan, the latter a "tailor-made" plan.

A prototype plan is just like choosing clothes off the rack at your local department store. Pick your size and your color, within the store's inventory, and then make a few minor alterations. Presto! A relatively good fit for a minimum of money.

The clothing stores of the retirement plan world are life insurance companies, banks, and other investment- or insurance-oriented entities. These companies are willing to offer their off-the-rack (prototype) plans for little or no money. Why the generosity? Because they normally expect that you will buy their products (life insurance, annuities, money markets, certificates of deposit) or that you will let them invest your funds for a fee. Nothing is wrong with the concept; it's classic capitalism.

Prototype plans are preapproved, for the most part, by the IRS. Because of the preapproval, there are limitations as to the provisions that can be inserted into the plan and trust. Usually, the plans are conservative and are not aimed at helping the owner-employee to any great degree. Traditionally, these plans have not been very aggressive or flexible; they could not be if IRS approval was expected. The IRS will only preapprove a handful of variables to be inserted in a prototype.

One advantage of these plans is their low cost, but be careful here. Remember, to get a plan for little or no cost, you most likely will have to buy something in return. If this something is expensive, either because of actual cost or because the investment return is inordinately low, the price may be more costly than you bargained for. Investigate all the costs of a prototype plan. Make sure that you are getting a good deal and are paying, directly or indirectly, a fair price.

Another advantage of a prototype plan is the ease of administration that is generally provided. Since these plans are preapproved by the IRS, no elaborate filings are required. Also, since all plans put out by an individual company tend to be similar in many of their provisions, these companies can maintain a low service fee to keep their plans running smoothly. Just like the clothing store with only a few lines of clothing, the off-the-rack retirement plan companies know their products well.

A last, and potentially major, benefit of prototype plans has to do with TEFRA. Now that retirement plan rules have been stan-dardized to a much greater extent, there should be few instances where a prototype plan will not offer you all the variables allowed by law. Only time will tell, but the prototype may be the wave of the future

Table 7-1. Pros and Cons of Prototype Retirement Plans

Pros	Cons
Inexpensive	Hidden costs for services and production
Simple	Simplicity makes for little flexibility
Pre-IRS approved	
May be more attractive after TEFRA	May be too IRS-oriented and *not* owner-employee-oriented

for most retirement plans, particularly defined contribution plans. (See Table 7-1.)

Tailor-made plans are plans which are specifically drafted to fit your particular situation. They are handcrafted to satisfy your needs and desires and can take advantage of as many of the liberal provisions of the Internal Revenue Code as is possible.

Because these plans are handcrafted, they tend to have high front-end costs; attorneys and tax accountants who know what they are doing seldom come cheap. There are not, however, any hidden product costs. Normally, these plans provide investment rules that are very broad, leaving those decisions entirely to you. Again, no one is trying to sell you a product to invest in; the professionals are selling their services in creating the plan.

Lawyers draft tailor-made plans and trusts. Usually, this is done with substantial input from you, as well as your accountant and other tax advisers. This broad base of input helps assure that all considerations are defined and planned for. *Do not let anyone, except a lawyer, draft your tailor-made plan.* To do otherwise is not only illegal on the part of the nonlawyer, it can also prove to be very costly if the job is not done right. Further, only use a lawyer who is a specialist in retirement plans, so that you will get your full money's worth. The plan must pass IRS scrutiny—both initially and upon an audit. Any mistakes will cost *you* money—lots of money.

Tailor-made plans fit your needs. They take best advantage of the retirement laws by providing access to every benefit allowed. Because of this process they can be expensive; in the long run they may very well be worth it. (See Table 7-2.)

You and your advisers must determine whether a prototype plan or a tailor-made plan best fits your circumstances. Inexpensive is not

Table 7-2. Pros and Cons of Tailor-Made Retirement Plans

Pros	Cons
Fit your needs	May be expensive, at least initially
You decide all the terms	IRS approval not assured
Takes maximum advantage of the law	May not be that much better than prototype plans because of TEFRA

always bad, if *all* costs are considered. That which at first blush appears expensive may, in the long run, be the most inexpensive. As a rule of thumb, the more complex your situation and the more you wish to accomplish, the more you should consider a tailor-made plan. Traditionally, prototypes were oriented toward the more mundane planning situation; however, under TEFRA they may be the better way to go.

Who Should Invest the Funds and Do the Paperwork?

The trustee is responsible for the investment of plan funds and the plan administrator is responsible for most of the paperwork involved in a qualified retirement plan. In practice, the difference between the two is so nebulous as to be nonexistent. When it comes to planning for the successful talent, it may be more convenient, less expensive, and less confusing to keep the players to a minimum.

Most of our clients who are successful talents act as their own trustees and plan administrators. They then hire a professional to take care of the paperwork associated with their plan. The reasons for this are fairly simple: They want to control the investment policy of the retirement funds and they want their own people, usually CPAs or actuaries, to keep the records. By doing this, it is their feeling that fees are kept to a minimum and their control is maximized. Our talented clients generally believe that they can invest as well, or better than, institutions and not have to pay the institution's fee to boot.

These clients hopefully understand that they have all the liability under the plan. As trustees, they will be judged as experts. As plan administrators, they will be judged as experts. There's no escaping the fact that *they* will be judged as experts.

**Table 7-3. Pros and Cons of
Being Your Own Trustee**

Pros	Cons
Control	Liability
Rate of return controlled by you	Probably need help
No fee	Lack of time and expertise

In the case of the true one-person talent, however, liability is kept to a minimum. If mistakes are made, the injured party is the talent, who is probably not going to sue himself or herself. Once any other people are involved, the situation dramatically changes. Liability does exist. All plans must follow standards set forth by the IRS, the Department of Labor, and other governmental agencies. These agencies may choose to make an issue out of a mistake, no matter how few people are affected, so liability in a one-person corporation cannot be completely eliminated.

Self-trusteeing a plan can be beneficial if you have the time or expertise to take on the job. If you lack either or both of these, you can still be your own trustee—you can hire investment advisers to do most of the work. This approach still allows you to retain control. Some of the pros and cons associated with self-trusteeing a plan are shown in Table 7-3.

Institutional trustees are used because it is assumed that they take on liability and that they specialize and will do a good job. Neither of these assumptions is necessarily correct.

Most institutional trustees, whether they be banks, insurance companies, or trust companies, have little liability under the retirement laws. First of all, you as the plan sponsor will be required to either name your investment strategies or to approve the institution's strategies. If these strategies go wrong, you will have little recourse. The institution will take the position that you approved the actions and were in actual control; the institution only did your bidding. In our experience, institutional liability only comes into place if there is an out-and-out case of fraud or if the mistake is monumental in scope.

Another liability-avoidance technique used by the institutional trustee is to call poor investments "conservative" investments. A trustee does *not* have to make any return on invested assets; a trustee is only charged with doing the best job possible in preserving the plan assets. Thus assets are normally invested in the same things as every other institutional trustee invests in. It's hard to call an institution

Table 7-4.   Pros and Cons of Institutional Trustees for Qualified Retirement Plans

Pros	Cons
Can have *some* liability	Disclaimer of liability
Conservative	May be too conservative
Good administrators	Bureaucracy

imprudent when it does everything its competitors are doing, particularly when those competitors are also so-called experts.

On the other hand, conservatism is not always bad. Because the funds that are contributed to a retirement plan are tax deductible and because the income that is earned is earned tax-free, there are generally more funds to invest when using a qualified retirement plan. Thus any investment return is increased, because it is tax-free. The income that is earned in a retirement fund does not have to be the highest available. Retirement plans are a government freebie; to lose this magnificent benefit in high-risk investments is a travesty. Preserving the capital of a retirement fund is very important.

Institutional trustees are usually very good administrators. They do a good job of providing all the information necessary to running a plan. A trained staff is usually available to give some personal attention, and timeliness of response is normally good. A good institutional trustee can considerably ease the administrative burden.

Table 7-4 summarizes some of the pros and cons of using the institutional trustee.

Your ultimate decision as to who will invest your funds and do the administration should be based on your particular comfort level. If you want to be involved, you can always act as your own trustee and hire investment expertise. If you do not want the burden of trusteeship, hire it out. The penalties for not having the expertise and ability to do the administration can be severe; choosing a proper trustee is the best way to assure that your liability is kept to a minimum.

How to Invest Retirement Money

This is not a book about investment. It is, however, a book which is concerned with practicality and bottom-line answers. The bottom line in the investment of retirement plan funds is to *avoid* risk. As we mentioned, retirement plans are a true tax-free benefit. Over a period of years you can double or triple your money, even *after* taxes are paid. There is absolutely no reason to jeopardize this benefit.

If you like to gamble in your investment portfolio, that is certainly your prerogative. But if you do, use personal dollars. At least if you lose your money, you can take a tax write-off. This is not so if your retirement plan loses money; the plan does not get to write off its losses. All losses only mean less tax-free dollars.

We have additional thoughts as to the use of retirement funds. Do not invest in tax shelters. The income in a retirement plan is tax-free; there is no need to shelter it. Buy secure investments which will always generate an income flow. Do not worry about capital appreciation; if you want to invest in land, do it personally. A capital gains tax, at least for now, is not that onerous. Also, a pension plan should not borrow, so if you need leverage to buy capital assets, do not use your plan to do it. And last, be concerned about inflation, but not consumed with it. Invest in assets which can, hopefully, at least match the inflation rate. If you do not, however, it is not the end of the world. Remember, you are delaying tax in your retirement plan; you have more principal to begin with and, as a result, are already ahead of the inflation game. Worry about keeping what you have.

Retirement plans are no place for speculators. When given a sure bet, it does not pay to risk it for a few additional dollars of return. In fact, it does not pay to risk it at all. Get good advisers who know how to preserve what you have while providing you with a reasonable return. By doing so, you will maximize the benefits provided by retirement plans under our income tax laws.

How Not to Invest Retirement Money

The retirement laws have been fashioned in such a way as to eliminate as much abuse as is possible in retirement plan investing. An area that has been continually abused in the past is the use of plan funds to benefit the administrators or participants in the plan illicitly.

These prohibited transactions encompass any dealings between the plan and a person who is involved with the plan, either as an administrator, as a provider of plan services, the employer, or the people covered by the plan. The rules for prohibited transactions are so broad that even related entities and personal relatives are covered.

Do not use the plan to skim money off to you, your company, your friends, or relatives. Do not try to skirt the rules. If you do, there are fines that range from 5 to 100 percent of the funds involved in the prohibited transaction.

Borrowing your own plan funds is a prohibited transaction. It is exempt, however, as long as the borrowing limitations are met. We bring this up to highlight a last point: If a participant in the plan receives a distribution of funds in a loan transaction which is a prohibited transaction, there may be an additional 10 percent tax to the talent *and* income taxes will have to be paid on, supposedly, income tax–free dollars.

Talk with your advisers before you make any investment which involves your retirement plan, your company, you, your relatives, or friends. A little advice beforehand can eliminate a big penalty after the fact.

How to "Discriminate" Legally

A qualified retirement plan must cover all eligible employees of a business enterprise. As the number of eligible employees increases, so does the amount of contribution that must be made. For example:

In 1984, Don James had a defined contribution plan which required a 15 percent contribution. Don was the only employee and made $100,000; the contribution was $15,000.

In 1985, Don added an employee who was eligible for his retirement plan. The employee's salary was $20,000. Don made $100,000. The total contribution was $18,000 for both Don and his employee.

The employee cost $20,000 to hire and $3,000 as far as a contribution was concerned. You can see that as the plan contributions increase for Don, they must do so for his employee as well. Our retirement laws do not allow very much discrimination between employees.

The best way to keep eligible employees out of your plan is not to have any. Obviously, this can be difficult, especially if secretarial assistance is required for your particular needs or if other help is needed.

There are a few ways to hire help which will not be eligible as an employee. The first is to hire only part-time employees. Part-time is defined by the retirement laws as working less than 1000 hours per year. A second, and less effective, method is to hire independent contractors. The concept of an independent contractor is fully explained in Chapter 10. Briefly, an independent contractor is an individual who hires out his or her services to a multitude of people on a fee basis.

Hiring independent contractors was used for many years as a way to escape covering eligible employees. Many businesses hired the same employee for so long that the relationship created was almost the same as the employer-employee relationship, except the names were changed to protect the not so innocent. A few well-drafted contracts usually did the trick in the pre-TEFRA days.

TEFRA, however, made things a little more difficult. Now, this type of relationship may be construed to be employee-leasing. If so, a plan must be set up for the leased employee. The requirements of this plan are not extremely onerous; the contribution must be 7½ percent of salary and must be mandatory. This may be a small price to pay for the talent who must use the services of other people.

Another plan element that can be used to keep otherwise eligible employees out of the plan for as long as possible is the minimum-age requirement. Employees under the age of 25 do not have to be included in a plan. Hiring these "youngsters" may be a way of keeping plan costs down.

Another age element applies strictly to defined benefit retirement plans. Since the contribution to these plans is normally less for young, lower-paid employees, it is possible to design a plan which either eliminates or reduces contributions for this type of employee. Careful and expert plan design is called for to make this work.

Other methods of reducing coverage include vesting schedules and waiting periods. Vesting, as discussed in Chapter 6, can take as long as six years. If employees leave before they are fully vested, the amount they leave behind will benefit those left in the plan. The amounts will either be given to those remaining in the plan or will be used as part of the employer's contribution at a later date.

Waiting periods simply allow the employer not to cover new employees. The maximum waiting period is one year, but it can be extended under the right circumstances. Again, careful planning by your advisers can help you implement the proper waiting period (if you have other employees).

Another method of legally discriminating is achieved by integrating your plan with social security. While TEFRA eroded this benefit in defined contribution plans, defined benefit plans can still use integration most effectively. Since social security benefits can be programmed in as part of the retirement benefit, a lesser contribution needs to be made for your other employees. Some complicated calculations are called for when it comes to making proper use of social security integration. Your advisers should help you decide whether or not to integrate your retirement plans with social security.

Legally discriminating is not easy, but it can be done. As is always the case for qualified retirement plans, following the rules is paramount to success. To review, discrimination can legally be accomplished by:

Having no employees

Hiring independent contractors, even if they are leased employees

Using minimum age requirements and hiring younger employees

Using the longest vesting schedule available

Having a waiting period for new employees

Using social security integration, especially in defined benefit plans

The Controlled Group

Avoiding having employees or, at least, not covering them in retirement plans has, as you can imagine, been in favor since Congress began to reform the retirement laws many years ago. We have shown you some of the effective methods of eliminating employees from coverage. The controlled-group rules are another congressional attempt to close the discrimination loopholes in our retirement laws.

Controlled groups are multiple businesses which are owned or controlled by one or more people. An example of a controlled group would be an incorporated life insurance agent who owns a restaurant as a sole proprietor. While there are two distinct businesses, a corporation and a sole proprietorship, the owner is the same.

If our life insurance agent decides to put a retirement plan in the corporation (no other employees) and not put one in the restaurant (five employees), the life insurance agent is going to have a potential tax problem.

Our tax laws consider all business entities owned by one person as being one single entity for purposes of determining whether or not a retirement plan covers who it is supposed to. Generally, a retirement plan must cover 80 percent of all employees who are eligible to participate. Assuming all the restaurant's employees are eligible for a retirement plan and the life insurance agent has put a retirement plan in the corporation, the life insurance agent cannot exclude them from a retirement plan just because they happen to be in a different business entity. If the law allowed this, then every business owner would attempt to create two businesses so that the employees in one business would have a retirement plan (the employee-owner) but the employees in the other would not (nonowner employees).

From time to time, we have clients who want to get around the controlled-group rules. They suggest that their spouses or children own one entity and that they own another. It is a creative thought, but Congress already had it. Members of one family are considered to be another type of controlled group. Family members are covered by certain rules that attribute ownership among them. For example, spouses are looked upon as one person or owner for tax purposes. So are parents and children.

There are, however, some ways to avoid the controlled-group rules. By setting up two or more businesses, all or a great part of which are owned by unrelated people, the ownership rules for controlled groups can be circumvented. A detailed discussion of how this is done is really not necessary for purposes of your understanding. If you are in a position where it is necessary to have employees but you do not wish to cover them in a plan, you must seek sophisticated advisers to help you. You may have a particular situation that lends itself to multiple businesses owned by separate individuals.

If you choose to attempt to avoid the controlled-group rules by divesting yourself of ownership, you should be cognizant of a few potential pitfalls. As soon as you lose control of a business, you may lose your business. Loss of control will probably create more headaches and expense than covering employees in a retirement plan. Unless you set up a veritable web of legal documentation, you may be the employee who is finally excluded from the plan. It may be that you have given someone else the perfect opportunity to carry off your prior business, employees, and your prior livelihood. Only take this course of action if a lot of money is involved and you are willing to risk the consequences.

Odds are that if you run up against the controlled-group rules, you are trying to accomplish exactly what they were intended to stop.

The road to tax heaven is paved with the tax assessments of failed schemes. Keep out of the controlled-group area if at all possible. Do not underestimate the IRS and Congress in this area. They have had more experience in it than you have.

This chapter does not purport to cover all the aspects of creating and maintaining a qualified retirement plan. We would need a volume many times as thick as this book to do that. If you understand the basics, you should be able to listen to your advisers and make the right retirement plan decisions.

Chapter

8

The Subchapter S Corporation
The Congressional Platypus

Prior to late 1982, a Subchapter S corporation was virtually ignored when individuals sought professional advice on whether or not to incorporate. In the main, individual talents have incorporated, and continue to incorporate, for retirement benefits. Traditionally, the shareholder-employees of S corporations could not take advantage of retirement benefits to the extent that shareholder-employees of regular corporations could. There could be no doubt that retirement plans for S shareholder-employees simply did not measure up! As a result, S corporations were ignored by incorporating talent.

In 1982, Congress changed many of the rules with regard to Subchapter S corporations. This change, coupled with the TEFRA pension law changes, makes the use of S corporations by individual talents potentially viable. Our recent experience seems to indicate that many professional advisers are considering the S corporation for their talented clients.

Given this new interest in the new S corporation, it is important to understand how it works, what it can and cannot do, and how it differs from regular corporations.

The Old Law

Subchapter S corporations have been around for years. Congress initially intended that the S corporation would be just like any other corporation except that it would be taxed as a partnership. By the time Congress passed its initial Subchapter S legislation, it had become a convoluted attempt at meshing corporate and partnership tax law, and as a result, the S corporation became a unique statutory creation: a hybrid, half-corporate, half-partnership entity that looked like a corporation but that was taxed (sort of) like a partnership.

Following is a description of the traditional S corporation, the congressional platypus:

It looked just like a regular corporation and was, in fact, created in precisely the same way as any regular corporation.

It had all the obvious attributes of a regular corporation: shareholders, directors, and officer-employees. It also had its choice of fiscal years and the usual limited liability. However, with the exception of certain trusts, its shareholders had to be individuals who were restricted to owning one class of common stock.

Its employees could take advantage of the usual nonretirement corporate fringe benefits: medical reimbursement plans, group term life insurance, and all the other benefits (discussed in Chapter 5) accorded regular corporate employees.

Shareholder-employees of S corporations could not take advantage of normal corporate retirement plan benefits. They were restricted to the same benefits that were allowed to self-employed taxpayers (Keogh or HR-10 plans).

The S shareholders were taxed on the ordinary income earned by the S corporation. This was true even when the corporate income never left the corporate bank account. The S corporation generally did not have a corporate tax bracket, nor did it pay corporate income tax, except for certain capital gain income. Its income (for income tax purposes) automatically flowed to its shareholders, and that income, whether received or not, was taxable to the shareholders in the same proportion as their ownership in the corporation.

Subchapter S losses, just like income, flowed directly to the tax returns of the shareholders. Shareholders could not, however, deduct losses that exceeded the value of their investment (cost basis) in the corporation. Losses that were generated in excess of one's investment were lost forever.

If income left in an S corporation was later taken out, the shareholders did not (usually) have to pay another tax. Since the income was previously taxed, it would not have to be taxed again.

If an S corporation earned more than 20 percent of its annual income from investments (passive income), it automatically became a regular corporation under the income tax law.

The S corporation was used by many taxpayers; a unique concept was used for unique reasons. Following are three major reasons people elected Subchapter S:

To pass through losses that would be (predictably) generated by a new business venture to the corporation's investors.

To utilize the corporation solely to limit one's liability.

To enable nonworking (passive) investors to take corporate income without paying double tax (typical regular corporation dividend).

The S corporation was not used by talents because:

Talents did not have losses. They were making money, lots of money; that is why they wished to incorporate in the first place.

Talents were not passive investors in a corporate enterprise. They incorporated their talent and employed that talent to generate income.

Talents incorporated to save taxes. The major tax advantages of incorporation were retirement plans. Subchapter S corporations did not offer these advantages to any greater extent than the unincorporated talent.

Table 8-1.   Comparison of Different Tax Entities with Subchapter S Corporations before the New Law

Income Tax Characteristic	Regular Corporation	Sub-chapter S	Partnership	Sole Proprietor
Separate tax bracket	Yes	Sometimes	No	No
Passive income a factor	Yes	Yes	No	No
Pass-through of losses	No	Sometimes	Yes	Yes
Double tax	Yes	Sometimes	No	No
Deductible fringe benefits for owners	Yes	Yes	No	No
Choice of fiscal year	Yes	Yes	No	No
Limitation on owners	No	Yes	No	No
Choice of accounting method	Yes	Yes	Yes	Yes
Limitation on types of stock	No	Yes	—	—
Owner limitations for retirement plans	No	Yes	Yes	Yes

In Table 8-1, we compare the income tax characteristics of different tax entities with those of Subchapter S corporations prior to the new (1982) law. We hope this overview proves helpful to your conceptualizing these congressional platypuses.

The New Law

The Subchapter S Revision Act of 1982 drastically changed the S corporation rules. Congress's avowed purpose in making these changes was to integrate the S rules more closely with the partnership tax rules. It partially succeeded, for there are still tax differences between S corporations and partnerships. Before we outline these changes, we must tell you that TEFRA had a massive effect on all of the retirement benefit rules including those with respect to S corporations. So please, do not jump to any conclusions with respect to the new S corporation until you have reread, at the very least, Chapter 6, "Retirement Plans." The changes to an S corporation are as follows:

It still looks like a regular corporation.

It still has most of a regular corporation's attributes: shareholders, directors, and officers. All S corporations incorporated after 1982 must adopt the calendar year as their tax year, but can have some leeway as to a fiscal year within three months either side of a calendar year.

Subchapter S corporations still have access to limited liability, and their shareholders must, with a few exceptions, be individuals.

Shareholder-employees of the new S corporation *cannot* take advantage of the usual nonretirement corporate fringe benefits. Medical reimbursement, group term life insurance, the $5000 employee death benefit, and other fringe benefits can no longer be provided to shareholder-employees tax-free.

Shareholder-employees of S corporations can now take advantage of *all* the retirement plans offered by regular corporations. Because of TEFRA, *all* business entities enjoy the exact same opportunities with regard to retirement programs and benefits.

Subchapter S shareholders are still taxed on the income earned by the corporation although the technical rules as to how the pass-through to the shareholders occurs have been changed. Subchapter S corporations are still without a corporate tax bracket, except for some capital gains.

Losses still flow directly to the tax returns of the shareholders. But now, shareholders do not lose their unused losses. They are carried to a year in which there is sufficient basis to use them, just like a partnership.

Previously taxed income (income left in the corporation) will generally be tax-free when taken out.

Subchapter S corporations that are formed after 1982 no longer have to worry about keeping their passive income below that historically important 20 percent. There is *no limit* on the amount of passive income that the S corporation may receive. The rules are different (and very complex) for preexisting corporations that elect Subchapter S.

In Table 8-2 we compare the income tax characteristics of different tax entities with those of the new S corporations. We hope this overview proves helpful.

Congress has certainly changed the rules! But people will still use S corporations to pass through losses and receive income without paying double tax while still maintaining limited liability.

Talents wishing to incorporate will certainly look at the new S model and will both favorably and not so favorably compare it to the older model it replaced.

On the positive side, they will find that they can have the same retirement benefits as anybody else.

Table 8-2.   Comparison of Different Tax Entities with Subchapter S Corporations after the New Law

Income Tax Characteristic	Regular Corporation	Sub-chapter S	Partnership	Sole Proprietor
Separate tax bracket	Yes	Sometimes	No	No
Passive income a factor	Yes	Sometimes	No	No
Pass-through of losses	No	Sometimes	Yes	Yes
Double tax	Yes	Sometimes	No	No
Deductible fringe benefits for owners	Yes	No	No	No
Choice of fiscal year	Yes	Sometimes	No	No
Limitation on owners	No	Yes	No	No
Choice of accounting method	Yes	Yes	Yes	Yes
Limitation on types of stock	No	Yes	—	—
Owner limitations for retirement plans	Yes	Yes	Yes	Yes

On the negative side, they will find that they generally must be on a calendar year and that nonretirement fringe benefits are no longer available.

In addition, one must also remember that incorporated talent seldom can take advantage of limited liability; the pass-through of losses is seldom needed by the incorporated talent; and incorporated talents have no real business reason to generate passive income.

We suppose that the question will no longer be, "To incorporate or not to incorporate?" but will become, "To incorporate (regular or S) or not to incorporate?"

Chapter

9

Corporate
Creation
In the Beginning
There Was Paper

Now that we have given you the corporate basics, you may be wondering how a corporation is formed and how one begins its activity. This chapter addresses these questions. First, however, let us review a few of the basics.

A corporation is a fictitious "person" with an identity all its own. Almost all corporations have a majority of the following characteristics:

The power to own assets in the corporate name

The ability to sue or be sued

Centralized management carried on by a board of directors

Ownership which can be readily transferred

Unlimited life

Limited liability

A corporation is brought to life by following formal rules set out in individual state laws. While the laws of all states differ in some respects, there are certain aspects of corporations which are almost always present. These include articles of incorporation, by-laws, and organizational minutes.

Articles of Incorporation

The articles of incorporation (or, more simply, articles) are the foundation documents of corporate existence. The articles (some states call them "certificates of incorporation") are usually filed with the secretary of state of the state in which you incorporate. A corporation's birth begins with the filing of the articles. Individual states oftentimes grant a formal charter, the birth certificate of the new, fictitious person. The articles usually contain the following information:

The name of the corporation

The names of the people who incorporated it

The purposes of the corporation

The period of duration (usually perpetual)

The number of shares that can be issued, their voting rights, and any other rights the shares have

The minimum capital the corporation is to have

The address of the initial office and the name and address of the person who is responsible for legal service of process (who gets handed lawsuits) against the corporation

The names and addresses of the first directors

Any other public information (the articles are a public document) that the incorporators want to include

The articles of incorporation provide the corporate foundation and overall framework. Just like a birth certificate, they give the vital statistics relative to the new arrival.

By-Laws
Your Very Own Rules

The by-laws of a corporation describe how a corporation is to be operated from both a legal and managerial point of view. By-laws take many of the articles' vital statistics and apply them to the corporation's everyday operations, just like *Robert's Rules of Order*. Included in the by-laws of most corporations are the following provisions:

How, when, and where shareholders meetings are held

How, when, and where directors meetings are held, and how long directors are to serve

The authority of directors and how they may or may not delegate their authority to committees or officers

The duties and responsibilities of the officers, the length of their service, and how they are elected

How stock is issued, its form and proper record keeping

Housekeeping provisions, including the form and use of the corporate seal; the fiscal year of the corporation; and information with regard to buy-sell agreements, employment contracts, and other contractual matters

The corporate by-laws can contain whatever provisions the shareholders and directors choose. They are, however, required to be consistent with the articles (if they are not, the articles will control). They cannot violate state law.

A corporate operation can go much smoother when all the operating rules are set forth; that is what by-laws are for. Careful drafting of the by-laws can eliminate considerable confusion when the shareholders, directors, and officers are trying to act within their given capacities.

First Minutes
Starting with a Clean Act

Articles of incorporation and by-laws establish corporate existence and the corporate rules. The first minutes, or "organizational minutes," as they are often called, pull all operating aspects of a corporation together and launch it as a going concern.

First minutes are a record of the proceedings of the initial meeting of the directors of the corporation. How did the directors already become part of the corporation? Let us review what the procedure has been up to the moment of the first meeting of the directors.

An incorporator, usually the lawyer of the talent who wants to incorporate, files articles with the appropriate state or local official. The articles name the initial directors of the corporation. These directors almost always include the talent who wants to incorporate.

It is the initial directors who have the first meeting. One of these directors is elected secretary of the meeting and keeps a record of the meeting by taking the organizational minutes.

The directors officially approve the articles and by-laws of the corporation so that corporate procedures exist. Next, the ownership of the corporation is addressed by issuing the stock certificates.

The articles authorize the directors to issue (sell) a certain amount of stock. All or some of the stock can be issued. Stock that is issued is called "authorized and outstanding stock." Stock which has not been issued is only "authorized stock."

Stock is sold to shareholders. It may either be sold for cash, for services, or in exchange for property. We will discuss how this is done later in this chapter. Enough stock is sold to capitalize (get money into) the corporation so that it can pay its initial expenses and have assets on which to launch its business endeavors.

Once stock is paid for, it is issued to the shareholder. The number of shares of stock owned by a shareholder divided by the total number of shares outstanding gives the shareholder his or her percentage ownership of the corporation. In the case of a one-person talent corporation, all the stock is generally owned by that person.

In the text so far, we have used three different terms: shareholder, director, and officer. We are continually surprised by the lack of understanding by most people as to the difference of each. This difference becomes quite important when addressing corporate formalities. Each of these functions must be properly differentiated; otherwise, the corporation may not be recognized as a legitimate and separate tax entity. This, as we shall see, can lead to disaster with regard to the one-person talent corporation.

Shareholders are investors. They invest their money or property in a business enterprise with the hope of receiving a return on their investment (either in the form of a dividend or appreciation in the value of their stock). Their function is limited by most state laws. Shareholders vote only on matters of liquidation (the ending of a corporation), sale of the corporation to third parties, and changing basic corporate documents like the articles or other major matters affecting the capitalization of the corporation. They also elect, usually each year, the board of directors.

Directors are the policy-setting members of a corporation They make the big decisions. It is important that the directors vote on matters that are not day to day. This is especially true in the one-person talent corporation. Any transaction not in the ordinary course of business is a matter upon which the directors must decide. The board elects corporate officers and delegates their duties. Corporate officers report to the board.

Officers are familiar to all of us. They usually consist of a president, vice president, secretary, and treasurer. The president reports directly to the board and is usually (but not always) the chief executive officer. The president runs the day-to-day operations of the corporation and is in charge of implementing the policies of the board. In most states, corporations need only two officers, the president and the secretary. A secretary is required because it is the secretary's duty to witness or verify the president's signature.

The duties of the shareholders, directors, and officers are separate and distinct, even if a shareholder is also a director and officer, which is almost always true in the case of the one-person talent corporation. Separating these functions is critical in keeping your corporation IRS-clean.

Shareholders and directors are required by state law to meet at least once a year and must keep minutes of their proceedings. They may meet more frequently if they choose. (Minutes must be kept of these special meetings too.)

After the stock is issued, the directors have to establish corporate bank accounts, approve initial fees and expenses, and set up the corporation's books and records.

Perhaps the most important function of the first meeting, other than issuing stock, is the adoption of benefits and contracts related to tax matters. Tax benefits which are adopted include a medical reimbursement plan and qualified corporate retirement plans. It is also important to adopt company expense and auto policies (usually done in employment contracts).

Your Employment Contract
An IRS Insurance Policy

An employment contract is one of the critical documents that is prepared for a one-person talent corporation. It establishes the fact that the incorporated talent is separate from the individual talent (employee). An employment contract can be a highly effective insurance policy to thwart an IRS attack.

Charles Laughton made sure that his corporation met every corporate formality. Charles even went to the extreme of not being an officer or a director of his corporation in order to highlight his employee status. The employment contract is critical to the successful running of a one-person corporation.

An employment contract is a detailed agreement between the employer (corporation) and the employee (talent) setting forth all aspects of the relationship. It should contain the following provisions:

Names of the employer and employee

Date of the agreement and how long the agreement is to last

The duties of the employee and the services to be performed

Salary and bonus structures

All fringe benefit programs, including insurance, cars, expenses, and the procedures for their use

A requirement that the employee exclusively perform services for the employer, along with a promise not to provide those services to others without the employer's written consent

Any "special" arrangements between the employer and the employee as to compensation, outside services, and the like

The employer's right to set working conditions, set fees to be charged, and delegate work assignments

There is a reason for all this apparent nonsense. One-person talent corporations are attacked by the IRS because the corporation and its talent appear to be the same in the eyes of the IRS. If the corporate formalities are ignored, the IRS will consider them the same, and the benefits of incorporation will be lost.

Remember, it is the taxpayer who has the burden of proving that his or her corporation is a viable, separate entity (this means that you are guilty until you prove yourself innocent); quite a reversal of constitutional rights in the minds of many people. The only way you can prove that you have played by the rules is to establish and follow them. Appendix A includes an example of what we consider to be a reasonable employment contract form for incorporated talent.

Fattening Up Your Corporation

Money or other property needs to be put in your corporation so that it can begin its operations. While the concept of putting things in a corporation (capitalizing) may seem simple enough, it can turn into a process that is both complicated and controversial.

Capitalizing a corporation usually is no more than a transfer of some types of assets into the corporation in exchange for stock of the corporation. It is really a sale by you of your assets for your corporation's stock. Done correctly, the whole transaction is tax-free. Oftentimes, the transfer becomes somewhat more complex. For example, some of the assets that are transferred into the corporation may have liabilities associated with them. In other instances, the shareholder chooses to transfer assets in the corporation in exchange for stock and debt. In this manner, the shareholder is giving some assets to the corporation and loaning others.

IRS agents can assert, often successfully, that a transfer of property, debts, or accounts receivable to your corporation is taxable. They can also take the position that the transfer is not effective and disallow it for tax purposes. They can even call the debt that the corporation owes you, the shareholder, "equity" and turn payments from the corporation to you into dividends! The following sections describe some of the problems you may encounter when funding your corporation.

Cash: The Easy Way

The easiest way to get money into a corporation is by transferring cash. The procedure is quite simple: You either write a check to the corporation or deposit cash in the corporation's bank account. In exchange, you should receive stock. This transaction is tax-free. Corporations do not have to pay an income tax when they sell their own stock, and you do not have to pay a tax to receive it.

Property: Another Matter

Property can be difficult to put into a corporation. The incorporated talent corporation is a personal service corporation. It has no need for a lot of equipment or other assets. At most, it will own office furniture and a car. The one-person corporation is merely an income conduit and is used to take advantage of fringe benefits and retirement plans. There is no reason to transfer major amounts of property to the talent corporation, nor is there a need to accumulate property after incorporation.

If you decide to capitalize your corporation with property, however, make sure that you or your immediate family owns 80 percent or more of the issued stock. A tax may result if you do not.

The Internal Revenue Code encourages incorporation (or at least purports to). Normally, if you exchange your car, as an example, for IBM stock, you will pay a tax. An exchange of a car for stock is considered tantamount to a sale; sales create tax. To encourage incorporation, the Internal Revenue Code states that an exchange of your property for stock of a corporation owned 80 percent or more by you, your spouse, your children, or your grandparents is not taxable.

You must also be sure that a formal exchange takes place. A formal exchange means either a bill of sale or a sales contract. Make sure that title to the property is actually transferred to the name of your corporation and that your minutes document the transaction.

Debts Can Spell Real Trouble

Some people transfer debt to their corporation. Their rationale is that since debt is paid back with aftertax dollars (the principal is not tax deductible, only the interest is), the corporation's lower tax bracket should be used to retire the debt. All things being equal, there is nothing wrong with this theory. Unfortunately, all things are not always equal.

In the event you choose to transfer debt into your corporation, make sure it is related to business assets. Trying to transfer your house mortgage—without the house, of course—to your corporation will not work. Any nonrelated or nonbusiness debt transferred to your corporation will create taxable income to you. Since the corporation is taking over your debt, it is the same as if the debt had been paid for you by someone else. This is called "forgiveness of debt" and causes you to receive taxable income to the extent of the transferred debt. It is not a gift; corporations cannot make gifts, except to charity, which shareholders aren't.

You will also receive taxable income if the amount of the debt transferred to your corporation exceeds the cost basis of the assets you transfer into your corporation. Cost basis is a term frequently used by tax professionals. It is the original cost of an asset, less any cost recovery (depreciation). For example, if you buy a car for $9000, that is its cost basis. If the car is used for business, it can be deducted over its life, which is usually three years. If an equal amount is written off each year, the cost basis of the car after two years would be $3000 ($9000 original cost less $6000 in write-off). However, the debt on the car may be higher than its cost basis. Let us assume the debt is $5000 and the cost basis of the car is $3000. When the car is transferred into your corporation in exchange for stock, there may well be a tax to you on $2000, the difference of cost basis ($3000) and the debt ($5000).

You must be careful of this potential tax trap. Always check with your accountant before a transfer of debt is made to your corporation. We have only given you some of the pitfalls of transferring debt. Let an expert guide you so that unnecessary taxes can be avoided.

Debt versus Equity

If you do not receive stock in exchange for cash, you have either made a loan or a capital contribution to your corporation. The corporation must pay back its loans, and when it does, the proceeds are not income taxable to the lender. A capital contribution is another matter. When a capital contribution is paid back, it can often result in dividend income. It will be a dividend to the extent that the corporation has retained earnings. An example may be helpful at this point:

> You put $1000 in your corporation. At the time, you don't think about the tax consequences. The corporation needs the money for office supplies. A year later, you need your $1000 back, so you have the corporation write you a check for the $1000. The corporation has retained earnings (earnings it has already paid tax on) of $1000. You, as a result, will have a taxable dividend of $1000.

For all intents and purposes, the $1000 looks like a capital contribution (there was no promissory note). A capital contribution is a gift to the corporation. The corporation cannot make a tax-free gift back to you ($1000); therefore, it must be a distribution of earnings and, consequently, a dividend.

The lesson to be learned is that when you put assets into your corporation, decide whether it is a loan or a capital contribution. If it is a loan, use a properly prepared promissory note. If it is a capital contribution, take back stock.

Sometimes even calling these payments into the corporation "loans" will not save you from problems with the IRS. Many people, when they incorporate, decide to put assets in the corporation in exchange for stock and debt. For example:

> You decide to incorporate your talent. You fund your corporation with $10,000, $5000 of which is cash and $5000 of which is property. Based on advice from your tax consultant, you take back $500 worth of corporate stock and $9500 worth of debt in the form of a note from the corporation. Why? So that later on your corporation can pay the $9500 back tax-free to you. In addition, your corporation can pay you interest on the $9500, income tax deductible to the corporation and income taxable to you.

> The Internal Revenue Code makes it dangerous to pursue this course of action. There is a chance that this sort of practice is allowing you to take money out of the corporation which really is profit, not debt. You may be disguising a dividend in the cloak of debt and avoiding the two taxes which are the cornerstone of corporate taxation.

> The IRS can, by law, "convert" what you thought was debt into equity. Just like our example above, this can mean a dividend. Worse yet, any interest paid on the debt can also be converted to dividends, creating even more hardship.

This ability to convert debt into equity by the IRS is in the midst of great controversy at the time of our writing this book. Taxpayers and professionals alike are trying to make this practice less onerous than it is now. Until it is settled, it is wise to get advice on how to treat your contributions into your corporation. Knowing the dangers can help avoid the pitfalls.

Accounts Receivable: A Special Problem

Accounts receivable are a problem associated with many professionals such as doctors, lawyers, accountants, and engineers. Any person who bills for services usually creates accounts receivable. When professionals make the decision to incorporate, their receivables become an important part of the tax-planning strategy.

Most of us are cash-basis taxpayers; we do not report income until we actually receive it. Therefore, a receivable is not income until collected. Incorporation gives us a chance to decide whether we should collect the receivables personally and be taxed on them or transfer them to our corporation and let our corporation collect and be taxed on them.

For some time, there was a controversy between the IRS and taxpayers as to the efficacy of transferring accounts receivable to a corporation. The IRS always wanted them to be taxed to the individual (higher tax bracket). The IRS also contended that income was generated when both accounts payable and accounts receivable were transferred into a corporation. Accounts receivable have a zero cost basis. Accounts payable, on the other hand, are liabilities. When both were transferred, income was created if the liabilities (accounts payable) were greater than the cost basis of the accounts receivable (zero).

Most of the problems with regard to accounts receivable have been laid to rest. You can now transfer accounts receivable into your corporation, and the corporation will take them into income. Accounts payable can be transferred into your corporation as long as they arose from the business to be incorporated and do not exceed the amount of the accounts receivable. When the payables are paid, the corporation gets the deduction, not the incorporator.

If you transfer accounts receivable into your corporation but retain your accounts payable (so *you* can take the deduction), you may have a problem. The IRS can take the position that this action "materially distorts" your income. That means you got too good a tax break. The IRS usually wins this argument. This method of getting rid of income and increasing expenses should be avoided unless you have special circumstances that warrant using it.

Proper planning when transferring receivables and payables can mean considerable tax savings—see a professional.

Getting a corporation ready for business is filled with all kinds of practical problems and traps for the uninformed talent. Learning as one goes can work but can be costly. The astute talent who intends to play the game would be far better off if he or she took the time to learn the rules before stepping onto the field.

Chapter

10

Problems Common to All Incorporated Talent
A Minicourse in Self-Defense

The IRS does not look fondly upon the one-person corporation. In the eyes of the service, it seems unfair that an individual in a relatively high income tax bracket (enjoying few tax benefits) can be transformed into another tax-paying entity with a low income tax bracket (enjoying substantial fringe benefits). Congress and the courts have, in some instances, agreed with this perception.

Traditional IRS resistance to decades of Laughtons, along with the willingness of Congress and the courts to expedite the service's position, has resulted in an arsenal of weapons that can be used by the service to attack the one-person talent corporation. This chapter discusses the tax problems associated with incorporating a talent and some very real defenses available to a talent to solve those problems.

Whose Income Is It?

The IRS and the courts have developed a legal doctrine called "assignment of income." This doctrine is fairly simple: If you earn the income, you are taxed on it. If you give or transfer your income to your corporation, you will not shift the income tax liability; it will remain with you.

Virtually every court case which has dealt with both the validity of the one-person talent corporation and the true income-earner issue has come down to one central theme: Was the corporation a real, operational, and functioning entity? In other words, if all, and not less than all, of the corporate formalities were followed to the letter, the courts have held that the corporation was the true income earner. This has been true even where the talent (Charles Laughton) performed all the services.

Much of our book is devoted to the discussion of the mundane process of record keeping. Our preoccupation with this point is valid and cannot be overemphasized: If you are not willing to follow all the corporate formalities, you probably should not have to go to the time and expense of incorporating because, odds are, your corporation will not stand up to IRS scrutiny.

There are five absolute rules for the one-person talent corporation to follow so that the corporation is the income earner; each must be assiduously adhered to: incorporate properly, have employment contracts with all employees, contract in the corporate name, act like a corporation at all times, and avoid income splitting.

Incorporate Properly

Make absolutely sure that your corporation is properly created under state law. Your best insurance policy in this regard is to hire professionals with an expertise in the one-person talent corporation area. Most any lawyer can incorporate a business. Most any accountant can help a business owner set up the corporate books. In our view, however, talent seeking to incorporate should hire specialists to facilitate their desires, attorneys and accountants who know what they are doing. Skimping in the beginning can cost enormous sums later on.

To us, proper incorporation means good articles of incorporation, by-laws, and first-class organizational minutes. Each, in its own way, provides the bedrock upon which the corporate edifice will be raised. We discussed the incorporation process in our previous chapter. Should you decide to incorporate, a quick review would help.

Have Employment Contracts

An employment contract, in our experience, is the most important corporate tax document available to the talent. Without a sound and professionally drawn employment contract, your chances of success when audited could be remote at best. It is so important that we will review it here once again to reinforce its use.

An employment contract establishes the employer-employee relationship. It is evidence to the world (though the IRS would suffice) that the talent is working for his or her corporate employer rather than personally free-lancing.

In a properly written employment contract, the talent should be specifically prohibited from performing services without the written consent of the corporation. Because the talent agrees to provide services "exclusively" to his or her corporation, the corporation becomes the real income earner. A good employment contract should, among other things, allow the talent corporation to accomplish the following:

Charge fees for its services, without employee intervention.

Determine what talent to use when filling a request.

Review and evaluate all aspects of employee performance.

Direct all aspects of employee performance.

Determine all employee salaries and benefits.

Ensure that employees devote their time and service exclusively to the corporation.

A special word needs to be said about the exclusivity requirement. The IRS is much more likely to ignore the corporate entity when the talent haphazardly runs some, but not all, income through the corporation. Taking some income personally and other income corporately suggests to the IRS that the corporation is a convenience used only to generate tax savings. In order to protect yourself, you should ask yourself, "If I were contracting with a totally unrelated party, what would the terms of our contract be?" The answer would contain the reality the IRS is constantly looking for.

"Exclusive services" does not necessarily mean all types of services that can be generated. It means services indigenous to a given field or profession. For example, a geologist may also be an accomplished musician; here, the two skills are so separated that exclusivity may not apply, and the musical income may be taken personally, the geology income corporately. One must be careful, however. When in doubt, opt for total exclusivity.

There is one single, dominant, and critical concept that we are trying to communicate: An employment contract should be between separate and independent parties. Such a contract should be perceived as negotiated at arm's length. A point worth remembering is the following: If there are additional employees, it would be wise to have employment contracts for everyone. This shows a consistent corporate policy and bolsters the corporate image.

Included in Appendix A is a sample employment contract. It is illustrative of the concepts we have been discussing and reflects many of the provisions that buttress the one-person talent corporation.

Contract in the Corporate Name

It is very frustrating to create a sound corporate structure, utilizing all the techniques we have discussed, only to find out that the incorporated talent did not use—much less recognize—the corporate entity. This occurrence happens all too often and can occur as follows:

Andrea Aines, a successful consultant, incorporates and becomes president of her corporation. The incorporation process is accomplished with perfection. Andrea then signs a contract to perform various consulting functions for a large conglomerate. All checks paying for Andrea's services are made out to her; she dutifully deposits them in her corporation's bank account.

Upon IRS audit, Andrea's corporation, perfect as it was, is ignored because Andrea contracted in her own name. Because she ignored her corporation, the IRS simply followed suit and ignored it as well. Andrea's corporate benefits could be lost; taxes, interest, and penalties could be assessed.

Andrea, as an employee of her one-person talent corporation, had no right to contract with the conglomerate. Because she did, all the income that was earned could be taxed to her rather than to her corporation.

All documents which relate to the performance of corporate services should be in the name of and signed by the corporation. Andrea should have signed all the conglomerate contracts as follows:

Andrea Aines, Inc.
By: Andrea Aines, President

The above signature shows that Andrea was only acting in her capacity as an officer of the corporation. It makes clear that the corporation is the contracting party and that Andrea is merely signing on its behalf. To fully sustain Andrea's authority to act on behalf of Andrea Aines, Inc., minutes of the board of directors of the corporation should reflect that the directors approved the contracts. To further strengthen this point, Andrea should have used corporate stationery, calling cards, and billing statements.

All these corporate "tracks" should make it clear to the world (again, the IRS will do) that Andrea is merely acting on her corporation's behalf.

Act like a Corporation

In Chapter 12, "Observing Corporate Formalities," maintenance of an ongoing corporation is discussed. That chapter reiterates a most important theme relative to the one-person talent corporation: Creating a formal paper trail may assure continued effective use of the corporation for tax purposes.

Avoid Income Splitting

Income splitting appears to rankle both the IRS and the courts (we discussed this at length in Chapter 5). Running income through a corporation to merely fund fringe benefits and retirement plans is "questionable" to the IRS but is permissible if done properly. The splitting of income is another matter!

Moving income from a high bracket to a lower bracket in the case of a one-person talent corporation appears to be a pretty clear indication that assignment of income may be occurring. This is especially true when there is no real business reason or purpose for accumulating income in the lower corporate brackets.

Let us take a look at two different examples of income splitting:

> Andy Anderson is a successful salesperson for Universal Gadgets, Inc. Andy has incorporated himself and operates as A.A. Sales Co. Because Andy deals with upper-income customers and must travel a great deal, A.A. Sales Co. provides Andy with an expensive car. A.A. Sales Co. must keep income in the corporation in order to pay for Andy's car. The corporation is taxed on the money that is used to pay for the car at substantially lower tax rates than Andy's, had he paid for it out of personal earnings.

> Barbara Bledsoe is a salesperson for Universal Gadgets, Inc. She is also incorporated. Her corporation, B.B. Enterprises, Inc., retains income on a consistent basis. Barbara does not need a corporate car; she uses her corporation's money to invest in mutual funds. The income in her corporation is taxed at rates lower than Barbara's personal bracket. The income earned from the mutual funds is also taxed at the lower corporate bracket.

In Andy's case, there is a bona fide business reason to retain income in his corporation. Barbara, on the other hand, is taking full advantage of income splitting. Neither Andy nor Barbara is breaking the law or doing anything inherently shady. Barbara, however, is more likely to be taken to task by IRS agents because of her income splitting. Will the agents prevail? They certainly may. Barbara, to buttress her defense, should make sure that her corporate minutes reflect a bona fide reason (or at least a pretty good fabrication) for keeping those earnings in her corporation. Without these records, there's a pretty strong chance that the tax result will not be to Barbara's liking.

The Independent Contractor Problem

One of the more difficult obstacles for the one-person talent corporation to hurdle deals with the concept of your talent corporation being construed as an employee rather than an independent contractor; the difference between the two is absolutely critical although oftentimes almost indistinguishable. This difference, however, may very well determine the tax validity of your corporation, particularly with regard to fringe benefit programs.

If an employer-employee relationship is found between the master corporation (the hiring corporation) and your talent corporation (the corporation which is hired), the IRS may disregard your corporation and determine that you are in reality the employee of the master corporation rather than your own talent corporation.

If the IRS agents are successful in finding this relationship, they will disallow all your corporation's fringe benefit deductions. This will result in additional tax to you and your corporation and the possible assessment of interest and penalties.

The independent contractor status of some types of talent was finally settled under TEFRA. Real estate agents and some commissioned salespeople are now clearly independent contractors. The granting of this status does not mean that these classes of talent should not try to follow at least some of the aspects discussed here. These two types of specific talent will be discussed in the next chapter, but be aware that a formal contract is required for these types of talent to qualify as independent contractors. A good reading of this chapter will help in understanding some of the provisions that are important to those contracts.

IRS agents look at a host of factors in making a determination as to whether or not an employer-employee relationship exists. Some of these include:

Degree of control exercised by the master corporation.

Right of your talent corporation to delegate work assignments.

Frequency of services performed for the same master.

Is your corporation really in an independent trade or business?

Who pays for services, expenses, and "tools of the trade"?

Who Controls the Talent?

The most important factor in determining whether an employer-employee relationship exists is the degree of control that the master corporation appears to exercise over your talent corporation. Items which can indicate excessive control include the setting of work hours, dominating the work environment, and setting the daily regimen.

An independent contractor is only expected to achieve certain results. How those results are achieved is, in essence, up to the independent contractor. The master corporation is not allowed to exercise supervision and control over the independent contractor.

In all contracts between the master corporation and your talent corporation, the anticipated results should be recorded. It should be absolutely clear that your talent corporation will decide how it will achieve those results.

Right to Delegate Work Performed

An independent contractor should be able to hire and fire its own employees. It should also be able to decide who will perform the work for which it has contracted. In order for your talent corporation to remain "independent," the contract between it and the master corporation should spell out that your talent corporation has the absolute right to delegate the requirements of the job among its employees. *Even if the talent corporation has only one employee, the contract should include this very important provision.*

A contract which specifically names the individual to perform the services or which gives the master corporation too much control over what individuals will perform the services runs the risk of creating the employer-employee relationship and the risk of personal holding company problems.

Frequency of Services

The more often your talent corporation performs services for a master corporation, the more likely it appears that there may be an employer-employee relationship. If your talent corporation seems to be critical to the success of the master corporation's business, the IRS will assert that the master corporation directly controls you. If your talent corporation depends too much on the master corporation's business, the IRS will also assert that the master corporation controls you, the talent.

Both IRS contentions, although frequently asserted, can be overcome. If the contract between the master corporation and your corporation allows your corporation the ability to perform services for others and you indeed render services to others, it would be difficult for the IRS to assert the "dependence" argument successfully. Freedom of choice is independence. Independence in the talent corporation results in independent contractor status—the desired result.

Maintaining an Independent Business

If a talent corporation is engaged in a business or profession which is traditionally rendered by nonemployees, an employer-employee relationship will normally not exist. For example, physicians, attorneys, dentists, and accountants are almost always engaged in independent business ventures. On the other hand, professional managers, some consultants, and technicians are usually thought of as employees.

To overcome the independent business hurdle, your talent corporation should be able to perform services for more than one master; the general public would do nicely. The services of your corporation should not unduly be restrained by the master corporation.

Your corporation could certainly choose not to offer its services to the general public or multiple masters; the fact that it does not may be a problem, but it is not as bad as a contract that restricts those services.

The IRS will also look at whether or not your corporation is taking any business risks. If it is, the service will rightly conclude that it is an independent business. If it is not, the IRS will perceive employer-employee status and move against you.

Who Pays the Bills?

Employers usually furnish employees with all the necessary tools of the trade: offices, furniture, secretarial services, telephone, and supplies. Independent contractors have like needs but generally pay for them directly.

Any agreement between master and talent corporations should directly set forth who pays for support services, expenses, and tools of the trade. This agreement should outline all billing and payment procedures.

If the master corporation furnishes the talent corporation with an office, secretarial support, supplies, or other services, it should bill the independent contractor for the legitimate costs of such. This is true in any situation where there is a close ongoing relationship between the master corporation and the talent corporation.

In order to maintain its independent contractor status, your one-person talent corporation should pay for its own services, expenses, and tools of the trade. If it elects not to, it runs the risk of being categorized by the IRS as an employee.

The subject of who pays for income tax withholding, social security, and unemployment taxes must be addressed in the agreement between the master and talent corporations.

An employer has the absolute responsibility to withhold social security taxes under the Federal Income Contributions Act (FICA), to withhold federal income taxes, to match FICA taxes paid by the employee, and to pay taxes under the Federal Unemployment Tax Act (FUTA). The agreement between the independent contractor and the master corporation should obligate each to pay these items for its own employees. Without such an agreement, if either of the parties neglected its withholding responsibility, the other most probably would be held responsible as well. If the IRS disallows the independent contractor status of your talent corporation, the master corporation would generally be liable for these items as to its talented employee(s). With a properly drawn agreement, the master corporation may well skirt this result.

It is important to remember that a one-person talent corporation is a business and must act like one. It should enter into contractual relationships with master employers which set forth, at a minimum, the following provisions:

Names of independent contractor and master corporation

Type, extent, and duration of services to be performed

Determining who pays for what services, including how these services are to be billed; when payment is due; and who is responsible for arrearages

A statement of nonexclusivity, so that the independent contractor may perform services for others

How the contract can be terminated

A statement of how FICA, FUTA, withholding, and matching FICA taxes are to be paid

There is no method that absolutely eliminates the risk that your personal service corporation will be considered an employee of one of its clients or customers. To reduce the risk, you should know what differentiates an employee from an independent contractor and then reduce that knowledge to carefully selected provisions in written contracts.

A sample independent contractor agreement is included in Appendix B. It will help show you what is expected in an independent contractor relationship. This is *not* a do-it-yourself form. Use it to learn more about independent contractors so that you can better visualize the relationship needed to qualify yourself as an independent contractor.

The Personal Holding Company Problem

Congress has long recognized that successful people create corporations to take advantage of lower income tax brackets. In an attempt to limit this bracket-splitting practice, Congress added the concept of a personal holding company (PHC) to the Internal Revenue Code. Initially, the PHC provisions of the law were directed to incorporated investments. Here is how incorporated investments worked:

John Rawlins owned $200,000 worth of certificates of deposit, the income on which amounts to about $20,000 per year. John had other income and didn't need the $20,000 for living expenses. His income tax bracket was 50 percent. John heard that corporate rates are substantially less than personal rates (let us assume 15 percent).

After reading several books on corporations, John incorporated. He transferred all his CDs into the corporation in exchange for its stock.

John's taxes, so he believed, were reduced from $10,000 (50 percent of $20,000) to $3000 (15 percent of $20,000). John was in for a rude awakening.

John created a PHC. A PHC is any corporation of which more than 50 percent is owned by five or less individuals and at least 60 percent of its income is from investments (other than sales of securities) or personal services. Since John owned 100 percent of the corporation and all the income was from investments, John's corporation was a PHC and was subject to a special tax.

The PHC tax treats investment or personal service income as if the shareholder (John) earned it personally. If John does not distribute the $20,000 in income by paying expenses or dividends, it will be taxed at a 50 percent tax rate. The 50 percent PHC tax applies *no matter what tax bracket John is in and no matter how much PHC income the corporation generates.* The PHC tax is a penalty tax. It punishes individuals who attempt to use their corporation's lower tax bracket for investment or personal service income. The same result would occur if John derived income from personal service contracts. For example:

> Maureen is an executive of a corporation and makes a substantial income, which is taxed in the 50 percent tax bracket. A hobby of Maureen's is playing the trumpet for a band. Maureen's contract with the band requires that Maureen and only Maureen can play for the band. The hobby is very lucrative and generates $20,000 of income per year.
>
> Hoping to lower her income tax burden, Maureen incorporates her musical talent. Odds are that Maureen will not save any taxes, because her "business" is based on personal service income. Since Maureen (not her corporation) is required to perform, the income derived from the band is PHC income.

There are several methods that can be used to avoid being construed as a PHC. The first is to make sure that less than 60 percent of the talent corporation's income is derived from investments or personal services.

Another approach, and the one which is most commonly used, is to avoid classifying service income as "personal" service income. If you are beginning to think that this technique sounds like word games or semantics, you are correct. Service income only becomes "personal" when someone other than the corporation can designate who is to perform the services, and the person who is designated to perform the services owns 25 percent or more of the corporation.

Following is an example of how to transform personal service income (PHC income) to service income by a change in contractual language:

> Sara James is an actress. Her corporation, James Acting Co., contracts with an advertising agency for the use of Sara in a

commercial. The contract between James Acting Co. and the advertising agency specifies that Sara must perform; no one else will do.

Under this scenario, the income that Sara's corporation receives from the advertising agency is clearly PHC income. Contrast this with the following example:

James Acting Co. is active in providing actors and actresses for various purposes, including films, advertising, and live performances. James Acting Co. is totally owned by Sara James, who is president of the corporation and its only employee.

James Acting Co. enters into a contract with an advertising agency. The contract states that James Acting Co. must provide an actress for a certain commercial. James Acting Co. has full authority to provide any actress it may choose.

The income received under this latter example is *not* PHC income and is therefore not subject to the 50 percent penalty tax. James Acting Co. can designate who is to perform under its contract with the advertising agency.

Two problems can arise under this approach: Either the advertising agency refuses to sign the contract because it insists that Sara must perform the services or the agency adds a contractual description of an actress who can only be Sara James. Designating the person to perform the services by name or by description creates PHC income.

In most cases, contractual language that does not designate, either by direct reference or by description, who is to perform should be used. However, it is our experience that an "eyewink" understanding as to who is going to perform is generally understood. Upon an IRS audit this eyewink understanding may come to surface; if it does, PHC status will be assessed on the income received.

The best way to avoid PHC status, even if you have PHC income, is to distribute all the PHC income. Time and again, we have shown that a one-person talent corporation (service organization) should not be used to split income or to accumulate earnings; if it is, you can add PHC to your list of problems. To distribute all the PHC income, remember the following:

A one-person talent (personal service) corporation is used to provide fringe benefits and retirement plans: Service income is earned by the corporation; benefits and retirement plans should be fully funded; and the remainder of the corporation's income distributed in salary to the employee talent.

Accumulation may properly occur; however, only for items such as cars, furniture, or equipment. These are permissible uses of PHC income and will generally not cause the PHC penalty tax to be assessed.

A method erroneously used to avoid PHC status is to have a family member own the stock of the talent corporation. Brothers, sisters, spouses, grandparents, and children are all considered one shareholder for purposes of the PHC stock ownership rules; having family members owning the stock will not avoid PHC status.

Having an unrelated person own your stock would work for tax purposes, but it might not be such a good idea. A falling out among friends has been known to happen; if it does, the talent may end up with a lawsuit, attorneys fees, and a worthless corporation.

The PHC problem is not insoluble as long as you understand its effect and how it can be avoided. Because of the PHC's planning importance, however, a review of its attributes should be helpful to you.

A personal holding company is a corporation which derives 60 percent or more of its income from investments or personal service contracts and has more than 50 percent of its stock owned by five or less people.

A personal service contract is a contract which allows someone other than the corporation to designate by name or description who is to perform the services under the contract.

If PHC income is not distributed from the corporation, it is subject to a 50 percent tax.

To avoid PHC income problems, enter into contracts which allow your talent corporation to designate the person who performs the services.

Another way to avoid PHC status is to have a nonfamily member own the corporation (not a good idea, in our opinion).

The best way to avoid the PHC tax is to distribute all the corporate income for necessary business expenditures, fringe benefits, retirement plans, or salary.

The Unreasonable Compensation Problem

Corporations which are owned by only a few shareholders have a common problem: whether or not the compensation paid to shareholder-employees will be fully allowed as a deduction to the corporation by the IRS. The service has taken the position that shareholders normally expect a return on their corporate investment. Since shareholder-employees normally receive only salary from a corporation (not dividends), the IRS and the courts have inferred that part of the salary is really a return of the shareholders' investment and, therefore, a dividend; this is called the "unreasonable compensation argument."

The unreasonable compensation argument generates more tax for the Internal Revenue Service. A salary is fully deductible by a corporation and income taxable to the employee who receives it. A return on investment is a nondeductible dividend payment to a shareholder. The dividend is subject to a double tax; it is income that will be taxed at the corporation level and taxed again to the shareholder receiving it.

In determining whether or not a salary is reasonable, IRS agents will try to ascertain whether or not funds are being paid for services or are really "disguised" dividends (a wolf in sheep's clothing). Factors which contribute to a positive determination (no dividend) include:

Qualifications and expertise of the employee

What services the employee provides

The state of the economy

Compensation paid to other employees in similar circumstances

Prior earning capacity of the employee

These factors are broad and can be broadly interpreted by the IRS agents. Factors which tend to show that a disguised dividend has been paid are just as broad:

Whether or not the corporation has paid dividends in the past

The availability of corporate funds, accumulated cash, and investments

Compensation as a percentage of gross and net income

The method actually used to determine compensation for employees

The amount of capital in the corporation

In a one-person talent corporation, the services of the shareholder-employee almost always generate most if not all of the corporate income. It may be difficult for the IRS agents to contend that compensation paid to the shareholder-employee is unreasonable, even if all the corporate income is paid to the shareholder-employee. There is generally little or no capital invested in the talent corporation—therefore a return on investment argument is not usually appropriate.

There are, however, instances where the unreasonable compensation argument may apply to a one-person talent corporation. Accumulating income for income-splitting purposes means that cash or investments remain in the corporation. The earnings from cash or investments create income which is not generated from services. This income, as well as the amounts accumulated, can be construed to be a dividend when later paid out as salary.

You should be aware of several actions that you should take with regard to the one-person talent corporation and the unreasonable compensation problem:

Do not accumulate income.

Do be consistent in your salary payments from year to year.

Do not overcapitalize your corporation.

Do make sure that you have an employment contract which sets out salary, bonuses, expenses, and fringe benefits, as well as the nature and scope of the services you will provide.

Do record minutes to reflect why and how compensation is paid and for what purposes corporate earnings, if any, are to be retained.

The Affiliated Service Group Problem

Imagine, if you will, an almost perfect incorporation scheme. It would involve the incorporation of a single talent, but the new talent corporation would have unlimited access to the employees of another organization. These employees would only be used by the incorporated talent when needed. They would not be eligible for any of the talent corporation's fringe benefits including retirement plans. This would be true even if the talent controlled their every function. The incorporated talent would work as an independent contractor for this other organization on an exclusive basis. There would be no need for large billing systems or the need to find other work. The incorporated talent would, in essence, be an employee of the other organization, except that the incorporated talent would be the master of all of his or her own fringe benefits.

Until a few years ago this tax scheme could be utilized by all talent. It was used by many. The first talents to adopt this incorporation scheme were partnerships of professionals, such as lawyers, accountants, and doctors. It worked like this:

> AAA Clinic is a partnership of seven doctors. Five of the doctors would like to incorporate and the other two do not. The clinic has fifteen other nondoctor employees who have few fringe benefits and no retirement plan.

> The five doctors each set up their own separate corporations, each with its own types of fringe benefits and retirement plans.

> The partnership now consists of five corporations and two individuals. All the nondoctor employees and the two unincorporated doctors are subject to the fringe benefits (few) and the retirement plan (none) of the partnership. The other five doctors are employees of their own respective corporations and are included in their respective corporations' fringe benefits (massive) and retirement plans (even more massive).

If that sounds like a very nice tax loophole, it *was*. It no longer works. The law considers all of the doctors, whether incorporated or not, and all the other employees as one big happy family, called an "affiliated service group." As one group, they all have to be covered by the same retirement plans. *Another loophole bites the dust.* The partnership of corporations to utilize fully fringe benefit planning on an exclusive basis is at an end.

The final curtain in the demise of the "perfect" talent corporation came in the early 1980s. Under TEFRA, Congress went even further:

> Stella Starr is a well-paid biochemist of Mammoth Industries. Mammoth pays very well but has few other incentives for employees. Its existing retirement plan guarantees that Stella will earn $100 per month when she retires. Stella is in a 50 percent federal income tax bracket and does not seem to have the discipline to put away any money toward her retirement.

Stella is advised by her tax lawyer to incorporate and to have the corporation work for Mammoth as an independent contractor. Her corporation can then implement a very sophisticated retirement plan and other fringe benefits for Stella.

Stella's plan no longer works. It has gone the way of the dodo and other extinct animals. The new mandate which must be followed under the affiliated service group rules as refined by TEFRA is that if an organization (whether a corporation, partnership, or individual) performs management functions primarily for another organization, they all belong to one big happy family. If Stella gets the benefits, all of Mammoth's employees must get the same benefits. Everyone in both organizations must play under the same fringe benefit rules—an obvious impossibility.

Here is a synopsis of the types of talent that may be subject to the new affiliated service group rules:

Any talent, whether in a corporation, partnership, or sole proprietorship, providing services to another service organization, if the talent owns part of that other service organization.

Any talent, whether in a corporation, partnership, or sole proprietorship, providing management functions to primarily one other organization

Only time will tell whether or not some very ingenious tax expert can figure out a way around the affiliated service group rules. Maybe someone will convince Congress of the need to allow successful professionals to have their own retirement plans with benefits commensurate with their salary during their active employment years. If you think you might be one of the unfortunates who fall under these rules, see your tax adviser right away. There are a few methods of avoiding the affiliated service group rules, although they are risky and expensive. You should also read Chapter 13, "Getting Out of Your Corporation." It may be the most graceful way of avoiding the affiliated service group trap.

The Social Security Problem

A minor but sometimes irritating aspect of incorporating, at least to our clients, is the double social security payment required by corporations. Corporations are required to withhold a certain percentage of an employee's base salary to pay FICA (social security tax). In 1983, this amount was 6.7 percent of the first $35,700 of wages. This amount has, of course, been scheduled to go up and will likely continue to do so.

Corporations are also required to match the amount of FICA withheld from their employees. The result is a 13.4 percent social security tax. For an employee who earned more than $35,700 in 1983, and most incorporated talents did, the cost was $4783.80.

Unincorporated owners such as partners of partnerships or sole proprietorships are not faced with this double whammy on their income. A different type of social security tax is assessed in their case, called the "self-employment tax." The self-employment tax in 1983 was 10.3 percent of the first $35,700 in income, or $3677.10. The $1106.70 difference between FICA and self-employment tax is a cost of incorporation. However, gradually the self-employment tax and the double FICA will be equal. This will occur after 1989.

Over a long period of time, the savings in social security tax between unincorporated talent and incorporated talent can be significant. To determine the actual effect in your situation, you should consult with your accountant or tax lawyer. This extra tax cost should be considered prior to making the incorporation decision.

Most of the weapons that the IRS and Congress have armed themselves with to combat the unfettered spread of incorporated talent can be overcome by good planning. The only one which cannot effectively be eliminated is the double FICA, and that is an anathema we all live with.

Armageddon

One of the first questions we are asked by clients after we have explained the incorporated talent concept is, "That sounds great. But what happens if the IRS audits me and determines that my corporation doesn't work?" It can happen. A one-person talent corporation is not invulnerable to a successful IRS attack. Every client should be aware of the consequences if this sad result does occur.

As we have discussed, there are many ways that a one-person talent corporation can be questioned by the IRS. The three theories most often used by IRS agents are:

The corporation is a sham and is only being used to avoid taxes.

The shareholder is the real income earner, not the corporation.

Reallocation of income between the corporation and the shareholder-employee.

The Sham Corporation

"Is the corporation real?" This question answered in the negative is the essence of the IRS sham corporation argument. This was the argument that the service made (unsuccessfully) in the Charles Laughton case.

To keep a corporation real (a separate legal entity) involves time, money, and effort. Taking the time, paying the money, and putting in the effort can almost always destroy the service's sham corporation argument.

If the IRS determines that the corporation is, in fact, a sham, all contributions made to retirement plans will be disallowed and subjected to income tax at the shareholder-employee's tax bracket. Fringe benefits such as a medical reimbursement plan will be subject to individual limits. Many of the corporate expenses may also be disallowed because they are construed to be personal in nature and not subject to personal deductions. All in all, such a result would be an income tax disaster. Taxes, penalties, and interest will be assessed. The time, money, and effort involved in this type of catastrophe will far surpass the time, money, and effort necessary to keep the corporation real.

Assignment of Income

The IRS has a multitude of weapons to determine who really earned the income that was passed through the corporation. If the IRS agents elect to attack on the assignment of income argument, the problems encountered can be expensive. When an individual assigns income to a corporation, it means that the individual earned the income and then contributed it to the corporation. The corporation becomes the legal owner of the funds, but the individual will be liable for the income taxes on those funds. The funds are still owned by the corporation, however. If the individual takes these funds out of the corporation, a dividend could ensue, potentially creating a double tax. Liquidation of the corporation is imperative when caught in the assignment of income argument. It is ultimately less painful as far as taxes are concerned.

Reallocation of Income

The IRS can also allocate income between the corporation and the shareholder-employee. This means that part of the income will be treated as personal and the balance as corporate. Under this attack, there would generally not be a double tax, and liquidation would not be necessary, although it would be wise. Once you are in the throes of this type of IRS attack, it is almost always better to cut losses and get rid of your corporation.

The sham corporation argument, the real income earner argument, and the reallocation of income theory can be parried through proper planning. Pursuing the corporate paper chase with vigor can create a wonderful IRS insurance policy.

Self-incorporation can provide an extraordinary cornucopia of benefits; it can also create massive income tax problems if it is not properly accomplished. In our opinion, every talent should seek out and use the very best of advisers. As we have discussed, these advisers should include a tax attorney and an accountant who specialize in the area.

Chapter

11

Problems of Specific Talent
Going an Extra Mile

While there are generic problems associated with incorporating talent, some specific talents usually have to go an extra mile. Either because of special state laws or particular IRS doctrines developed for particular areas of talent, it is just tougher to successfully incorporate some talent. Just because the road is a little rocky does not mean that these talents are not ripe for incorporation. It does mean that a road map can help those specific talents to find their way better.

Statutory Professionals

Most states have their own laws with regard to the incorporation of certain designated professionals. These statutes are a relatively recent phenomenon, products of professionals taking advantage of the tax benefits afforded by incorporating.

Traditionally, states have not allowed professionals who perform services to incorporate. The main reason for this prohibition was the legislative feeling that such professionals as doctors, dentists, lawyers, certified public accountants, architects, and engineers should be totally responsible and, therefore, liable for their professional acts. In the opinion of our elected officials, it was not good public policy to allow such professionals the opportunity to limit their liability by using the corporate structure. State legislatures also seemed to manifest the belief that professional services were personal in nature and should remain so. To allow corporations to provide these services would be callous and unprofessional.

To combat this legal inability to incorporate, many professionals would create "associations" that were, in reality, corporations. They were much like the trade guilds of the Middle Ages. These associations were not corporations under state law but were taxed as corporations under the Internal Revenue Code.

Traditionally, business entities which possessed the characteristics of a corporation have been taxed as corporations. To qualify as a corporation, an association had to have a majority of the following attributes:

Ownership separate and apart from the entity itself

Centralized management

Continuity of existence (Death of an owner would not terminate the entity.)

Free transferability of interest (Ownership could be bought and sold.)

Limited liability

There was no federal requirement that these associations should qualify as corporations under state law in order to be taxed as corporations. As a result, it was fairly easy for these associations to adopt corporate characteristics, not be in violation of state law, and be federally taxed as corporations. In reality, these associations were no more than partnerships which elected to be treated under the Internal Revenue Code as corporations.

These associations were recognized as corporations for many years and were allowed to take full advantage of all the corporate benefits. The problem was that an individual professional who did not want to join an association could not take advantage of the corporate tax laws. State law stood in the way. Professional loners either changed their ways (became joiners) or paid more tax than many of their peers. A sole and independent practitioner was truly discriminated against in the good old days!

In the midsixties, the IRS adopted rules aimed at halting the use of associations. This action was followed by a tremendous outcry from the professional community. Not only did professionals scream, they also took aim at changing the federal tax laws. They caused a great number of state legislatures to enact special incorporation laws which gave corporate status to professionals.

The outcome of the tripart battle between the professions, states, and the IRS was victory for the professions. Today, almost all professionals, whether in groups or as individuals, may incorporate in one form or another. They may make full use of the favorable income tax treatment afforded corporations.

This unique evolution of statutory professionals has created some interesting quirks in their corporate existence. These quirks can present potential problems if not understood.

Limited Liability

Because of the strong legislative belief that traditional professionals should be responsible for their own acts, virtually all state statutes on professional incorporation provide for full professional liability. Professionals cannot limit their professional liability by incorporating. They may, however, limit their liability as to creditors just like any nonprofessional. If a professional makes an error which adversely affects a client, the client may sue both the professional corporation and the professional who erred. Professionals who practice together do have some limited liability. If one professional makes an error, the other professionals are usually not personally liable for that error, but the employer-corporation's assets as well as those of the professional who erred are subject to the client's claims.

Creditor liability is the same for professional corporations as it is for regular corporations under the laws of most states. Since state laws vary so much, local counsel must be used to ascertain local law. This is particularly true with regard to professional corporations.

Specific Laws for Specific Professions

State laws vary on almost all aspects of regulating professional corporations or associations. For example, some state laws require shareholders, directors, and officers of professional corporations to be professionals who are licensed to practice that particular profession. In these states, nonlicensed professionals cannot own, operate, or control a professional corporation. There may also be special state-licensing requirements that must be met before incorporation is permitted. Notification to a professional regulatory body that incorporation is desired is almost universally required.

Other typical state restrictions include the type of business activities that may be conducted and specific requirements for the buying and selling of professional corporation stock.

Any professional wishing to incorporate should seek out an attorney who is well-versed in professional corporation or association law. Violation of a state statute, regardless of whether it was inadvertent or not, could lead to severe penalties and actions. Particular care should be exercised in the structuring of any professional corporation or association so that all statutory requirements are meticulously followed.

Accounts Receivable

The most troublesome tax problem facing a statutory professional wishing to incorporate is the assignment of his or her accounts receivable into the new corporation. Under the current provisions of the Internal Revenue Code, this receivable problem is much improved; it is not, however, totally solved.

A few "receivable" pointers may be helpful to you if you are considering incorporation.

Transfer accounts receivable to your corporation by bill of sale or contract.

List all receivables to be transferred, and make sure this list is part of the corporate minutes authorizing the transfer.

Only transferring receivables without accounts payable may lead to trouble with the IRS. The IRS says that you cannot distort your income by juggling payables and receivables.

Have your accountant predetermine the amount of the receivables and payables that should be put in your corporation in order to maximize your tax and financial benefits.

Remember, there is the potential of extraordinarily bad tax results if receivables are not properly handled.

Sales Professionals

Commissioned salespeople are oftentimes excellent candidates for incorporating their talents. Their ability to generate large amounts of income along with their independent nature gives them a unique ability to take advantage of the best features of corporations. However, sales professionals have two unique problems with respect to incorporating their talents: where and how their commissions get paid and trying not to serve two masters.

Commissions

Salespeople get involved in a wide variety of compensation arrangements. These are usually in the form of a commission which is paid upon the successful consummation of a sale. In our experience, only a minority of these commission arrangements are in writing. Those that are in writing are, of course, between the company which provides the product and the salesperson.

Upon incorporation, it is absolutely necessary to reduce all compensation agreements to writing. These agreements must be between the product company and the one-person talent corporation. The sales contract should not mention the individual salesperson by name or by description. It should specifically state that the sales corporation can designate who will do the selling.

Assigning preexisting sales contracts into a corporation is not advisable. Existing contracts usually name the salesperson and can generate personal holding company (PHC) income. Assigning these preexisting contracts to a new corporation may be construed as an assignment of income, something anyone can live without. New sales contracts should be drafted so that there is no question as to who is involved in the sales relationship and who is the true earner of the income.

Many salespeople wish to incorporate and still keep some of their old company's fringe benefits. These benefits include pensions, medical insurance, and expense allowances. In most cases, this cannot be done. Incorporating your cake and eating it too is very difficult. The cost of incorporating and providing your own benefits may well be the loss of existing master-company benefits. There are times when a carefully drawn agreement can continue some of the old benefits, but they are few and far between. Taking the double-benefit course should be tried only after careful investigation and upon the best of professional advice.

Life insurance agents, in particular, face some unique assignment of income problems. In the life insurance industry, agents are not only paid an initial commission when they sell a policy but are also paid renewal commissions. These renewal commissions are paid over a period of years on a predetermined schedule as long as the original policy is still in force and premiums are being paid on it. Over the years, renewal commissions can become rather substantial. If preexisting renewal commissions are transferred to the life insurance agent's talent corporation, they will be considered the income of the agent—*not* the corporation (assignment of income). Even though the corporation collects the renewals, the agent is taxed on them. This is not true of renewal commissions generated by policies the agent sells as an employee of his or her talent corporation. These renewals are income to the corporation.

There is a potential unreasonable compensation problem if renewals are paid out to the agent-employee in addition to other commissions. Since renewals are for prior contracts, they may be considered income from an asset (just like income from corporate investments in mutual funds). The asset would be the business previously written by the corporation. Renewals would then be "extra" income earned from actual assets of the corporation. Paying them out to the agent-employee on top of current income could lead to the IRS conclusion that the renewals are disguised dividends.

This problem can be avoided by simply stating in the employment contract between the agent and the talent corporation that renewals are part of the agent's regular compensation package. *Without this language there could be a major tax catastrophe.*

We cannot overemphasize the importance of formal written contracts between the talent corporation and the company which provides the products sold by the talent corporation as well as a formal employment contract between the talent corporation and the salesperson. With these agreements properly written, signed, and implemented, virtually all assignment of income, sham corporation, and PHC problems can be eliminated. Paper, paper, and more paper identify you as a legitimate talent corporation and will help ward off an IRS offensive.

An Independent Contractor Opportunity

TEFRA conferred a potential boon to many individuals engaged in the sale of real estate or who sell on a commission basis. It cleared up the question as to whether or not they could act as independent contractors. Unfortunately, it did not reach all those salespeople who wanted to have a clear shot at being an independent contractor.

It has always been difficult for most commissioned salespeople to qualify as independent contractors for the purposes of incorporating and setting up their own benefit programs. The reason for this difficulty was that, more often than not, the employer wanted to restrict the sales activities of its salespeople. Good salespeople are valuable commodities, and the companies for which these salespeople sell wanted their services on an exclusive basis. Since independent contractor status can rarely be used by those who work for only one company, salespeople often lost out on the opportunity to have their own corporations.

Recognizing this problem, Congress now allows real estate agents and "direct sellers" to maintain independent contractor status. The criteria which must be met by real estate agents and direct sellers to become an independent contractor are:

A real estate agent must be licensed to sell real estate.

A direct seller must be engaged in selling consumer products out of the home or otherwise outside a permanent retail establishment.

The services of each must be performed pursuant to a written contract with the company for whom the services are performed. The contract must provide that the salesperson is not an employee of the master company.

Substantially all of the salesperson's compensation must be received because of sales, not hours worked.

These rules will cover a multitude of salespeople and do represent a giant step forward. Many salespeople, especially those working out of a company headquarters, will still have to continue fighting the battle for independent contractor status. We have some suggestions to help these people in their struggle.

The Real Independent Contractor Problem

Salespeople are often prohibited from competing with the company they sell for. This presents a problem with respect to the independent contractor relationship that is necessary to successful incorporation.

A salesperson who signs an agreement not to compete (covenant not to compete) with a particular business is captive to that business. That person is locked in, and looks like an employee. One of the tests for determining independent contractor status is the ability to render services to competing firms. A salesperson's inability to perform services for competitors is often a stumbling block to his or her desires to incorporate.

One way to circumvent the restricted competition problem is for the salesperson to sell products other than those which are considered competitive. For example, a salesperson who sells automotive fan belts, tires, or related accessories may be able to also sell unrelated vendor goods, such as small tools for a different manufacturer. A one-person talent sales corporation selling several different types of products, some of which are exclusively sold for one company, stands a much better chance of being classified as an independent contractor than an exclusive-product one-person sales corporation.

There is no single format or equation to distinguish ironclad planning from dangerous planning. However, with diverse sales products and few, if any, master-company restrictions, the one-person sales corporation should prevail on the independent contractor argument.

Some salespeople have given verbal covenants not to compete, promises that they will not sell the products of competing companies. These types of arrangements are not overlooked on IRS examination. If there is a history or pattern of selling exclusively for a single company, that alone may be enough to embroil the sales corporation in an independent contractor dispute with IRS agents. However, the fact that there is no written prohibition as to other manufacturers may help. Please remember, you may be asked to testify as to your verbal agreements and pattern of doing business—and perjury means jail.

If you are an employee-salesperson now but tomorrow you incorporate, what has really changed? The IRS says "nothing" has changed. If, in fact, the only thing that changed was salesperson to Salesperson, Inc., the IRS will prevail. Incorporation, in and of itself, does not create independent contractor status. There must be more than just a tax reason to incorporate. Simple incorporation, even if done with the maximum attention to corporate formalities, may not be enough to create a real business purpose to incorporate. Some change in business, other than form, tends to demonstrate other purposes for incorporation.

Establishing a business purpose and independent contractor status is definitely tough for many salespeople to accomplish. In reality they want to incorporate to lower their taxes, not to change their business habits. This attitude, if not disguised, may very well lead to the IRS's not recognizing the new talent corporation. Even if one's business purpose and change in business format are cosmetic, that will be better than no change at all.

If there is no way for you to avoid total exclusivity as to your services, you should know that there is little chance of your sales corporation succeeding. Serving one master is a fast way for a one-person sales corporation to lose its corporate tax status.

Authors, Composers, and Artists

Copyright royalties are a form of personal holding company income. A PHC, as discussed earlier, is a corporation which has *personal* service income. The PHC rules force corporations to distribute their income, rather than have it taxed at the more favorable corporate income tax rates. All PHC income which is not distributed is taxed at a 50 percent rate, regardless of what tax bracket the corporation or the incorporated talent is in.

Many literary and artistic works are copyrighted under the federal copyright laws. A copyright, as thousands of authors, composers, and artists have found out, is a marketable item. There are two basic methods to market a copyright: licensing or selling.

Licensing the Use of a Copyright

A license is almost the same as a lease. When authors or artists license a copyright, they are allowing someone else to use (lease) their copyrighted work for a limited period of time. The fee charged for licensing a copyright is called a copyright royalty and may be paid all at once, over a period of years, or based on the number of books, scores, or prints sold.

Copyright royalties are PHC income, which can be used to pay for expenses, fringe benefits, retirement plans, and salary. To the extent that copyright royalties are not spent for these purposes and are retained in the corporation, the 50 percent penalty tax will be imposed. It is important to know that if your corporation licenses copyrights, the royalties are PHC income and can be subject to the PHC penalty tax.

Selling the Copyright

Many people who hold copyrights actually sell or assign them, rather than leasing them. The income received from the sale or assignment of a copyright is *not* PHC income. The income from selling a copyright may be received in the form of one payment, a series of fixed payments, or can be determined based on the number of books, scores, or prints sold, which is no different than when a copyright is licensed. The only difference between the two is that under a license, the ownership of the copyright is retained by the creative talent or the corporation, while a sale means that the ownership of the copyright is sold.

A copyright developed by the creating talent or the talent's corporation is not defined as a capital asset. That means that the sale proceeds are ordinary income and not capital gain income. The only tax benefit from the sale of a copyright is that the proceeds are not PHC income.

Both copyright royalty income and sales income can create an unreasonable compensation problem. This is especially true if the income is received in a lump sum. Lump-sum income received and paid out in the same year by the talent's corporation can certainly resemble a dividend. In such a case the IRS will most likely ask, "Did the talent (employee) receive this lump sum for services, or is it a return on his or her investment?" This question should be anticipated and preanswered in the talent's employment contract. Language that can be used is as follows:

> Because most of the employee's efforts are expended in the creation of the works contemplated in this employment contract, the employee should be paid for that effort. Since there is no way to measure such effort, the employee will receive 100 percent of any advance royalty or proceeds from the sale of a copyright of a work created by the employee.

Language of this type should be effective in rendering an unreasonable compensation argument ineffective. The payment for services under the employment contract is exactly the same payment the employee would have received had the employee been unincorporated. There should be no ground for unreasonableness.

There may be one more troublesome area if you are a talent that receives income from copyrights. Many times, you will want to contribute existing copyright royalties or sales agreements to your corporation at the time you incorporate. These are receivables, just like those of statutory professionals. The same care should be exercised when transferring them into the corporation as for accounts receivable. Copyrights, royalty, and sales agreements must be formally contributed into your corporation by contract; not to do so could make you and your corporation prime candidates for assignment of income problems.

Business Executives

Corporate executives were, for many years, the orphans of incorporated talent. While their professional cohorts—doctors, lawyers, and accountants—were reaping the benefits of having their own corporations, the executives of our world received more and more income and, consequently, paid more and more taxes. The corporations which employed them wanted, in many cases, to provide them with tax benefits but were statutorily prohibited from putting benefit packages together solely for executives; the Internal Revenue Code prohibits discrimination in favor of executives.

Finally, in the late 1960s and early 1970s, executives began to strike back. The more aggressive executives sought expert tax advice. They found that there was a chance that they, too, could incorporate.

They found that the one-person corporation did not have to be the exclusive bailiwick of doctors, lawyers, accountants, authors, and the many other professionals who had taken advantage of their own corporations.

Executives also learned, to their dismay, that their road to incorporation was not as easy as that of other talented people. The obstacles put in the executive's way were numerous and fraught with tax problems. The hurdles that had to be overcome were, in fact, a magnification of the more significant problems faced by other talents in their quest to incorporate.

Through perseverance and sheer numbers, executives slowly began the process of transforming the traditional employee-manager into the incorporated executive. No longer was this class of professionals tied to the fringe benefit apron strings of their master corporations. All the benefits available to one-person corporations often became theirs.

TEFRA has provided a rude awakening to executives. Whether Congress feared that too many Americans were incorporating or whether Congress was lobbied by the large corporations, fearful of losing control over their executives, we do not know. We do know, however, that TEFRA dealt a severe blow to the one-person corporation as far as its availability to executives is concerned. Many people believe, as we do, that the day of the incorporated executive working for a master company is gone.

Because the executive corporation movement is so important to executives and their business employers and because the problems they faced epitomize the general problems faced by many talented people who are or wish to incorporate, we will highlight some of their more significant incorporation roadblocks for you. With this perspective, you should better understand the many issues involved in incorporating talent. You will also better understand the clever way that Congress dealt the potential deathblow to the incorporated executive. If we are wrong in our assessment, the following material is even more critical to the executive reader.

Traditional Problems

Incorporated executives, as well as executives who wished to incorporate, before the instigation of the TEFRA rules had five major problems to overcome before becoming IRS-recognizable one-person corporations: business purpose, business activity, change in employment arrangement, permission from the master company, and loss of employment benefits.

Business Purpose

To be a true corporation, it was best for the executive to have reasons other than tax for incorporation. Incorporation for only tax reasons has always been a practice that has galled the IRS. Be that as it may, the IRS has traditionally made it easier on the incorporating talent who can manufacture a good nontax reason for incorporating.

Executives have found this task particularly difficult. Chapter 3 has some of the nontax reasons that are available to those who wish to incorporate. An additional reading of this chapter will highlight how others have filled their first minutes with every conceivable form of nontax reason, hoping that at least one would suffice. In our opinion, the best nontax reason was ego because it seemed to work. Can you come up with some more?

Business Activity

A corporation is not necessarily tax viable if it has articles, by-laws, and minutes. Under state law it is a fictitious person, but its tax life comes into existence when it performs real business functions. Business activity is simply a tax manifestation attributed to corporate life. The IRS has long maintained that corporations must actually engage in business activity.

Business activity encompasses many functions, one of which is the providing of corporate facilities such as office furniture, supplies, secretarial services, and other elements of the traditional business enterprise. You can see that this was difficult for the executive's one-person corporation. The master company provided everything. There was no need for the one-person corporation to provide anything.

Happily, this was one obstacle that could be overcome by a lawyer's stock-in-trade: paper. Contracts were established between the master corporation and the executive corporation. These contracts provided that the executive corporation would lease all the facilities it needed from the master corporation. The master corporation would, of course, charge for these services. This presented no problem. These costs were charged right back to the master corporation by the incorporated manager. The net effect was no effect at all, other than the tax effect, of course.

The secret of making these contracts work, in order to provide for business activity, was the fact that the corporation was doing something. In the worst case one could argue that the corporation was at least making contracts. In the best case it was making contracts which gave the executive facilities and services in the style to which the executive had become accustomed. If that could be done, the business activity test necessary for corporate tax existence was met.

Change in Employment Arrangement

One day the executive was an employee, the next an incorporated independent contractor. Everything else remained the same. This continuance of the status quo struck the IRS as another factor which indicated that the employee status of the executive still remained and that the corporation was merely a shell.

Overcoming the lack of change in the employment arrangement was a hurdle not easily vaulted. Neither the master corporation nor the newly incorporated executive really wanted any change. It was traumatic enough that the executive was now in a corporation. Any more change was adding chaos to an already confused relationship. Nevertheless, changes had to be made.

One of these changes included a change in the corporate title of the manager. Corporations are usually not allowed to be vice presidents or general managers. Only real people fill those jobs. The executive may have been Joe Fisk, vice president, before talent incorporation but became Joe Fisk, president, Fisk Management, Inc., after he incorporated.

Another change that was required and was extremely difficult to overcome was the ability of the executive corporation to provide management services for other master corporations. This freedom in the marketplace is an important element of becoming an independent contractor. Successfully making this change and memorializing it in the independent contractor agreement between the master corporation and the incorporated manager was usually enough to create the arm's length environment the Internal Revenue Service was looking for.

Getting Permission from the Master Company

Closely related to the issue of obtaining independent contractor status was the task of getting permission from the master company for the executive or manager to incorporate. Allowing executive incorporation was always difficult for most corporations and particularly those who were paternalistic.

Establishing a legitimate independent contractor relationship necessitates a loss of control over the executive by the master corporation. An independent contractor is only told what has to be accomplished, not how it is to be accomplished. Corporate employers want to control not only results but how those results are reached, and they are not apt to give up their control.

Of great concern to the master corporation was its liability with regard to FICA, FUTA, and unemployment liabilities. The master company would have to pay these amounts to the federal government in the event that the executive's corporation did not. These amounts could be quite large, especially when interest and penalties were assessed. Usually, the master company insisted on ongoing proof that these obligations were paid.

Perhaps the most difficult concession that a master corporation was asked to make was in the area of personal holding companies. To avoid PHC status, the corporation's incorporated manager had to ensure that the manager was not actually named or described in the contract between the two corporations. More often than not, this was the last straw for the master company; most would not give on this point. In our experience, the master companies wanted to know who was going to be showing up for work. They were not about to sign a contract that would allow the incorporated executive to send just anyone to work!

In order to receive permission to incorporate, the executive usually gave in on this issue. The PHC issue never arises if all the corporation's income is paid out in salary, fringe benefits, and expenses. Paying out all the earnings was a small price to pay to achieve the overall results of incorporation for most executives.

Loss of Employment Benefits

Perhaps the most underrated consideration, when an executive considered incorporating, was the loss of his or her current benefits with the master company. Sometimes the benefits being received prior to incorporation were superior to those finally adopted by the manager's corporation. In the zeal to incorporate, many individuals got caught in the "grass is always greener" syndrome. Care had to be taken by the executive's professional advisers to make sure that incorporation was really the best course of action in light of the benefit comparison.

In addition, there was usually no consideration given to the fact that most master companies provided certain very real unemployment benefits. Few executives considered what would happen if their employment was terminated, or, should we say, if their corporation was terminated. Terminated corporations generally do not receive severance pay or unemployment benefits.

Most executives making good salaries are optimists, at least in our experience, and seldom considered what would happen if they and their corporations were terminated. The incorporated executives were not always better off in their new corporations, but they did not find out in many cases until it was too late.

The problems associated with the incorporation of the executive epitomized the problems of all incorporated talents, but it was the executive who received the short end of the stick. Last of the professionals to take advantage of incorporation, the executive was the first to lose it. And lose it the executive did; Congress passed TEFRA and closed the executive corporation door.

The Demise of the Incorporated Executive

Congress, with the passage of TEFRA, made no attempt to define executives as employees rather than independent contractors, nor did it attempt to blatantly disallow executive corporations. It used a more subtle method.

In Chapter 10 we addressed affiliated service group rules. These rules exist to prohibit partnerships of professional corporations from avoiding covering all employees in a retirement plan. The essence of these rules is to prevent a professional who owns an interest in a partnership or a corporation from incorporating himself or herself and establishing a private retirement plan. The rule effectively includes all members of a service organization in one big family. Everyone must be covered in the same or similar plans.

These same affiliated service rules now apply to executives. If, as a result of TEFRA, an organization's principal business is performing management functions for another organization on a regular basis, both organizations are considered to be a single employer. Because they are considered to be a single employer, all employee benefits of one must be provided to the employees of the other.

The result is that the executive's corporation and the master company are considered to be part of one big happy family. Everyone in that family has to be covered by the same fringe benefits. The executive is back at ground zero: same benefits, same income taxes, no corporation.

Congress did not even leave room for other tax maneuvers. The law speaks to organizations, not corporations. Even if the executive liquidated his or her corporation and attempted to take advantage of TEFRA's liberal retirement plan changes for Keogh plans, there is still no relief from these rules. TEFRA defines organization as any corporation, partnership, or individual. Sound the funeral dirge; executive corporations and independent contractor status for executives are dead.

The new law adds insult to injury. There is one other provision of TEFRA which has an adverse effect on incorporated executives as well as any other incorporated talent. This provision states that any personal service corporation which provides services to only one other organization and is formed principally for the purposes of taking advantage of taxes can be totally overlooked by the IRS. As a result, IRS agents can ignore a properly formed corporation and allocate its income and deductions wherever they please.

The days of executive incorporation have gone the way of the brontosaurus. Tax-conscious executives will be singing the blues over their three-martini lunches. On the bright side, their employers will show nothing but smiles. Executive corporations were a thorn in their sides; perhaps that is why Congress abolished them. The executive corporation, at least for now, is no more.

Individual talents certainly have individual problems when it comes to putting their talents in the corporate structure. We have not covered all the problems indigenous to specific incorporated talents but have highlighted those problems that manifest themselves most frequently. Every talent's situation is generally as unique as his or her talent, and as a result, each talent should seek out the very best of professional advice.

Chapter

12

Observing
Corporate
Formalities
How Not to
Embarrass Yourself
at Your Own
Dinner Party

Throughout this book, we have berated you with the paramount mandate of the personal service corporation: *Corporate formalities are the keystone of successfully incorporated talent; they must be followed.*

Corporate formalities do not end with the incorporation process; they just begin. It is easy for most of us to be precise in our initial corporate dealings. We have a brand new "toy" that is going to provide us with tax benefits, a new image, and pizzazz. But the newness wears off and we are back to the old grind. Soon forgotten are our minute books, our employment contracts, and the bevy of paperwork that we paid so dearly for.

Then we receive a short, nondescript letter from the IRS. "We are being audited! They want our minute book, all our corporate books and records!" We frantically try to get everything together; some things we can, some we cannot. We look for our last three years of minutes and then remember that meetings were never held; no meeting, no minutes! We think of doing the minutes on an old typewriter and using old pens to backdate them. Visions of San Quentin pass before our eyes.

We have not exaggerated the scenario. It happens somewhere, every working day, year in and year out.

Paperwork takes time, effort, and money. It is an unpleasant task that is readily ignored. If you are not willing to conduct this corporate paper chase actively, think twice about incorporating your talent. Without paperwork, you are as vulnerable as a lone turkey in a very big turkey shoot.

Let us review some of the necessary evils of maintaining the corporate existence and then develop some practical guides to fulfilling ongoing corporate necessities. Maybe we can show some of the lone turkeys how to shoot back.

Staying Out of the Personal Holding Company Trap

The PHC 50 percent penalty tax is a great disincentive for either receiving PHC income or not distributing PHC income that has been inadvertently received. To review, PHC income in a personal service corporation is usually in the form of income received when someone other than the corporation designates, by name or description, who is to perform services. Generally, where PHC income is 60 percent or more of all income, a PHC exists and a penalty tax is assessed on all the undistributed PHC income. This forces the shareholder of a PHC to either take the income as salary or expenses or pay a dividend.

When faced with a PHC, always pay out all PHC income in the form of salary, fringe benefits, or retirement plans. These are deductions of the corporation and eliminate any undistributed PHC income problems. A dividend is another method of distributing PHC income. Avoid this method. Dividends are subject to double taxation and may be more expensive than the PHC penalty tax.

The desire to income-split (use one's corporate and personal tax brackets to lower income tax rates) should be avoided. Income splitting may cause PHC income to be retained in the corporation. Do not keep income in your corporation unless there is a legitimate business reason for doing so.

Assuming there is a reason to income-split, you should structure your income so it does not fall under the PHC rules. Make sure all contracts between your corporation and the companies that hire its services make clear that your corporation can designate whomever it chooses to perform its services. Do not let the master company have any say in who is to perform. Constant monitoring by your accountant, coupled with using the services of your tax attorney (to review contracts), can help assure you that your corporation is not a PHC.

Remaining an independent contractor is also very important to the success of your personal service corporation. Always make sure that your contracts maintain your independent contractor status. Never perform services without some kind of written document which sets forth the agreed-upon relationship. Many of our clients have us draft a form, or "boilerplate," contract that can be used in most instances. While this method is not as surefire as doing a contract tailored to each job, it at least assures that basics are covered. Independent contract agreements that have a long duration (over six months) or include larger than normal fees should always be professionally written. Attorneys' fees are cheap in comparison to the adverse consequences and expenses incurred through losing an independent contractor issue with the IRS.

An independent contractor must make sure that all FICA, FUTA, and withholding requirements are met. These requirements include timely payment of the correct amounts due and the filing of the appropriate tax forms. Failure to comply with these provisions can create personal tax liability for the officers and directors of the corporation as to the original tax plus penalties and interest and, in the worst case, conviction of a misdemeanor or felony!

Generating Paper

Paper is the lifeblood of a corporation. Running out of paper is like running out of blood—the corporation dies. Minutes, contracts, and government forms are three areas in which paper plays an important part.

Minutes

Minutes are a contemporaneous record of the dealings of the shareholders and directors. They are the formal reflection of the suggestion, discussion, and approval or disapproval of corporate acts. Both shareholders and directors are required to hold at least one meeting a year. They can, however, hold special meetings during the year for corporate matters that cannot be postponed until the annual meeting.

Shareholders are responsible for electing the board of directors. The shareholders normally meet and vote on changes in the articles of incorporation, a major sale of the assets of the corporation, mergers, liquidations, and most other matters which directly affect their stock. Because shareholders vote only on these items, a meeting once a year is generally enough. This is almost always true in a one-person talent corporation.

The board of directors elects the officers of the corporation. Directors also vote on almost any transaction which is not in the ordinary course of business, and as a result, they normally meet more than the shareholders. The directors can delegate a lot of their authority to the corporate officers. This delegation, done in minutes, allows greater flexibility for the officers and tends to reduce paperwork. The directors must approve the acts of the officers at the annual meeting, because even though the officers have authority to act, the ultimate responsibility lies with the directors.

In our experience, owners of one-person talent corporations do not keep their corporations up to date. They do not have meetings of either the shareholders or the directors. There is no written and separate recognition of the shareholder, director, and officer roles. The talent figures that he or she *is* the sole shareholder, chairperson of the board, president, and, in addition, the sole employee, of course. Any decision the talent makes is gospel, and no number of meetings are going to change it.

The reality and the formality do, however, have to be separated. To be a corporation is to act like a corporation. Just because decisions at the various management levels are a foregone conclusion does not eliminate the need to follow the rules. Form is important and should be followed.

Many state laws recognize the inability of most smaller corporations to cope with stringent legal requirements. These enlightened states include a provision in their corporate laws allowing for "consent minutes," or "minutes of action."

Consent minutes, as we will call them, are minutes of meetings that never happened. If a major corporate action is to be taken or has already been taken and the directors and shareholders approve of that action, then a meeting is not necessary. To give approval, the directors or shareholders merely sign the consent minutes. Their signatures give affirmative consent to the action taken or to be taken. These minutes which evidence the directors' or shareholders' approval of certain corporate actions when signed by all the directors or shareholders have the same exact force and effect of full-blown meeting minutes.

We suggest to our clients that they keep an annual notebook, highlighting the date and description of each transaction which they consider to be out of the ordinary. We also supply them with a checklist of examples. They are asked to keep copies of any documents or records associated with these transactions.

At the end of the year, either a meeting is held in our offices or the notebook is sent to us for review. Consent minutes are prepared from this information. The result is less fuss, fewer meetings, and lower fees! The minutes will stand up and are usually complete and effective.

Keeping minutes is as easy or hard as you choose to make it. They are a necessary evil and can be a helpful management tool. They can help you remember what you did during the year and, more importantly, why. Minutes, when approached with a positive attitude, are a useful management tool. They are absolutely critical to continued corporate existence.

Contracts

When contracts are used between your corporation and other people or businesses, several objectives are met:

Contracts in your corporation's name indicate that the required corporate formalities are being carried on.

Contracts demonstrate a business purpose and a continuing corporate function.

Contracts with master companies reduce the likelihood that you have assigned your income. They show that your corporation is the real income earner.

Contracts between you and your corporation help assure the IRS that you and your corporation are dealing on an arm's length basis and that you are an employee eligible for corporate benefits.

Your corporation should be a party to the contract. You personally should never be a party.

All your corporate contracts should be reviewed by your lawyer so that the likelihood of a mistake can be reduced. If you are not a lawyer, do not practice law.

One last reminder with regard to contracts. Approve all of them in the directors' minutes. This action will give formal recognition and validity to the corporation's contracts. Not only will the IRS be on notice that all formalities are being met, but in a later contract dispute, it may help to prove that the contract was legally binding.

Government Forms

Almost all levels of government, from federal to state to county to city, require some type of formal reporting. Make sure that your corporation, through its advisers, complies with all these requirements. Noncompliance can lead to fines as well as other penalties. Failure to file any of these forms may lead to nonrecognition of the corporate existence. All your planning will go for naught if you forget to file a critical form which affects your corporate existence.

Self-Dealing with Legal Propriety

Nothing is more questionable to IRS agents than the dealings between the sole shareholder and that shareholder's corporation. Because it is sometimes difficult to differentiate these two alter egos, dealings between them are apt to be questioned.

Some transactions which are likely to be the subject of more than cursory IRS scrutiny are salaries, bonuses, fringe benefits, and expenses, especially for travel and entertainment.

Before we discuss each of these items, it would be helpful for you to remember that you must prove to the IRS that what you have done is legal and does not violate any tax rule. The IRS does not have to prove that you are wrong. You have the "burden of proof" that what you have done is right.

Salaries

Your salary may be deemed excessive or unreasonable. If it is, the excessive amount will be taxed twice; it will be considered a dividend. A carefully drafted employment contract can help you meet your burden of proof and can justify the salary taken. Your salary should also be approved, at least yearly, in minutes of the directors.

Salaries can also be subject to IRS attack if they are not paid properly. For example, if you have a year in which your noncorporate income is high, you may wish to defer receiving your corporate salary until your next tax year. In most cases, this can be done because the corporation's fiscal year is different than your tax year (calendar year). Thus if your corporate year-end is January 31, you can delay paying your salary until after December 31 but before January 31. Your salary is taxed in the next calendar year, and your corporation receives a deduction for the salary in its corporate year.

The IRS knows that even though your corporation is a separate legal entity, you have total control of when its income is paid. If you delay paying income in the manner we just described, IRS agents can allocate the income back to the prior year. They can make a good case that since you control the corporation, you had the right to receive your salary in the prior year. Since you had the right to receive it, the IRS will tax it in the prior year.

We know of no fail-safe way to avoid this problem. However, a properly drafted employment agreement allowing the corporation to defer salary payments, plus directors' minutes stating a business purpose for this deferral, can be very helpful.

One other word on deferral: Greed will get a tax planner in trouble almost every time. The feeling that if some is good, more is better is *not* a basic tenet of tax law. Taking some salary and deferring some is much wiser than deferring all of it.

The biggest danger to incorporated talent as far as unreasonable compensation is concerned is the "big year." From time to time, the shareholder-employee of a personal service corporation may have an exceptionally lucrative year. For salespeople, it may be a particularly large sale bonus; for a lawyer, a contingent fee. Whatever the reason, a large amount of income may occur in one tax year.

Forward planning is desirable so that such an event can be anticipated and planned for on the front end. Anticipation can very well reduce the exposure of a successful unreasonable compensation argument by the IRS. Without a written agreement, a sudden increase in salary resulting from a good corporate income year can be the subject of an IRS audit. However, if payment for such an event is contemplated and agreed to before it is paid (through provisions in the employment contract), IRS agents will find it much more difficult to assert their unreasonable compensation argument. Make sure that this type of contingency is part of your employment contract.

You must remember that transactions between a shareholder-employee and the corporation are always suspect from the IRS's point of view. The IRS agents want to make sure that you are not, somehow, disguising a dividend. One of the most frequently used methods of disguising a dividend is to add it to compensation. Proper adherence to corporate formalities, coupled with the advice of your tax professionals, can allow you to avoid the problems associated with unreasonable compensation.

Bonuses

Bonuses are a favorite IRS target. A bonus is normally paid at or near the end of a corporation's fiscal year. Many people use a bonus as a way to defer income to another calendar year or to reduce the corporation's taxable income at its year-end. Some people pay a bonus for exceptional or outstanding services; this rarely happens in a one-person talent corporation.

A bonus looks very much like a dividend payment. Dividends are payments to shareholders as a return on their investment. As such, they are paid from profits. However, unlike a bonus, they are not deductible. Since bonuses resemble dividends, IRS agents are fond of treating them as dividends. If they do, the corporate bonus deduction is disallowed, but the payment is still income to the shareholder-recipient. The net result is double tax.

Again, an employment contract, good directors' minutes, and restraint of greed present a good first-line defense. The best defense, however, is not to pay a bonus. If you choose to defer salary until the end of the corporate year, call it what it truly is, deferred or accrued salary. As long as you have a business reason to hold this salary until the end of the year, you should not face tough IRS resistance. What's in a name? Well, the name "bonus" spells big trouble; the name "accrued salary" is good business. Get the picture?

Fringe Benefits

Almost all corporate fringe benefits are subject to rules promulgated by either the Internal Revenue Code or the IRS. Simply follow these rules and your benefits will be protected. We have discussed many of these rules for fringe benefits in earlier chapters. They include medical reimbursement plans, retirement plans, and the like.

Always insist on formally written benefit plans. These reflect a desire to follow the rules. Always adopt the plans in directors' minutes and enumerate them in your employment contract. Putting fringe benefits in your employment contract is a means of showing that they are part of your employment package and were subject to arm's length negotiation. It also demonstrates to IRS agents that the benefits were not intended to be dividends but were part of your compensation package. Again, potential dividend problems can be alleviated by use of a written employment contract.

Expenses

Deductions are allowed for ordinary and necessary business expenses incurred in the running of your trade or business. To qualify, these expenses must be directly related to your business. What is ordinary, necessary, and related to your business is often a matter of conjecture and controversy.

Upon IRS audit, you can expect that your expenses will be examined in great detail. This scrutiny is based on the often valid assumption that the shareholder-employee has incurred at least some expenses for personal rather than business use. Areas which are particularly vulnerable to this commingling of personal and business records include travel, entertainment, and automobiles.

When expenses of a shareholder-employee are found to be personal rather than business-related, the corporation's deductions for those expenses are disallowed. The total amount is then treated as income to the shareholder-employee. The expense was incurred for personal use and is therefore not deductible to the corporation. The result is a dividend: double tax.

To reduce your exposure to the disallowance of expenses, keep good records; record keeping is vital, remember? As long as you have a record, which is kept at or about the same time the expense is incurred (a contemporaneous record), showing the amount of the expense, what it was for, and the circumstances under which it was incurred, there should be little or no problem in your justifying the expense as business-related. There are somewhat tougher rules for travel and entertainment. The circumstances must be delineated in much greater detail, outlining who was involved, what business was discussed, and even how much of the time spent was business-related.

Our clients, every one of them, claim that this record keeping is a royal pain in the neck, and they are, of course, right. But when compared to the alternative—a long, hard, expensive IRS audit—it is really not so bad and should become a habit. There is no substitute for paper; its long-term benefits usually outweigh the short-term neck pains.

Other protective measures can be used to justify expenses. A corporate credit card is an excellent method to track expenses. Merely write on the receipt all information with regard to the expense: who was there, what was done, or what the expense was incurred for. A monthly expense voucher, coupled with all receipts, can definitely save IRS-related headaches and let you know where the money went.

Make sure that your employment contract allows for expenses, such as travel and entertainment. Also include a procedure as to expense vouchers and reimbursement procedures. As to reimbursement, avoid it if you can. Use corporate funds and credit cards to make corporate expenditures.

Make sure that the directors' minutes reflect any extraordinary expenses, such as expensive business trips, seminars, or the like. The minutes should reflect the purpose of the expense and specific approval of it.

Please, remember one last point: If you incur an expense which is personal and charge it to your corporation, do not let the corporation expense it. You should take it into income or, better yet, simply reimburse your corporation. This demonstrates to the IRS that you are playing straight. On the other hand, don't be afraid to deduct a legitimate business expense. When in doubt, deduct it. If you are wrong, your employment contract can help you avoid the double tax trap. If you are right, you get a deduction that you otherwise would have lost. The IRS rarely finds a personal expense that should have been deducted. If you do not take the deduction, it is definitely lost.

To self-deal with legal propriety means that you must follow strict corporate formality. Ask yourself what you as an owner of a business would expect from one of your employees. Odds are, you will not allow any expense which is not business-related. If you treat yourself as that employee and make sure all transactions between you and your corporation are based on this employer-employee relationship, few questions will arise when the IRS agents come knocking at your corporate door.

Accumulated Earnings

Unreasonable accumulated earnings occur when a corporation does not distribute its income in either salaries, expenses, or dividends. The result is that aftertax corporate profits build inside the corporation.

As we have discussed in earlier chapters, Congress determined early on that allowing income to stay in a corporation meant that the lower income tax brackets were being used. To counteract this "abusive" use of the corporate tax bracket, Congress passed several sections of the Internal Revenue Code, all of which define what accumulated earnings are, how they can be justified, and what the penalty tax is for those improperly accumulated earnings. These sections are aimed at forcing the corporation to distribute unneeded earnings or face a stiff tax.

The penalty tax on unreasonable accumulated earnings is 27½ percent on the first $100,000 of those earnings and 38½ percent on those earnings in excess of $100,000. *This amount is in addition to normal federal income taxes already paid.* Some adjustments are allowed to lower accumulated earnings, but these adjustments are usually not too effective.

The only good news is that the penalty tax only applies to earnings retained in the year or years of IRS audit. If you have gotten away with accumulating earnings for prior years, good for you. You are one of the lucky ones.

There is a base amount of accumulated earnings, which is allowed for all businesses. This amount is $250,000, *except for certain personal service corporations.* Personal service corporations in the areas of health, law, engineering, architecture, accounting, actuarial science, performing arts, and consulting are limited to a $150,000 base amount. Why this additional penalty for personal service corporations? Because that is where most of the abuse has occurred. Income splitting has been historically prevalent in personal service corporations.

The penalty tax will not apply to all corporations which have accumulated earnings in excess of the base amount if they can show that the accumulations are reasonable. Some acceptable reasons are business expansion, inflation (be careful here—inflation is only good for *some* accumulated earnings), and wide fluctuations in income and contingent liabilities. In almost all cases, the one-person talent corporation has great difficulty in proving that its earnings are not unreasonable.

Knowledgeable advisers recommend that earnings should not be accumulated. The potential problems are generally greater than the benefits derived. Upon an IRS examination, accumulated earnings stick out like an African elephant's ears. Not only are they obvious, they are normally almost impossible to defend against. This is particularly true with regard to the one-person talent corporation.

If you are a one-person talent corporation that is accumulating earnings, you ought to do at least two things. The first is to choose top-notch tax advisers; the second is to start preparing for that audit right now. Get together minutes and other documentation to justify and explain the actual reasons for those accumulated earnings. Remember, you have the burden of proving that the earnings are reasonable for the needs of the business.

A PHC cannot have accumulated earnings. If you are willing to pay the 50 percent PHC penalty, you can accumulate earnings to your heart's content. The federal government will appreciate your generous support.

Creating a corporation can be analogized to a dinner party: The table is set and the food prepared. Maintaining a corporation requires excellent table manners. Too many people forget or are not apprised of the expected etiquette. They get too comfortable at their own tables. Their corporate manners either are never learned or simply degenerate over time.

Unfortunately, IRS agents are more than willing to critique anyone's corporate etiquette at the time they audit. The service is a stern taskmaster that is generally unforgiving. Discipline is the mandate, not forgiveness.

If one is going to incorporate, one must learn to follow the formalities necessary for creating and maintaining the corporate existence: Not to do so would be a costly and time-consuming mistake. Sloppy corporate manners can be costly as well as embarrassing.

Chapter

13

Getting Out of Your Corporation
Breaking Up May Be Hard to Do

The changes in our tax law precipitated by TEFRA have made many incorporated talents question the viability of their staying incorporated. As the word with respect to the new law gets out, most incorporated talents will probably be asking their advisers, "Should I stay incorporated, and if not, how do I get out?" Since the corporate structure no longer provides the exclusive haven for major retirement planning, many talents may initially opt to do away with their corporate existence.

The knowledge in this chapter is critical to your economic well-being, whether you are already incorporated or are considering doing so. Talent corporations are killed, or liquidated (the proper term), for many sound and good reasons, other than a reaction to new tax legislation. They are liquidated because their talents retire, change careers, or die.

Liquidating a talent corporation can be a tricky affair. Like so many other things in life, getting into a corporation can be much easier and less expensive than getting out. The complications inherent in liquidation are brought about by certain provisions of the Internal Revenue Code. Congress determined long ago that it would attempt to tax the corporation or its shareholders on corporate dissolution.

Why Congress decided to punish liquidating corporations, we will never know, but we can speculate. You will recall from our various references to corporate history that Congress has traditionally viewed corporate existence as preferred existence. Since corporations have enjoyed favorable tax status, Congress must have reasoned that it would tax these entities on the cessation of their business, in effect creating a rear-end penalty. This theory even makes more sense when one considers that Congress took no political risk in doing so. Taxing a terminating business is not likely to raise the ire of American business because, in our experience, most businesspeople cannot envision their own eventual business demise. Taxation without political risk is good political strategy.

The key to liquidating your talent corporation is for you to know and understand the various types of liquidation approaches and to ascertain which approach is best in your circumstance. Our experience tells us that few talents ever give any thought to the consequences of eventually ending their corporations. This lack of foresight is regrettable because the end can be, and almost always is, more significant than the beginning. Knowing how to escape from a situation is every bit as important as knowing how to get properly into one, at least when tax is involved.

There are two basic types of IRS-sanctioned liquidation approaches that are commonly used by one-person talent corporations. The first we will refer to as a straight liquidation, the second as a calendar-month liquidation. There is a third type of liquidation which is part and parcel of a straight liquidation. It is called a one-year liquidation and, although used infrequently by talent, will briefly be discussed by us.

The Straight Liquidation

A straight liquidation is treated under tax law as if the shareholder-employee sells all his or her stock to the corporation in exchange for all the assets and liabilities of the corporation. This type of liquidation is taxable to the extent that the shareholder has a gain that results from that exchange. The amount of gain is the difference between the cost basis of the shareholder's stock and the fair market value of the assets received in exchange for the stock, less any liabilities assumed. The legalese in our previous sentence can be better understood through the following example:

Farthingill Corporation is owned totally by a famous Shakespearian actor, Thomas Aquinas Farthingill, III, also know as Tom. Tom has decided that his corporation is no longer what it used to be, and he wants to get out of it. The corporation has assets and liabilities valued as follows:

Cash	$20,000
Accounts receivable	10,000
Furniture	5,000
Bank note	(10,000)
Total	$25,000

Tom started his corporation many years ago with a cash investment of $1000.

Under a straight liquidation, Tom is taxed on the difference between the cost basis of his stock and the fair market value of the corporation's assets, less the corporate liabilities. The taxable gain is $24,000. This will be taxed at the favorable capital gain rate, a maximum of 20 percent.

Fair market value of assets	$35,000
Less: Bank note	(10,000)
Less: Cost basis	(1,000)
Total taxable gain	$24,000
Less: 20% tax	(4,800)
Net to Tom	$19,200

The result under Tom's corporate liquidation would be the same if Tom paid off his $10,000 liability and then sold his stock to someone else for $25,000. Tom would have a $24,000 gain ($25,000 less his cost basis of $1000), less $4800 of capital gain tax ($24,000 times 20 percent tax).

There is generally no corporate tax when a straight liquidation is used. Under a straight liquidation the shareholder pays tax at capital gain rates on the amount he or she receives after the cost basis has been subtracted.

There are, however, some major exceptions to the general rule (that the corporation suffers no tax upon liquidation) which you should be aware of. If a corporation has taken depreciation (cost recovery under ERTA) on assets, it may have to take some or all of this depreciation into income. This will occur if the fair market value of the asset is greater than its depreciated value on the books of the corporation. For example:

> The equipment in Tom's corporation consists of an old desk and chair acquired by Farthingill Corporation for $1000. They have been depreciated down to zero for quite some time but, in the interim, have become valuable antiques. They are now worth $5000. Upon the liquidation of the corporation, the $1000 in depreciation previously deducted must be taken into income by the corporation and corporate income tax must be paid on this amount. The $4000 difference between original cost and fair market value does not have to be taken into income by the corporation. It will be taken into income by Tom.

This concept is called recapture of depreciation, or recapture of cost recovery. Depreciation or cost recovery is a tax benefit bestowed on businesses by the Internal Revenue Code. Each is a term which allows the cost of an asset to be written off over a period of time. This write-off is supposed to represent the fact that the asset is wearing out and therefore has less value for each year it has been used.

The theory behind recapture is that if upon the sale of the asset (a liquidation is considered to be a sale) the asset did not really depreciate in value, then the corporation got the advantage of a tax deduction it did not really deserve. Since the amount written off was wrong (the asset did not wear out like it was supposed to), this amount will have to be taken back into income by the corporation. The amount that the corporation takes into income upon liquidation is the total amount of the cost recovery, or depreciation, that was taken and returned to the corporation through appreciation, not to exceed the fair market value of the asset.

In our example of the Farthingill Corporation, the depreciation taken was $1000. The fair market value was $5000. Since the fair market value exceeds the depreciation, Farthingill Corporation must take the full $1000 into income. The remaining $4000 is not subject to corporate tax. It will, however, be taxed on Tom's personal tax return. If the chair and desk were worthless at the time of liquidation, there would be no recapture. Likewise, if the chair and desk were worth $500, there would be $500 of recapture to the corporation. If the fair market value of an asset is less than the basis of the asset, there will be no recapture and no tax at the corporate level.

Recapture also applies to investment tax credit. Investment tax credit recapture can be more complex and expensive than depreciation recapture. A detailed explanation of all the aspects of recapture is beyond the scope of this book, but you must keep this tax concept in mind if you are thinking about liquidating your corporation. Recapturing depreciation (cost recovery) and investment tax credit can be very expensive. If you are considering a straight liquidation, consult with your accountant and tax lawyer and be sure that they calculate the amount of recapture in your corporation before the liquidation decision is finally made.

As you can see from our examples, the valuation of the corporation's assets becomes critical when a talent is thinking of using a straight liquidation. The more assets in the corporation and the higher their value, the more potential for recapture and for capital gain tax to the shareholder. The IRS defines fair market value as the amount that a willing buyer would pay a willing seller when neither the buyer nor seller is under any compulsion to either buy or sell and both have knowledge of the marketplace. This rule can certainly maximize value, which is, of course, the reason why the IRS uses it.

Before you attempt a straight liquidation, you should have a very good grasp of what the fair market value of your corporation's assets is. For some assets such as cash or marketable stocks and bonds, this may be quite easy. For other assets such as equipment, copyrights or real estate, the valuation may prove to be very difficult. If the amount of the assets is of any substantial size, it is always in your best interest to get them appraised by an independent appraiser. An appraiser who knows the purpose of the appraisal is sure to be more sympathetic to your case than an appraiser hired by the IRS. If the IRS agents do not like your values, they will hire their own appraiser, who will certainly not be very sympathetic toward you. You have the burden of proving that your appraiser's valuations are correct. A good appraisal will help meet this burden of proof and will help reduce your exposure to IRS attack. Your own appraisal will also enable you to isolate the true tax cost of a straight liquidation so that you can make a good decision as to its efficacy before the liquidation occurs.

Another liquidation consideration, which can be as important as recapture, is the amount of accounts receivable owned by your corporation prior to liquidation and the corporation's accounting method. We discussed methods of accounting in Chapter 5. A rereading of that material may help you understand how accounting methods relate to liquidation.

Let us assume that Tom's corporation is on the cash method of accounting and that at the time of liquidation it has $10,000 of uncollected receivables. If they are uncollected, no income tax has been paid on them under the cash method of accounting. Upon liquidation, the corporation is required to pay income taxes on these receivables, whether or not they have been collected! The only way the corporation can escape paying taxes on them is if the corporation can prove that they are worthless. This is very difficult to do. If your corporation has receivables that may be collectible, you will probably want to hold off on liquidating until they are paid down to some reasonable amount. Paying tax on income you do not receive is not indicative of good planning.

Now that we have some idea of the true picture of Farthingill Corporation's tax situation, we can analyze the total cost of a straight liquidation. With the elements of recapture and accounts receivable, the taxes have gone up considerably. We are going to assume that Farthingill Corporation is in the *lowest* corporate income tax bracket of 15 percent and that Tom is in the maximum personal tax bracket of 50 percent.

The Farthingill Corporation has the following income with its consequent tax:

Income:	
Accounts receivable	$10,000
Recapture	1,000
Total	$11,000
Tax (15%)	$ 1,650

Following is the total amount remaining to be distributed to Tom starting with his corporation's $20,000 in cash less the above-mentioned 15 percent tax of $1650, or $18,350.

Cash	$18,350
Accounts receivable	10,000
Furniture	5,000
Bank note	(10,000)
Less: Cost basis of stock	(1,000)
Total	$22,350
Tax to Tom at 20%	4,470
Aftertax balance	$17,880

The income tax paid by Tom, when recapture and accounts receivable are taken into account, is 20 percent of $22,350, or $4470. The total tax cost of liquidating is $6120. Tom ends up with cash and furniture of $8880 and the task of collecting his $10,000 of accounts receivable.

A straight liquidation can be an expensive way to liquidate the one-person corporation. To do it at the lowest tax cost takes considerable planning and thought. It is another area where the use of knowledgeable professionals can mean the difference between a large tax bill and one that is more palatable.

To summarize the elements of a straight liquidation:

A straight liquidation is almost as if the shareholder has sold his or her stock back to the corporation.

The amount of taxable gain to the shareholder-employee is the difference between the cost basis of the stock and the fair market value of the corporate assets, less liabilities.

The income generated to the shareholder-employee is generally taxed at the capital gain rates.

The corporation may have to recapture and pay income tax on depreciation (cost recovery) and investment tax credit it had previously taken.

The One-Month Liquidation

A one-month liquidation was invented for the benefit of corporations holding appreciated real estate. As we saw in the prior section, when the value of corporate assets is particularly high, a straight liquidation can generate significant income taxes. The congressional real estate lobby, aware of the disastrous results of straight liquidations for real estate corporations, was able to get temporary legislation passed to allow liquidations to occur at a low tax cost. This temporary measure, like many, many others, was never repealed and remains with us today.

The concept of a one-month liquidation is the same as a straight liquidation: A shareholder's stock is exchanged for the assets and liabilities of the corporation. The method of taxation and the time restraints with regard to each of these types of liquidations are entirely different.

To qualify under the provisions of the one-month liquidation, the whole process of liquidation must occur in any one calendar month. You can pick your month, but the IRS and the Internal Revenue Code are very precise about the fact that the entire process can only take one month. If the month is missed by even one minute, the liquidation is treated as if it was a straight liquidation. In some instances, the difference in taxes can be enormous. A one-month liquidation is absolutely no place for do-it-yourselfers or for inexperienced advisers.

Instead of a tax on the difference between the fair market value of the corporate assets, less liabilities, and the shareholder's cost basis in the stock, as is the case in a straight liquidation, the one-month liquidation causes the retained earnings of the corporation to be taxed as a dividend and may generate a capital gain tax on the cash in the corporation, in some instances.

Retained earnings of a corporation represent the aftertax earnings of the corporation. The Internal Revenue Code calls retained earnings "earnings and profits" and has a special method for calculating them. For our purposes, earnings and profits and retained earnings will be considered to be the same so that we can facilitate your understanding.

Given this background, let us examine why this special interest legislation was so apropos for shareholders of real estate corporations. Subsequent to World War II, many real estate entrepreneurs incorporated their real estate holdings or directly acquired real estate through their corporations. As we all know, real estate appreciated at phenomenal rates in the postwar years. If these entrepreneurs elected to liquidate their corporations under the straight-liquidation rules, they would have paid tax on the highly appreciated value of their real estate.

A one-month liquidation taxes corporate earnings and cash. Real estate corporations do not generally have either. As a result, the moguls of real estate could and would continue to acquire real estate in their corporations. Should they desire to get that property out of their corporations, they simply liquidate under the one-month approach. In doing so, they do not pay any tax on the appreciated value of their real estate holdings. For example:

> Joe Bob King acquires significant raw land in a corporation he created only for that purpose. King, Inc., paid $10,000 for the land. The corporation got the $10,000 because Joe Bob exchanged $10,000 for all the stock in the corporation. On liquidation that land has an appraised fair market value of $110,000.
>
> If Joe Bob liquidated under the straight-liquidation approach, he would pay a capital gain tax on the $100,000 difference between his stock's cost basis and the fair market value of the property.
>
> However, if Joe Bob liquidated pursuant to a calendar-month liquidation, he would not pay any tax, because King, Inc., did not have any retained earnings or cash. What a deal for Joe Bob.

The news of people liquidating their corporations, under scenarios very much like Joe Bob's, quickly spread in the country's locker rooms and social clubs. As a result, many people, including incorporated talents, assumed that they could do likewise with their corporate liquidations. In order to determine whether this approach works in the typical one-person talent corporation, let us take another look at the corporation of Thomas Aquinas Farthingill, III. Table 13-1 shows the book value of the Farthingill Corporation on the cash method of accounting.

Book value is a concept that simply shows the cost or face value of assets minus cost recovery (depreciation) and liabilities. No accounts receivable are shown because under the cash method of accounting they are merely expectancies and are not considered an asset until collected. You can see that the earnings of Farthingill Corporation are $9,000. This represents the taxable income left in the corporation after federal income taxes and does not include the $1000 Tom originally put in his corporation (cost basis). You will also see that while the fair market value of the furniture is $5000, its book value is zero because the original cost has been written off as depreciation, or cost recovery.

Tom will initially be taxed on the earnings of his corporation, if he chooses a one-month liquidation. You would think that this would be $9000. It is not, and that is where the complications in a one-month liquidation arise. Upon liquidation, the accounts receivable of a cash-method corporation have to be taken into income. Thus the $10,000 of receivables becomes taxable income to Tom's corporation. In addition, Tom's corporation will have to recapture depreciation of $1000. This is the amount which was depreciated in past corporate

Table 13-1. Book Value of Farthingill Corporation (Cash Method of Accounting)

Assets		
Cash	$20,000	
Furniture*	–0–	
Total assets		$20,000

Liabilities and Net Worth		
Bank note	$10,000	
Total		$10,000
Stock (cost basis)	$ 1,000	
Earnings	9,000	
Total		10,000
Total liabilities and net worth		$20,000

* The furniture has been totally depreciated, but it still has a fair market value of $5000.

years. Since the value of the corporate furniture ($5000) is greater than the recapture amount ($1000), all $1000 must be taken into income by the corporation.

The $10,000 in receivables plus the $1000 in recapture mean that the corporation will be taxed on a total of $11,000. Assuming that Farthingill Corporation is in a 15 percent tax bracket, there is a tax of $1650, leaving $9350 to be added to earnings. The earnings are then $18,350 ($9000 original earnings plus the $9350 created by the liquidation).

Tom is responsible for paying personal income taxes on $18,350. While Tom has received a total of $23,350 from the corporation—$33,350 in cash, receivables, and furniture less the $10,000 liability—he is only taxed on the $18,350 of earnings. The other $5000 is taken tax-free.

The $18,350 taxable gain is taxed as ordinary income with a maximum tax bracket of 50 percent. Since the earnings of the corporation have already been taxed once, the effect of Tom's electing a one-month liquidation is the creation of a sizable dividend.

There is one more tax quirk in a calendar-month liquidation. If Tom receives cash or certain stocks or bonds in excess of the earnings of the corporation, then they will be subject to tax to the extent that they are greater than the earnings. Farthingill Corporation has cash of $18,350 ($20,000 originally, less the $1650 paid in income taxes) and earnings of $18,350. Because the cash is equal to the earnings, there is no additional tax. In cases where cash exceeds earnings, the excess amount is taxed at the capital gain tax rate.

Table 13-2. Comparison of the Personal Tax Effects of a Calendar-Month Liquidation and a Straight Liquidation

	Straight Liquidation	Calendar-Month Liquidation
Ordinary income	$ –0–	$18,350
Tax (50%)	–0–	9,175
Capital gain	22,350	–0–
Tax (20%)	4,470	–0–
Total tax	$ 4,470	$ 9,175

Table 13-2 compares the tax to Tom under a straight liquidation and a calendar-month liquidation and assumes that Tom is in the highest personal income tax bracket: 50 percent on ordinary income and 20 percent on capital gain income.

In the case of Farthingill Corporation and Thomas Aquinas Farthingill, III, it is quite obvious that the straight liquidation is far better, from a tax point of view, than a one-month liquidation. Tom is no Joe Bob; of that, we are quite sure.

But wait! TEFRA, for once, may come to the rescue—or at least help the situation just a little. There is a special provision in TEFRA that gives some relief to personal service corporations. If a personal service corporation is liquidated under the provisions relating to calendar-month liquidations in either 1983 or 1984, there is no additional corporate tax on the accounts receivable. The corporate income tax on the receivables in the Farthingill Corporation can be avoided, but Tom will pay income tax on them when he collects them. While in our example of the Farthingill Corporation there is no significant relief (the tax saved is 15 percent of the receivables, or $1500), there may be instances where it will be extremely helpful in reducing tax.

There are many more rules and regulations surrounding the one-month liquidation. We have only scratched the surface as far as all the tax, legal, accounting, and practical considerations. A well-versed tax expert can go into all the lurid details and give you a complete analysis of your particular situation. You should be aware of the general concepts unique to one-month liquidations so that you can better understand exactly what your advisers may be telling you with regard to liquidating your corporation. Here is a short summary of the one-month liquidation:

A one-month liquidation must be accomplished, from beginning to end, within any calendar month.

While the premise that the exchange of stock for all the assets and liabilities of the corporation is the same in a one-month liquidation and in a straight liquidation, each is taxed in an entirely different manner.

The shareholder is taxed at ordinary rates to the extent of the earnings of his or her corporation. This essentially results in a dividend.

The shareholder may also be taxed at the capital gain rate to the extent that the corporation's cash exceeds its earnings.

The corporation is subject to recapture of depreciation and investment tax credit, which increases corporate taxes and earnings.

The corporation has to take its receivables into income if the corporation is on the cash method of accounting: This increases corporate earnings and taxes.

TEFRA gives relief as to the accounts receivable of personal service corporations liquidating under the provisions of calendar-month liquidations for 1983 and 1984.

The One-Year Liquidation

There is one additional type of liquidation which affects the one-person corporation in some very special instances. It is known as a one-year liquidation and is also a product of legislation designed to offer relief from a particularly onerous tax situation. The situation arises only in the case of a straight liquidation.

In a straight liquidation, the shareholder is taxed on the fair market value of the assets taken out of the corporation, less debts, and the cost basis of the shareholder's stock. What happens if the corporation sells some of its assets and then liquidates? This often happens when real estate or other capital assets are retained in the corporate name. If these assets are sold by the corporation, the corporation pays one tax upon the sale of the assets and the shareholder pays a second tax when the proceeds from the sale are taken out upon corporate liquidation.

This double tax seems quite unfair, especially if the reason the assets were sold was to reduce the corporation's assets to cash before liquidation. Congress recognized this unfair tax result and invented a one-year liquidation to alleviate the tax burden.

Under a one-year liquidation, assets which the corporation sells under a plan of straight liquidation are not subject to the corporate capital gain tax. However, the assets must be sold and the corporation liquidated within one year from the date that the corporation decides to liquidate. *The provisions of the one-year liquidation do not apply to a one-month liquidation.* A sale of assets in a one-month liquidation will create a corporate tax and a tax to the shareholder of the corporation.

Like almost all the corporate law provisions of the Internal Revenue Code, the one-year liquidation has some technical provisions which must be met. The most important of these provisions deals with the one-year period. If the corporate assets are not sold within one year of the date of the adoption of a plan of liquidation and if the corporation is not liquidated within that one-year period, there will be a double tax. This means that your corporation must formally adopt a plan of liquidation leaving no question as to when the one-year period begins. Adopting a formal plan is done by minutes of the board of directors and shareholders. There is also a form that you file with the IRS which will virtually assure that there is no question as to the date the plan was adopted.

Once this is done, the only other requirement is that the assets be sold and the corporation liquidated within that one-year period. We have seen situations where all the front-end requirements were met in a one-year liquidation. The plan of liquidation was formally adopted, the proper form sent to the IRS, the assets sold, and the cash and all other assets taken out of the corporation. Nobody bothered to take steps to properly liquidate the corporation, however, and a double tax resulted. It takes only one small error to cost someone a lot of tax.

The essence of a one-year liquidation is that the law is treating the sale of assets by a liquidating corporation as if the shareholder has already liquidated and is selling the assets immediately afterward.

An example will help you understand the one-year liquidation:

Centurion Real Estate Corp. is a company which was intended to be the personal corporation of Peggy Schuneman, a real estate broker. Peggy was advised, wrongly, that it is good business to acquire assets in a corporation at the corporation's lower tax bracket. Peggy contributed $10,000 to the corporation when it began and received stock back. Over the years, the corporation has ended up owning some raw ground and a company car, among other assets. The corporation has a few accounts receivable and has retained a substantial amount of earnings.

The real estate was purchased several years ago for $10,000 and is now worth $50,000. All of Peggy's advisers agree that it is best for the corporation to sell the property. They also feel that the corporation is no longer viable because Peggy has gotten out of real estate and is no longer active in the corporation. They advise her to adopt a plan of liquidation, sell the land, and liquidate the corporation pursuant to the provisions of a one-year liquidation. It is the feeling of Peggy's advisers that this course of action will generate the fewest tax dollars because of the marketability of the land and because the high amount of earnings make using the one-month liquidation impractical from a tax standpoint.

The shareholder (Peggy) and the board of directors (Peggy, her husband, and her accountant) sign minutes adopting a straight liquidation and stating that the corporation is to be liquidated within one year. They also authorize the officers of the corporation to sell the land and any other assets that can be sold prior to liquidation. The accountant sends the proper form to the IRS.

If the corporation sells its assets in the one-year period, there will be no capital gain tax to the corporation. There will be recapture of depreciation and investment tax credit, however, if assets are sold which are subject to those rules. There is no getting around the recapture rules in liquidations. When the corporation is ultimately liquidated, Peggy will pay taxes under the straight-liquidation rules. The only thing that will be different is that the corporation will pay no capital gain tax on the sale of its assets.

Assuming some or all of the assets are not sold, Peggy will still be taxed as if the liquidation was a straight liquidation. Just because there is no sale of assets does not mean there is a penalty or an extra benefit.

One of the characteristics of a one-year liquidation is that it is automatic. If you adopt a plan of straight liquidation and you liquidate within one year, you will fall under the provisions of a one-year liquidation. It is important, however, to document the one-year period. The IRS has been known to try to show that assets were sold either before the plan of liquidation was adopted or after the one-year period in order to garner an additional tax. A little caution is required to nake this type of liquidation work.

A one-year liquidation is used to avoid a double tax upon the sale of assets pursuant to a liquidation. It is most often used when an incorporated talent has accumulated extraneous assets in a personal corporation and the talent wishes to sell one or all of those assets without incurring the double tax. You must be aware that the price of paying one tax is the total liquidation of the corporation. Avoid having to use the one-year liquidation; do not acquire investment assets in your corporation.

The characteristics of a one-year liquidation are:

It is only used in conjunction with a straight liquidation.

It is used to avoid a double tax on the sale of assets within one year after the corporation decides to liquidate.

A formal adoption of a plan of liquidation by the shareholder and directors of the corporation is helpful to establish the beginning of the one-year period.

All the other rules of a straight liquidation apply, including recapture of depreciation and investment tax credit.

A one-year liquidation is automatic if the corporation adopts a plan of liquidation and liquidates within one year from the date of the plan.

Getting out of a corporation may present some very complex tax and legal problems, and there is no easy way out of your one-person corporation. The liquidation process takes a lot of forward planning and a complete understanding of the liquidation provisions of the Internal Revenue Code and the laws of your particular state. If you are considering the liquidation of your corporation, seek expert advice at the earliest possible time. By doing so, you will save a lot of money and time. *Getting out of a corporation is not easy to do.*

Chapter

14

A Corporate Précis
The Final Curtain of the Charles Laughton Story?

The world of the one-person talent corporation has been turned completely upside down with the passage of TEFRA. No longer are there pat formulas or rules as to whether one should incorporate, not incorporate, stay in a corporation, or get out of a corporation. The only thing that is for sure is that every person with talent must reexamine his or her situation. It is as if all of us, professional and nonprofessional, are just beginning our corporate walk: learning the rules and reassessing the position that we now find ourselves in. Interestingly enough, we are almost in the same position as was Charles Laughton when he became an incorporated talent pioneer.

We have tried to familiarize you with the massive changes in the law with regard to the one-person corporation. We have also attempted to highlight many of the tax issues which we have inherited from the days of Charles Laughton or which have arisen in the evolutionary process of tax law and legislation. Like a giant snake, the law has twisted and turned in every direction imaginable, leaving confusion and uncertainty in its path. Today, even the most astute professionals seem to be waiting for some type of direction as to whether or not incorporation remains a viable planning alternative for successful talent.

To discuss the relative pros and cons of corporations for talent, two points of view must be considered. The first concerns those of you who are not now incorporated and who would like to determine whether you should incorporate. The second relates to those of you who are already incorporated and who want to know whether you should "stay the course" or liquidate your corporation. This chapter will be devoted to addressing these two situations in light of the recent changes in our laws.

"Should I Incorporate My Talent?"

Before TEFRA was passed, incorporation and tax savings were synonymous terms for successful talent. Most people looked upon a corporation as a private tax haven. In our experience, only a very few people considered the real postretirement benefits that could be provided through the use of a corporate retirement plan; most looked only to the immediate tax savings that could be generated by making a retirement plan contribution. In our experience, talent used their corporations to reduce their current income tax burdens in much the same manner as Charles Laughton.

Today, it is not necessary for a person to incorporate in order to make a nice contribution (tax deduction) to a retirement plan: A corporation, a partnership, and a sole proprietorship are all in the same boat when it comes to retirement plans; TEFRA made them equal. All qualified retirement plans, whether in a corporation or not, are subject to almost identical rules. No longer does one business entity have the edge over others when it comes to retirement planning.

The limit on all defined contribution plans is now $30,000. For a profit sharing plan, the limit is 15 percent of compensation, not to exceed $30,000, and for a money purchase plan, 25 percent of compensation, not to exceed the $30,000 maximum. The $30,000 maximum deduction will be adjusted for inflation beginning in 1986.

There is no limit on the tax deduction for defined benefit plans. The only limitation is on the retirement benefit that is taken, which is now $90,000 per year for each year after retirement. While these limitations are far lower than those prior to TEFRA, they will still generate a nice tax deduction for overtaxed talent, and in the case of older talent, the tax deduction will continue to be substantial.

Why should you or any other talent incorporate? That question can only be answered by you and your advisers. The reason for our response is basic: There is no longer one dominant or exclusive reason to incorporate. Individual talents will look to combinations of tax and nontax benefits when considering the incorporation issue. The following is a synopsis of the pros and cons that we believe attach to the one-person talent corporation. They should assist you in making your incorporation decision.

Incorporating Your Talent: The Pros

Ego.   People enjoy having their names in lights. Being the president and chairperson of the board of their own corporation can mean good business. An incorporated ego reflects more than a name. It reflects a little bit of a corporate monument and a little bit of being a shareholder, director, officer. It manifests a bit of true salespersonship. It can be easier to open important doors when you have an important title. For many of our clients, ego has been a definite pro, a benefit greater than all the tax benefits combined.

Limited Liability.   We only put this under the pros of incorporation in great hope that it is true for someone. Limited liability rarely exists for the one-person corporation. The world has wised up to the corporate entrepreneur hiding behind the corporate veil. It is sad that so many people believe so strongly in a limited liability that rarely exists.

Separating Business from Your Personal Life.   Are you one of those people who have a hard time getting organized? If you are, do not rely on a corporation to make you more organized by some sort of magical metamorphosis. It will not happen. However, if you are concerned about cleaning up your act and are serious about separating your business and personal lives, a corporation can fit the bill. But you must keep your corporate and personal lives separate or face problems with the IRS upon audit. The penalty for not keeping them separated could very well be dividend treatment for many of the dollars taken out of your corporation. We consider this separation of lives a definite pro. But you must be willing to take the time and effort (or at least hire the expertise) to clean up your business act.

A Separate Tax Year.   Having your corporation on a different tax year than you are is truly a tax benefit. The added flexibility of timing income from one year to the next has the potential of saving a lot of taxes. This is especially true if your particular talent creates income which is not consistent from one year to the next. While this benefit can create tax problems if abused, its prudent use can consistently and substantially reduce tax over the years.

Accounting Method.   All businesses get to choose their accounting method. A corporation is not unique in this respect. There are people, however, who have not chosen their accounting method wisely and are not incorporated. These individuals can incorporate and have the corporation choose a new accounting method, eliminating the burden of the old method.

    If you incorporate, you can choose the method of accounting you wish to be on. Usually, the cash method offers the most flexibility for incorporated talent.

Ordinary and Necessary Business Expenses.   This is another pro which is not the exclusive property of the corporation. It has been our experience that taking business expenses on any sort of personal tax return lights up the IRS computers. The corporate tax return is better suited to accommodate these expenses without creating as much exposure. This may be very important to you if you or your advisers are aggressive with respect to your tax planning.

Medical Reimbursement Plans.   Being able to deduct medical expenses is extremely important to many a taxpayer. Medical care and supplies are expensive enough without having to pay for them with aftertax dollars. TEFRA made this even more significant by increasing the base amount of medical expenses which have to be paid before a deduction is allowed. A corporate medical reimbursement plan allows the corporation to pay for the medical expenses of its employees with before-tax dollars. The effect of this type of plan is for the corporation to take a full deduction for all health-related expenses without the talent having to report the same amounts as income.

While this plan represents a major boon to many talents who are considering incorporating, it may not apply to others. Some people just do not have enough medical expenses to justify incorporation. Others may have employees who would have to be covered under the plan, making it too expensive to operate. In the main, however, this is a major and splendid pro of incorporating.

Group Term Life Insurance.   Deducting life insurance premiums sounds attractive to most everyone. As a practical matter, it rarely happens in a one-person corporation. The rules for group term life insurance just are not very compatible to a one-person talent corporation. Consider this a quasi pro, but make sure that you check with your life insurance professional before you attempt to implement this benefit.

Putting Your Family on the Payroll.   Splitting income with members of your family, who are in lower tax brackets, makes a lot of sense, especially if you are paying for many of their expenses with your aftertax dollars. The process of putting them on the payroll is not difficult if done properly: It is important that they be paid a fair wage for services actually performed; this has not been too difficult for most of our clients over the years.

Writing Off Your Home as Corporate Headquarters.   Anyone who has an office at home may deduct the expenses associated with it if he or she meets strict IRS rules. If the write-off occurs, they can expect Uncle Sam's revenue agents to come knocking at their doors. A corporation may, however, lease office space in your home from you. This can be legitimately done with far less IRS exposure. A corporation looks very good when you are presented with this alternative.

Separate Tax Bracket.   Corporation tax brackets can be substantially lower than those of its shareholder-employee. The temptation is to use these lower tax brackets to accumulate lower-taxed dollars. There is nothing wrong with giving in to this inclination if the money is accumulated for legitimate reasons. These reasons include the purchase of a company car or other assets used in the business. Paying for items which are not currently deductible with corporate aftertax dollars makes sense when done in moderation. Talent corporations can accumulate up to $150,000 in earnings without suffering any penalty.

Borrowing Money from Your Corporation.   In the event that your corporation does accumulate money at lower tax brackets, borrowing from the corporation can be a method to use these dollars personally without paying a second tax. As long as proper documentation is prepared and the loans are paid off, there should be no problems with this tax strategy. Bad bookkeeping, with respect to loans made to you or your family members, will almost certainly result in a dividend.

Turning Vacations into Board Meetings.   Do you like to travel but find that it is pretty expensive when the costs are not tax deductible? A corporation is used from time to time to pay for the expenses of directors attending a board meeting. The meetings can be held virtually anywhere, as has been shown by the boards of many of our country's large public corporations. The expenses of these meetings can be paid by your corporation but only if substantial business is transacted. This is another area where good record keeping can be the difference between a nice inexpensive vacation and a very expensive one.

Driving a Company Car.   The purchase price of a car is a nondeductible expense. The price must be written off over a period of time. Because a car is purchased with aftertax dollars, it makes good tax sense to use lower-taxed corporate dollars to pay for it. A lot of income can be saved by using this technique. But keep in mind that there is inevitably personal use by the shareholder-employee of the company car. A cheap IRS insurance policy is to charge yourself a small fee for personal use each month.

Incorporating Your Talent: The Cons

Accumulating Earnings Unreasonably.   The phrase "accumulation of earnings," although a term of art among tax specialists, covers a multitude of sins. The first is using the lower corporate income tax brackets to such an extent that an accumulated earnings penalty tax is generated. Unreasonable accumulation of earnings, in excess of $150,000 in most talent corporations, generates a penalty tax of 27½ percent on the first $100,000 of unnecessary earnings and a penalty tax of 37½ percent on any earnings considered unreasonable above the first $100,000. *Do not use your corporation to accumulate aftertax dollars.* If accumulating aftertax dollars is the reason why you would like to incorporate, do not waste your time or money.

Paperwork. A corporation needs lots of paper to nourish it from birth to death. Paper creates a corporation and gives it the substance it needs to convince the IRS that it is real. Paper is also the lifeblood of the corporation as it grows and matures. Our tax laws make it plain that the taxpayer must prove that all his or her transactions are legitimate. This burden of proof requirement makes it quite easy for the IRS agents to disallow any transaction which they find to be the least bit suspicious. If they do, you must prove to them that what you did was aboveboard. The paperwork requirement extends to all areas of corporate existence.

An employment contract is a must to legitimatize the transactions between the corporation and its shareholder-employee. Independent contractor agreements are necessary to show the IRS separate corporate existence. All sorts of governmental reports are also required to be filled out and filed by corporations; they extend from the federal government all the way down to cities and municipalities.

You must be willing to play the paper chase if you want to incorporate. If this makes you uncomfortable or if it intimidates you, do not incorporate. You are the prime player in your corporation. The paperwork must be taken care of under your direction. No paperwork means no corporation. No corporation may mean massive taxes. Paperwork takes both time and money.

Unreasonable Compensation. The amount of compensation that you take out of your corporation, as well as the method used by you to take it out, can be questioned by IRS agents. This is a danger not found in other types of business organizations. The cure? You guessed it: *paperwork.* Documenting compensation both in an employment contract and in directors' minutes can help alleviate these problems. Also, a dose of moderation will help. Getting too greedy, when using the corporate form, is a quick path to tax disaster.

Personal Holding Company.   A one-person corporation stands a good chance of being classified as a personal holding company. The income it derives is almost always from personal services, and the people on whose behalf the services are performed usually want to be assured that a particular talent performs on their behalf. A PHC is not that big of a deal. As long as all the corporate earnings are paid out in salary, expenses, or fringe benefits, there is no problem.

Social Security.   A corporation and its employees have a high social security (FICA) and unemployment (FUTA) burden. The cost of the corporation's payments and the employee's payments is higher than if the employee paid self-employment tax. This ends, however, in 1990. Frankly, if this short-run cost seems to be prohibitive to you, do not incorporate.

Dividends.   Corporations are one of the few places in our tax laws where double taxation exists. The double tax on dividends is always a risk in a one-person corporation. Almost any disallowed expense, paid to or on behalf of a shareholder-employee, is subject to this double tax. Be prepared for this result when entering into the realm of the one-person corporation, and be prepared to take preventive action (paperwork) to avoid it.

Employees.   By definition, a one-person corporation has but one employee. Having more than one employee, who is not a family member, creates problems. Employees, more often than not, must be included in fringe benefit programs. They make planning much more complex and less effective. If at all possible, use legitimate methods of avoiding employees; this would include the use of independent contractors, part-time employees, and younger employees. Do not try to create chains of corporations in order to eliminate employees. Most of those loopholes have been closed. Anticipate future need for employees and plan accordingly. Employees are hard to plan around and will cost you extra time and money if they are in your corporation. Incorporation will definitely be less attractive for those talents who have full-time employees.

Expense.   All the paperwork and planning that we have discussed takes money. Professional fees are not inexpensive, especially if you hire top-notch professional advisers. Before incorporating, do a financial analysis of the costs, vis-à-vis the savings, generated through incorporation. Only then will you have an idea of what you are getting into from a cost standpoint.

Type of Talent.   Some types of talent cannot derive any benefit from incorporation. For example, under most conditions, corporate executives are no longer allowed tax breaks when they incorporate. The same is true for professionals who are in partnerships or corporations with other professionals. Some state laws still prohibit some types of talent from incorporating. Meet with your advisers, and determine if you fall into one of these categories. If you do, incorporation is obviously not for you.

Getting Out Is Hard to Do.   Liquidating a corporation is not the easiest and most inexpensive of tasks. Congress has made the process relatively painful by creating some intricate sections of the Internal Revenue Code. Most talents never anticipate the fact that they may have to get rid of their corporations some day. Liquidation problems are unique to corporations and are seldom anticipated. This, in our book, represents a significant con to their use.

Table 14-1 sets forth the pros and cons of incorporation in a straightforward and concise manner. At first glance, the pros and cons seem to be pretty even. But that is not necessarily so. We must stress that the motivation to incorporate will differ with every talent. There is no clear-cut answer to the question "Why should I incorporate my talent?"

We feel that, in most cases, the benefits of incorporation outweigh the detriments. (We are incorporated and intend to stay so.) Just having a staggered fiscal year and a medical reimbursement plan (at least in our situations) is worth the other aggravations associated with being

Table 14-1.   Pros and Cons of Incorporating Your Talent

Pros	Cons
Ego	Accumulating earnings unreasonably
Limited liability	Paperwork
Separating business from your personal life	Unreasonable compensation
A separate tax year	Personal holding company
Accounting methods	Social security
Ordinary and necessary business expenses	Dividends
Medical reimbursement plans	Employees
Group term life insurance	Expense
Putting your family on the payroll	Type of talent
Writing off your home as corporate headquarters	Difficulty of getting out
Separate tax bracket	
Borrowing money from your corporation	
Turning vacations into board meetings	
Driving a company car	

incorporated. It has been our experience that a good businessperson always has paperwork to do and rules to follow. The burden of maintaining a corporation is really not too great once you get the hang of it. And besides, it is nice to be the president of your own corporation.

"Should I Stay Incorporated?"

The answer to this question is much easier than the one for those talents considering incorporation. The first step toward deciding if you should stay incorporated is to make sure you read the prior section, aimed at the pros and cons of incorporation. You can bet that if there were more than a few surprises in that section, you will need to either do a cleanup job on your own corporation or terminate it.

You should also reread Chapter 13, "Getting Out of Your Corporation." Getting out may be much more expensive than you had previously thought, making the decision to stay in a great deal more attractive by comparison.

Regardless of your initial inclination toward keeping or terminating your corporation, you should pursue a more detailed analysis of the respective pros and cons.

Staying Incorporated: The Pros

Qualified Retirement Plans.   A qualified retirement plan is a definite pro for an existing one-person corporation. Liquidation of your corporation means that your existing retirement plans must be formally terminated. Formal termination generally necessitates IRS approval and the approval of one or two other governmental agencies. And to what end? After liquidation, you will probably set up a new retirement plan program anyway. That just means more expense, more time, and more effort. In our opinion, it will be far less costly to amend your retirement plans to conform to the new rules under TEFRA than to liquidate your corporation and start all over again. There would certainly be far less exposure to the IRS, and there would be no chance of having your retirement funds taxed on a current basis if you choose the amendment route. Already incorporated talent is in the best position to minimize expense while continuing to enjoy the plans.

You Already Know the Rules.   A novice who wants to incorporate has to jump through all the hoops to incorporate. You have suffered through the battles of being an incorporated talent and are probably fairly familiar with the rules. With any luck, you have learned to do all the necessary paperwork and have become familiar with all the routine corporate tasks. Getting out of your corporation may be far more traumatic than maintaining the status quo.

Your Major Expenses Are behind You.   Creating a corporation can be expensive, as you have no doubt found out. Odds are that the expenses of operating your corporation have been reduced, because the initial start-up costs and confusion have been virtually eliminated. Your retirement plans are in place, either put there by an institution or hand-crafted to your needs. In either event, the major expenses are out of the way. The only costs you have to look forward to are those necessary for maintaining your corporate plans.

There should be no reason to incur more expense through liquidating your corporation.

The Changes in the Law Can Be Effected without Liquidation.
Even if the changes made by TEFRA affect you adversely, changes can be made to your corporate structure without going through the time and expense of a liquidation. For example, if you have acquired

employees and the cost of covering them under the TEFRA retirement plan rules is prohibitive, your retirement plan or plans can be terminated without liquidating. The same can generally be said for the other changes under TEFRA: Liquidation is not the only solution to changes in the law. It is, however, one of the most expensive solutions.

Liquidation May Be Too Expensive.   Many one-person corporations have accumulated too much in the way of earnings or assets to make liquidation a viable alternative. This is a great incentive to stay incorporated. There are alternatives to liquidation. With foresight and planning, a corporation can, over time, run its assets down and alleviate the high tax cost of liquidation.

Staying Incorporated: The Cons

The New Law Makes Your Corporation Impossible to Carry On.   If you happen to be an incorporated executive or a professional who is an incorporated member of a partnership or corporation of coprofessionals, staying incorporated would not be wise. However, before you liquidate, check with your advisers as to the viability of remaining incorporated for a different or changed purpose. You may be able to use your corporation for some other business enterprise. Alternatively, you may want to slowly wind down your corporation by using up its assets. When the assets are finally used up, then there would be no need to liquidate the corporate shell. Either way, consult with your advisers as to which solution would be most practical in your case.

Other Circumstances Make Corporate Existence Impossible.
Your corporation may have problems other than TEFRA. Earnings may have accumulated to such an extent that liquidation is cheaper than the accumulated earnings penalty. There may be salable real estate that makes liquidation attractive under a one-year liquidation. Or the relief provisions of a one-month liquidation may be attractive enough to warrant liquidation. All these possibilities should be explored if your corporation no longer seems to fit your needs.

Table 14-2. Pros and Cons of Staying Incorporated

Pros	Cons
Qualified retirement plans.	The new law makes your corporation
You already know the rules.	impossible to carry on.
Your major expenses are behind you.	Other circumstances make corporate
The changes in the law can be effected	existence impossible.
without liquidation.	
Liquidation may be too expensive.	

Table 14-2 sets forth the pros and cons of staying incorporated. While there may be other reasons, either to stay incorporated or to liquidate, these pros and cons cover the major issues. A search and analysis of all alternatives is necessary before the expensive and irrevocable decision to liquidate is made.

The corporate entity is still viable for the person who has a talent to incorporate or who has already incorporated his or her talent. The final curtain has not fallen on the Charles Laughton story. You can count on one thing: The law will continue to change. You can only do what seems right today and try to anticipate what will occur tomorrow. The one-person corporation will remain as a monument to Charles Laughton and those like him who starred in the original production of the one-person talent corporation. Who knows, you may be the Laughton of tomorrow.

Appendix

A

Employment Contract

Your employment contract is perhaps the most important document in your corporate arsenal. Because the IRS is constantly concerned about disguised dividends, you must always be ready to prove that all transactions between you and your one-person corporation are not really dividends. Your employment contract represents an arm's length agreement, setting forth those items which your corporation and you have negotiated as part of your compensation package.

The employment contract in this appendix is representative of those we have used for our one-person corporation clients. While this employment contract is representative, it is here for reference only; it is dangerous to use a form for your particular situation. It will, however, help familiarize you with the contents of an employment contract so that you can help your lawyer tailor one that fits your particular situation.

To facilitate your understanding, we have listed, following the contract, annotations of some of its more important provisions. Each annotation consists of a brief explanation of the reason for the particular provision. Keep in mind that it is difficult to put too much in an employment contract. Your employment contract should contain *every* feature and *any* unique provision of your compensation arrangement. It might be helpful for you to write down your thoughts, as to your situation, as you read our hypothetical employment contract

EMPLOYMENT AGREEMENT

[1]

This Agreement dated _____, 19__, is by and between *Professional Service Corporation,* a Delaware Corporation (Corporation), and _____ ("Employee").

The Corporation desires to employ the Employee and the Employee desires to be employed by the Corporation upon the terms and conditions set forth in this contract.

The parties hereby enter into this Agreement to set forth their mutual promises and understandings and mutually acknowledge the receipt and sufficiency of valuable consideration in addition to the mutual promises, conditions, and understandings set forth below.

The duration of employment, the compensation to be paid the Employee, and other terms and provisions of this Agreement were approved and authorized on behalf the Corporation by action of its Board of Directors at a meeting thereof held on or by unanimous consent dated and effective as of the ____ day of ____, 19__.

ARTICLE I
EMPLOYMENT DUTIES
AND RESPONSIBILITIES

Section 1.1 Employment. The Corporation employs the Employee as a tax consultant, speaker, and author with all the requisite privileges and duties thereof. The Employee accepts such employment and agrees to abide by the Articles of Incorporation and By-Laws of the Corporation.

Section 1.2 Director of Corporation. The Employee shall, if elected or appointed, serve as a director of the Corporation. Nothing in this Agreement shall be construed as requiring the Corporation, its shareholders, or agents to cause the election or appointment of the Employee as a director.

[2]

Section 1.3 Duties and Responsibilities. The Employee is employed pursuant to the terms of this Agreement to act on behalf the Corporation and agrees to devote all the time and energies necessary to accomplish the duties hereunder. During the term of this Agreement and any renewal, the Employee shall not, without the written consent of the Corporation:

A.   Render professional tax consulting, speaking, or writing services to or for any person, firm or corporation, or other organization for compensation, or

B.   Engage in any activity that competes with the interest of the Corporation whether the Employee is acting alone or as an officer, director, employee, shareholder, partner, or fiduciary.

Any consent granted to the Employee shall be revocable by the Corporation at any time upon ten days' notice, and the Employee agrees to cease and desist upon receipt of such notice. The Employee does not presently engage in any such activities other than those set forth in this Agreement.

Section 1.4 Related Activities.   All income generated by the Employee for professional services and related activities such as consulting, lecturing, and writing shall belong to the Corporation regardless of to whom paid unless the Corporation agrees, in writing, that such proceeds belong to the Employee. Any checks made payable to the Employee which represent income belonging to the Corporation shall be endorsed over by the Employee to the Corporation.

Section 1.5 Copyrights.   All copyrightable material generated by the Employee along with any copyrights shall belong to the Corporation, except that the Corporation and the Employee may, by mutual consent, determine that such copyrightable material belongs to the Employee.

[3]

Section 1.6 Workweek.   For purposes of this Agreement, the Employee shall be considered as being paid on a seven-day week basis, since the Employee is available for call to work on Saturdays, Sundays, and holidays as well as the remaining five weekdays.

[4]

Section 1.7 Working Facilities.   The Employee shall be furnished with facilities and services suitable to the position and adequate for the performance of the duties of the Employee under this Agreement.

Section 1.8 Vacations. The Employee shall be entitled each year to a reasonable vacation, during which time the Employee's compensation shall be paid in full. Each vacation shall be taken by the Employee over a period meeting with the Corporation's approval.

Section 1.9 Expenses.

A. Employee Reimbursed for Expenses. During the period of employment, pursuant to this agreement, the Employee will be reimbursed for reasonable expenses incurred for the benefit of the Corporation in accordance with the general policy of the Corporation as adopted from time to time by the Corporation's Board of Directors.

B. General Expense. These expenses shall include but shall not be limited to entertainment and promotional expenses; automobile and/ or transportation expenses; educational expenses incurred for the purpose of maintaining or improving the Employee's professional skills; and dues and the expenses of membership in civic groups, professional societies, and fraternal organizations.

[5]
C. Additional Expenses. In addition to such reimbursable expenses, the Employee may incur in the course of the employment by the Corporation certain other necessary expenses for which the Employee will be required to pay personally but which the Corporation shall be under no obligation to reimburse or otherwise to compensate the Employee, including, but not limited to, the cost of maintaining office facilities in the Employee's home and all other items of reasonable and necessary professional expense incurred by the Employee in the course of employment.

[6]
D. Professional Activities. The Corporation recognizes that the Employee has an obligation to engage and take part in attendance at professional seminars and conventions and other related activities. The Corporation shall from time to time pay for reasonable expenses of the seminars, conventions, and related activities. The Corporation shall compensate the Employee fully for such times the Employee may be engaged in appropriate seminars, conventions, and other related activities which are approved by the Board of Directors.

E. Employee Shall Account Expenses to Corporation. With respect to any expenses which are reimbursed by the Corporation to the Employee, the Employee agrees to account to the Corporation in detail sufficient to entitle the Corporation to an income tax deduction for such paid item if such item is deductible.

[7]

Section 1.10 Assignment of Work. The Corporation shall direct and control the assignment of work to the Employee. Such determination shall be made solely by the Corporation. The Employee agrees to perform all the professional services assigned by the Corporation. The Employee recognizes that the work assigned may be subsequently assigned to other Employees.

Section 1.11 Fees. The Employee recognizes that the Corporation shall have complete authority with regard to the establishment of the appropriate fee for all professional services.

Section 1.12 Review by Corporation. The Employee agrees that all work performed pursuant to this Agreement shall be subject to the review and study of the Corporation.

Section 1.13 Performance of Services. The performance of services by the Employee on behalf the Corporation shall be performed at such times and at such places as shall be determined by the Corporation and in accordance with such rules as the Corporation may establish.

[8]

Section 1.14 Leave of Absence. The Corporation may from time to time approve leaves of absence with full or partial payment of salary and other expenses for other reasons in its sole discretion.

Section 1.15 Employee Benefit Plans. In accordance with their terms, the Employee shall be entitled to participate in any plans, arrangements, or distributions by the Corporation pertaining to or in connection with any retirement, health, disability, life insurance, bonus, pension, profit sharing, or other similar benefits.

ARTICLE II
COMPENSATION

[9]

Section 2.1 Basic Salary. The Corporation shall pay to the Employee a basic salary during the term of this Agreement as established from time to time by the Board of Directors of the Corporation.

The Corporation and the Employee recognize that the Board of Directors of the Corporation may from time to time review the compensation to be paid under this Agreement during the term of this Agreement and increase or decrease said compensation to such amount as the Board of Directors may deem proper. The criteria which the Board of Directors may take into consideration in providing for such increase or decrease are the Employee's ability, any increase in the difficulties involved in the offices filled and responsibilities assumed by the Employee, the success achieved by the Employee, the matters and accounts under the Employee's jurisdiction, the earnings and profits of the Corporation, the increase in volume and quality of business of the Corporation, and such other criteria as the Board of Directors may deem relevant.

Section 2.2 Director's Compensation. The Employee may receive additional compensation, if elected or appointed a director of the Corporation, upon approval of such additional compensation by the Board of Directors of the Corporation.

Section 2.3 Bonus. In addition to the basic salary, the Employee may receive a bonus or bonuses if voted by the Board of Directors. The Board of Directors in determining the amount of bonus, if any, shall endeavor to make the total compensation on an annual basis paid to the Employee equal to the reasonable value of the services performed as an employee of the Corporation, and shall base such bonuses on the Employee's services considered to be an outstanding contribution to the Corporation. Such bonuses, if any, shall be paid to the extent that the Employer has the financial ability to pay such compensation without incurring losses.

Section 2.4 Death during Employment. In the event of the Employee's death during the term of this Agreement, the Corporation shall pay the Employee's estate the compensation which otherwise would be payable to the Employee through the end of the year in which the Employee's death occurs.

[10]

Section 2.5 Reimbursement for Disallowed Expenses and Compensation. If as a consequence of an audit of the income tax returns of the Corporation by any federal or state agency, any compensation paid to the Employee, any expenses paid for the Employee, or any reimbursement for expenses paid to the Employee shall be disallowed in whole or in part as a deductible expense, and if the Corporation does not contest such disallowance or if the disallowance becomes final and binding, the Employee agrees to repay the Corporation all amounts of disallowed compensation and expenses. This provision for repayment shall not be waived by the Corporation.

The Corporation, in this regard, recognizes its duty and obligation to the Employee to employ competent tax consultants.

ARTICLE III
TERM OF EMPLOYMENT
AND TERMINATION

[11]

Section 3.1 Term. This Agreement shall be for a period of one year commencing on its effective date, subject, however, to termination during such period as provided in this Article. This Agreement shall be renewed automatically for succeeding periods of one year each on the same terms and conditions as herein contained unless either the Corporation, by its Board of Directors, or the Employee shall, at least forty-five days prior to the expiration of any one-year period, give written notice of the intention not to renew this Agreement.

Section 3.2 Termination by the Corporation without Cause. The Corporation without cause may terminate this Agreement at any time upon thirty days' written notice to the Employee. In such event, the Employee, if requested by the Corporation, shall continue to render the services required under this Agreement and shall be paid the base compensation in effect at the time of the notice until the date of termination.

Section 3.3 Termination by the Employee without Cause. The Employee without cause may terminate this Agreement upon sixty days' written notice to the Corporation. In such event, the Employee shall continue to render the services required under this Agreement and shall be paid the basic compensation in effect at the time of notice until the date of the termination, and no severance allowance shall be paid to the Employee.

Section 3.4 Termination with Cause. The Board of Directors of the Corporation may terminate the Employee at any time without notice by reason of misconduct by the Employee or for other cause contrary to the best interests of the Corporation.

Section 3.6 Termination upon Sale of Business. The Corporation may terminate this Agreement upon ten days' notice to the Employee upon any of the following events:

A. The sale by the Employer of substantially all of its assets to a single purchaser or to a group of associated purchasers;

B. The sale, exchange, or other disposition in one transaction of two-thirds of the outstanding corporate shares of the Employer;

C. A bona fide decision by the Employer to terminate its business and liquidate its assets; or

D. The merger or consolidation of the Employer in a transaction in which the Shareholders of the Employer receive less than 50 percent of the outstanding voting shares of the new or continuing corporation.

ARTICLE IV
SICK PAY AND DISABILITY

[12]

Section 4.1 Sick Pay. The Employee shall be paid full salary for time absent from work as a result of sickness or personal injury, as provided herein.

Section 4.2 Disability and Salary Continuation.

A. Definition of Disability. For purposes of this Agreement, the terms "totally disabled," "disabled," and "disability" shall mean continuous disability as defined in, and for the period necessary to qualify for, benefits under any disability income insurance policies paid for by the Corporation on the life of the Employee.

If no disability insurance is in effect on the life of the Employee, the terms "totally disabled," "disabled," and "disability" shall mean continuous disability which prevents the Employee from performing the normal duties of the Employee pursuant to this Agreement as shall be determined by two physicians, one designated by the Corporation and the other by the disabled Employee. If these two physicians cannot agree on whether the Employee is disabled within the meaning of this Section, they shall appoint a third physician, and the opinion of the majority shall be final, binding, and conclusive. The cost of all examining physicians shall be a cost to the Corporation and not to the Employee.

B. Salary Continuation.   If the Employee becomes totally disabled during the term of this Agreement, the Employee's full salary shall be continued for the period of time for which the Employee remains totally disabled.

If the Corporation pays premiums on a disability income insurance policy on the life of the Employee, then any proceeds paid directly to the Employee under such disability income insurance policy during the period of disability shall be offset against salary continuation payments due from the Corporation to the Employee.

ARTICLE V
NONDISCLOSURE OF INFORMATION

[13]

Section 5.1 Employee Shall Not Disclose Information.   The Employee recognizes and acknowledges that the list of the Corporation's clients, as it may exist from time to time, is a valuable, special, and unique asset of the Corporation. The Employee will not, during or after the term of employment, disclose the list of the Corporation's clients or any part thereof to any person, firm, corporation, association, or other entity for any reason or purpose whatsoever.

Further, all files and all records therein shall be the property of the Corporation, and the Employee shall not remove these files, or any records in them upon the termination of the employment with the Corporation, except pursuant to a specific request in writing with respect to and from the person to whom the file applies. In no event shall the Employee be permitted to take any file or the records therein of any person that the Employee did not directly work with while an employee of the Corporation.

[14]

Section 5.2 Covenant Not to Compete.   For a period of two years after the termination of this Agreement, the Employee agrees not to engage in any activity which competes, directly or indirectly, with the activities of the Corporation within 100 miles of the office of the Corporation.

Section 5.3 Breach of This Article. In the event of a breach or threatened breach by the Employee of the provisions of this Article, the Corporation shall be entitled to an injunction restraining the Employee from disclosing, in whole or in part, the list of the Corporation's customers or from rendering any services which may compete with those of the Corporation. Nothing herein shall be construed as prohibiting the Corporation from pursuing any other remedies available to the Corporation for such breach or threatened breach, including the recovery of damages from the Employee.

ARTICLE VI
GENERAL MATTERS

[15]

Section 6.1 Delaware Law. This Agreement shall be governed by the laws of the state of Delaware and shall be construed in accordance therewith.

Section 6.2 No Waiver. No provision of this Agreement may be waived except by an agreement in writing signed by the waiving party. A waiver of any term or provision shall not be construed as a waiver of any other term or provision.

Section 6.3 Amendment. This Agreement may be amended, altered, or revoked at any time, in whole or in part, by filing with this Agreement a written instrument setting forth such changes, signed by all the parties.

Section 6.4 Benefit. This Agreement shall be binding upon the Employee and the Corporation, its successors, and assigns.

Section 6.5 Construction. Throughout this Agreement the singular shall include the plural, the plural shall include the singular, and the masculine and neuter shall include the feminine, wherever the context so requires.

Section 6.6 Text to Control. The headings of articles and sections are included solely for convenience of reference. If any conflict between any heading and the text of this Agreement exists, the text shall control.

Section 6.7 Severability. If any provision of this Agreement is declared by any court of competent jurisdiction to be invalid for any reason, such invalidity shall not affect the remaining provisions. On the contrary, such remaining provisions shall be fully severable, and this Agreement shall be construed and enforced as if such invalid provisions never had been inserted in the Agreement.

The effective date of this Agreement shall be _____, 19__.

Professional Service Corporation

By: _____
                  President

Attest: _____
                  Secretary

Employee: _____

[1]   The heading and introduction should designate the corporation and where it was incorporated. The employee should have his or her full legal name listed, as well as an address. This constitutes a proper designation of the parties to the contract.

Briefly state the purpose of the agreement. This will help any reader (the IRS) identify the nature of the agreement.

[2]   Setting forth the duties of the employee is important, especially if there is a possibility of unreasonable compensation. The more duties and responsibilities that you have, the more your salary can be justified. You should also make sure that you cannot perform these services

for any other organization. You are an employee, not an independent contractor, and as such you are expected to work for only one employer.

Duties and responsibilities are also important if you have more than one talent but only one is incorporated. This will help keep your incomes separate and demonstrate to the IRS that your incorporated business is separate and distinct from your other ventures.

[3] The workweek provision is added to an employment contract to take advantage of a wage continuation plan. An employee who becomes totally disabled before retirement may receive up to $100 per week, tax-free, if the amount received is pursuant to a wage continuation plan. A seven-day workweek allows the maximum benefit of $100 a week tax-free.

While this may not seem like a big benefit, it can help in a one-person corporation. If the talent becomes disabled, this provision can help in getting tax-free income out of the corporation. The amounts paid are also income tax deductible to the corporation. Appendix C, "Health and Accident Plan," has a further provision which allows the corporation to enter into such a plan.

[4] Working facilities, vacations, and expenses are all very important to the disguised dividend issue. To justify an expensive car, beautiful office trappings, and other first-class facilities, you must make them part of your employment contract. Our agreement recognizes the need for this. Your advisers can expand yours to fit your needs.

The IRS has a propensity to try to show that too much vacation time and a high salary do not mix when claiming unreasonable compensation. Setting forth the vacation time or how it is determined will help in fighting the issue if it should occur.

Expenses of shareholder-employees are always questioned on an IRS audit. Allowing a wide range of expenses will help justify them to the IRS. Not keeping good records will jeopardize the deduction, however, and this provision will be meaningless. You must keep excellent records of business expenses if you hope to justify them on an IRS audit.

[5] There are some expenses that talent incurs which we do not, for one reason or another, encourage our clients to run through their corporations. This provision attempts to allow you to take a deduction for those expenses. If an employee is required by an employment contract to expend some of his or her own money in the line of business, then there is a good argument for the personal deductibility of expenses.

Requiring, or at least alluding to, an office in the home may bolster a personal deduction. An office in the home, as we discussed, does not automatically come with a tax deduction. There must be reasons for the office. This provision, we have found, helps if the IRS begins to question the purpose of a home office.

[6]   Conventions and seminars are a great way to get away from the pressures of business, to visit nice places, and, hopefully, take a tax deduction for the trip. They offer a built-in business purpose and offer a good way to mix business with pleasure. Recognizing the advantages of these tax deductible trips, we have always included a provision in our employment contracts to help assure that the corporation can pay for the trips (conventions) of our clients.

[7]   A one-person talent corporation is a prime candidate for a personal holding company. It is important to contract with the corporation, not the talent, to avoid a possible PHC problem. This portion of the employment contract helps demonstrate that the corporation, not the employee, is providing the talent of its choosing.

[8]   Many of the talented people that we represent choose to take a sabbatical from time to time. It may be business-related or may be for the purpose of recharging their talented batteries. Often, the talent wants to continue taking a salary from his or her corporation, even though work is not being performed. Leaves of absence are often a part of executive employment contracts in the public sector. They should also be allowed in the one-person talent corporation. We have found this to be true, if the proper steps are taken. This provision in an employment contract is the first such step.

[9]   A detailed description of your compensation arrangement can eliminate a lot of explaining if you are audited. Remember, you must justify your salary. Here is the place to do it. It is also the place to describe any quirks in how your salary is paid. For example, if your corporation has income which is high in some years and not so high in others, that should be mentioned here. Then when your big income year hits, it will be easier for you to defend your extraordinarily high compensation. If you try to anticipate those areas where you may be vulnerable to IRS attack and explain your position in your employment contract, you should stand a much better chance of surviving an IRS audit.

The word "bonus" causes IRS agents to lick their lips and smile.

A bonus inevitably means that there is a good case for a disguised dividend. A bonus properly instituted, however, can generally be justified. The language in this employment agreement is language which has been effective in past IRS audits that we have participated in. If you must pay a bonus, this language and proper minutes of the board of directors may very well save a double tax.

[10] One method for alleviating the burden of two taxes is shown here. By paying the disallowed amounts back to the corporation, pursuant to a binding contract, an employee can avoid being income-taxed on the amounts disallowed. The amounts are still not deductible to the corporation, but because these amounts must be repaid by the employee, there is no second tax. In our opinion, this provision should be included in all employment contracts.

[11] When you are creating an employment contract, its length should be comparable to those contracts in other business situations; all provisions that are standard are necessary. It is important that the employment contract be complete in every respect, including the specific terms it is designed to cover.

[12] We mentioned earlier that a wage continuation plan is a good method of paying deductible salary out of a one-person corporation upon the total disability of a shareholder-employee. This whole article is devoted to that end. While only $100 a week is income tax–free, the whole amount paid is income tax deductible to the corporation. Until the corporation runs out of cash, a wage continuation plan offers an opportunity to take advantage of some good tax planning for a normally unplanned for event.

[13] A nondisclosure provision in an employment contract for a one-person corporation is only needed for window dressing. It makes it look as if the agreement reached is truly that of an employer and an employee.

[14] A covenant not to compete is also for window dressing. We highlight this provision as a warning. Do not use this particular provision for other employees, that you may have, without first checking with your lawyer. Each state's law is different with regard to the enforceability of a covenant not to compete. *Never use one without professional advice.*

[15]   General matters are where lawyers put everything that does
not fit into one of the previous agreement categories. Our legal matters
article covers some provisions which are found in many legal
documents. There is nothing here of great import to you. It is more
of that window dressing which makes the employment contract an
effective tool when the IRS agents come knocking.

Appendix

B

Independent Contractor Agreement

The independent contractor agreement is to a talent corporation working for a master company what an employment contract is to the individual talent employee. Under TEFRA, many talent corporations cannot use retirement plans and other fringe benefits unless they can show that they are providing services for others. The independent contractor agreement is evidence of other work performed. The independent contractor agreement provides a method to illustrate that the one-person corporation is providing a real business function and is not merely a sham. It is a contract between a master company and the talent corporation—not the talent—which hopefully also circumvents the PHC problem. In short, it is a good insurance policy, insuring that your talent corporation is separate from your talent.

We are going to annotate some of the provisions of the typical independent contractor agreement, as we did with the employment contract. This will give you a better idea as to why these provisions are found in the independent contractor agreement.

INDEPENDENT CONTRACTOR AGREEMENT

[1]

This Agreement, dated _____, 19__, is by and between Personal Service Corporation, incorporated under the laws of the State of Delaware (Independent Contractor) and Master Corporation, incorporated under the laws of California (Company).

[2]

The Company is engaged in publishing various legal, financial, and tax periodicals as well as the editing and illustration of such periodicals. To compete successfully in the publishing business, the Company needs to employ, from time to time, the services of certain contributors to its periodicals. These contributors furnish articles and information which are vital to the content and expertise provided by the publications. The Company also is engaged in providing financial planning services to a highly select group of corporations, partnerships, and individuals. These clients are the product of many years of successful financial planning on the part of the Company and have become a profitable part of the business of the Company. Because of the sometimes unique needs of these clients, it is necessary for the Company to provide additional financial services which are outside the expertise of the Company.

The Independent Contractor is well known in the area of financial planning. The experience and reputation of the Independent Contractor are such that the association of the Independent Contractor with the Company will mutually benefit each of them. The Independent Contractor employs authors of some reknown and has expertise in many areas of financial planning that the Company would like to utilize. Both the Independent Contractor and the Company realize that their association could be profitable to each of them and they wish to establish a relationship which will benefit them both.

The Company and the Independent Contractor hereby enter into this Agreement to set forth their mutual promises and understandings.

ARTICLE I
DUTIES AND RESPONSIBILITIES

[3]

Section 1.1 Engagement of Independent Contractor. The Company hereby engages the Independent Contractor as an independent contractor to perform the duties and responsibilities as set forth in this Agreement. The Independent Contractor will have all the rights and privileges incidental and necessary to the services contemplated under this Agreement.

Section 1.2 Specific Duties and Responsibilities. The Independent Contractor is engaged pursuant to this Agreement to perform the following services on behalf of the Company:

Provide at least one typewritten article of no less than 3000 words to the Company for each of the twelve months following the month of this Agreement. The articles can be on any subject that the Independent Contractor chooses as long as they deal with an aspect of financial planning.

Provide on a periodic basis an outline of current issues in the financial-planning field that the Independent Contractor feels are of interest to those readers of the type who historically read the periodicals published by the Company. These outlines will be furnished by the Independent Contractor within thirty days after the request in writing of the Company.

Provide consulting to the Company with regard to its own financial-planning services when requested to do so. These services may be rendered directly to the Company or may be rendered to the clients of the Company if so requested by the Company.

Provide any other services to the Company as may reasonably be requested by the Company from time to time.

ARTICLE II
COMPENSATION FOR SERVICES

[4]

Section 2.1 Compensation for Articles. The Company will pay the Independent Contractor $1000 for each article submitted by the Independent Contractor which is actually used in a publication of the Company. Payment will be rendered one-half upon written notification that the Company has determined that such article is to be used and the remaining one-half at the time of publication of the article. In the event that the Company notifies the Independent Contractor that an article is to be used and the article is not subsequently used, the Independent Contractor will retain the initial payment.

Section 2.2 Compensation for Outlines. The Company will pay the Independent Contractor $250 per outline submitted by the Independent Contractor pursuant to the written request of the Company. An outline will consist of at least five pages. There shall be a minimum of twenty-seven lines on each page consisting of an average of seventy characters per line. If the Company requires a shorter outline, the compensation shall remain at $250. If, however, the Company requires an outline of more than five pages, the Independent Contractor shall be paid an additional $75 per page.

Section 2.3 Compensation for Consulting Services. The Company shall compensate the Independent Contractor $100 per hour of time for each hour or part of an hour that the Independent Contractor provides financial-planning services on behalf of the Company. The Independent Contractor is required to keep a record of the number of hours or parts thereof provided either to the Company or each client of the Company, as well as a detailed description of the services provided, including the tasks performed, the reason for such performance, and the results of the services rendered, if possible.

The Independent Contractor will be paid for the number of hours submitted within ten working days of the receipt, by the Company, of the required records. The Independent Contractor shall not submit more than three such sets of records in any calendar month so that the Company can reduce the administrative time required to process such payments.

Section 2.4 Compensation for Other Services. Other services performed by the Independent Contractor for or on behalf of the Company shall be compensated for based on mutual agreement. The Independent Contractor agrees to perform additional services upon the reasonable request of the Company as long as the compensation shall be agreed upon prior to the commencement of the services so performed. If the Independent Contractor chooses not to perform additional services for the Company, the Company agrees that this Agreement shall continue to be in full force and effect and that such decisions by the Independent Contractor shall affect no other rights of the parties under this Agreement.

ARTICLE III
TERM OF AGREEMENT

[5]

Section 3.1 Initial Term. The initial term of this Agreement shall begin _____, 19__, and continue for one year subject, however, to termination during such period as provided in this Article. At the end of the term of this Agreement, all of the parties' duties hereunder shall cease and all amounts due to the Independent Contractor will be paid pursuant to the terms of this Agreement. In the event that all the services that were begun under this Agreement have not been completed at the time this Agreement is terminated, it is agreed by both the Independent Contractor and the Company that these services will be completed as soon as is reasonably possible after the termination of this Agreement. Services rendered after the termination of this Agreement for projects begun prior to the termination of this Agreement will be compensated for under the terms of Article II.

Section 3.2 Continuation of Agreement. The Company and the Independent Contractor contemplate that the relationship under this Agreement shall continue for some time. To this end, the parties agree to meet at least thirty days prior to the termination of this Agreement under Section 3.1 in order to either extend this Agreement or modify such terms and conditions as the parties mutually agree.

Section 3.3 Termination upon the Bankruptcy or Liquidation of the Independent Contractor. This Agreement shall terminate upon the adjudicated bankruptcy or the liquidation of the Independent Contractor. Adjudicated bankruptcy shall be defined as the date of any decree of bankruptcy issued by a court of competent jurisdiction. Liquidation shall refer to the sale or other disposition of more than 50 percent of the stock of the Independent Contractor, the sale or other disposition of more than 50 percent of the assets of the Independent Contractor, or the formal acceptance by the state of incorporation of the Independent Contractor of Articles of Dissolution or equivalent documentation.

Section 3.4 Voluntary Termination.   Either party to this Agreement, for any reason whatsoever, may terminate this Agreement upon thirty days' written notice. In such event, all services under this Agreement shall be completed pursuant to Section 3.1.

Section 3.5 Termination for Cause.   Since the quality of the services to be performed under this Agreement are of paramount importance to the Company, the Company is vitally concerned with the expertise of those employees, agents, or servants of the Independent Contractor performing such services. If, at any time, the Company ascertains that the expertise of the Independent Contractor's employees, agents, or servants is not of the high quality and expertise that the Company deems necessary to satisfactorily complete the services under this Agreement, the Company can terminate this Agreement. Termination under this provision may be accomplished only in writing. Upon receipt of the written termination notice, the Independent Contractor will cause all services to immediately cease. The Company shall only be liable for payment of services which it determines to be beneficial or of sufficient quality to warrant payment.

ARTICLE IV
WORKING FACILITIES AND EXPENSES

[6]

Section 4.1 Working Facilities.   The Company shall provide secretarial services to the Independent Contractor for purposes of typing, copying, and reviewing all written material contemplated under this Agreement. The Company agrees that these are services provided to other independent contractors on an industry basis as part of a working independent contractor relationship and therefore will not charge the Independent Contractor for such services. The Company will also provide the Independent Contractor with temporary offices for the employees of the Independent Contractor when they are working on projects related to this Agreement. There will be no charge for this service.

In addition, all acceptable travel, entertainment, and other incidental expenses incurred by the Independent Contractor or its employees, when providing financial-planning services for clients of the Company, will be paid in full by the Company. Expenses which are incurred by the Independent Contractor or its employees are to be submitted to the Company for its approval and payment. Only expenses which are submitted in writing, with a description of the purpose of the expense, the client on whose behalf it was incurred, and the parties involved in the expense, and, if in excess of $25.00, which are accompanied by a receipt will be paid by the Company. Expenses incurred by the Independent Contractor or its employees shall be paid within ten days after receipt of the expense information outlined above.

Section 4.2 Expenses. Notwithstanding anything in this Agreement to the contrary, the Independent Contractor hereby agrees to reimburse the Company for any and all expenses incurred by the Company on behalf of the Independent Contractor for services performed under this Agreement which are not set forth in Section 4.1. The Independent Contractor also understands and agrees that expenses which are not covered by Section 4.1 are the sole expenses of the Independent Contractor and that the Company shall have no liability for their payment.

ARTICLE V
RELATIONSHIP OF THE PARTIES

[7]

Section 5.1 Independent Contractor Status. The parties' intention is that the relationship between them is that of employer and independent contractor. Neither the Independent Contractor nor any agent, employee, or servant of the Independent Contractor shall be deemed to be the agent, employee, or servant of the Company. Furthermore, the Independent Contractor shall have no real or apparent authority to bind the Company in any manner. Benefits provided by the Company to its employees, including, but not limited to, compensation insurance or unemployment insurance, are not available from the Company to the Independent Contractor, its agents, employees, or servants. The Independent Contractor shall be responsible for the payment of all federal, state, and local taxes or contributions imposed or required under any unemployment insurance, Social Security, income, or any other laws with respect to the Independent Contractor's employees.

Section 5.2 Employees of the Independent Contractor. The Independent Contractor may hire any employees deemed necessary by the Independent Contractor. The Company shall have no duties or obligations with respect to any of the Independent Contractor's employees, agents, or servants. The Independent Contractor has full authority and control as to its employees, agents, and servants, and the Company will exercise no control over the personnel policies of the Independent Contractor, including hiring, supervision, or termination.

Section 5.3 Supervision.   The Independent Contractor shall have full authority to control and direct the performance of the details of the services provided by the Independent Contractor to the Company. The Company is only interested in the results achieved. All work performed by the Independent Contractor shall, however, meet the approval of the Company and shall be subject to the Company's general right of inspection and supervision to secure the satisfactory completion of the services under this Agreement. The Independent Contractor warrants and agrees to assign only qualified personnel to perform services on behalf the Company and that failure to do so may cause immediate termination of this Agreement under Section 3.5.

Section 5.4 Compliance with Law.   The Independent Contractor agrees to comply with all federal, state, and municipal laws, rules, and regulations that are now in effect or may be in the future applicable to the Independent Contractor, its business, and its personnel.

ARTICLE VI
NONDISCLOSURE OF INFORMATION

[8]

Section 6.1 The Independent Contractor Shall Not Disclose Information.   The Independent Contractor recognizes that technical information, operating procedures, and client information, as well as financial information, of the Company are highly confidential and are the sole property of the Company. The Independent Contractor, its employees, agents, or servants agree not to disclose, during or after the term of this Agreement, any information relative or pertinent to the Company's financial condition or operating procedures. In addition, the Independent Contractor, its employees, agents, or servants shall not disclose any information that relates to clients of the Company, including the name of the clients.

All files and all records with respect to the Company's clients or the Company itself shall be the property of the Company, and the Independent Contractor shall not remove these files or records without the specific written consent of the Company. The Independent

Contractor agrees that all these files and records are the property of the Company and that upon the termination of this Agreement, they will be promptly returned to the Company.

Section 6.2 Clients of Company. The Company and the Independent Contractor agree that the clients of the Company are unique assets of the Company. The Company is giving the Independent Contractor the opportunity to work with these clients. While the Company expects that the Independent Contractor will render financial-planning services to other organizations, it also expects that the Independent Contractor will not continue relationships with the clients of the Company after this Agreement is terminated. Therefore, the Independent Contractor agrees that it, its shareholders, directors, officers, employees, agents, or servants will not render any financial services to a client of the Company for one year after the date of termination of this Agreement.

Section 6.3 Breach of this Article. In the event of a breach or threatened breach of the provisions of this Article by the Independent Contractor, the Company shall be entitled to an injunction restraining the Independent Contractor, its shareholders, directors, officers, employees, agents, or servants, whichever the case may be, from disclosing, in whole or in part, any information or documentation intended to be covered by this Agreement or from rendering services to any client of the Company. Nothing herein shall be construed as prohibiting the Company from pursuing any other remedies available to it for such breach or threatened breach, including the recovery of damages.

ARTICLE VII
GENERAL MATTERS

[9]

Section 7.1 Delaware Law. This Agreement shall be governed by the laws of the State of Delaware and shall be construed in accordance therewith.

Section 7.2 No Waiver. No provision of this Agreement may be waived, except by an agreement in writing signed by the waiving party. A waiver of any term or provision shall not be construed as a waiver of any other provision.

Section 7.3 Benefit.   This Agreement shall be binding upon the parties, their successors, and assigns.

Section 7.4 Amendment.   This Agreement may be amended, altered, or revoked at any time, in whole or in part, by the written agreement of the parties hereto.

Section 7.5 Construction.   Throughout this Agreement, the singular shall include the plural, the plural shall include the singular, and the masculine and neuter shall include the feminine, wherever the context so requires.

The headings of Articles and Sections are included solely for convenience of reference. If any conflict between the headings and the text of this Agreement exists, the text will control.

Section 7.6 Severability.   If any provision of this Agreement is declared by a court of competent jurisdiction to be invalid for any reason, such invalidity shall not affect any other provision of this Agreement. On the contrary, such remaining provisions shall be fully severable, and this Agreement shall be construed and enforced as if such invalid provision had never been inserted in this Agreement.

Section 7.7 Notice.   Any notice required to be in writing under this Agreement shall either be sent by certified mail, return receipt requested, or by personal delivery and shall be considered as received from the party delivering such notice as of the date of the signing of the return receipt in the case of certified mail or upon the date of the signing of a receipt upon delivery in the case of personal delivery.

The parties to this Agreement have signed this Agreement as of the day and date first written above.

Personal Service Corporation

By: _____

Master Corporation

By: _____

[1]   In the heading of the agreement it is important to identify who the contract is with. It demonstrates a corporate agreement, not an agreement with the talent itself.

[2]   Sometimes, it is good for your contract to tell a story. This story will help explain to you, the company hiring your corporation, and the IRS just what the contract is all about. It also reinforces the proposition that the agreement is corporate, not personal.

[3]   The master corporation and your corporation are going to want to make sure of the services to be provided. This section should be as clear and comprehensive as possible to avoid future problems with the master corporation. The provisions dealing with the duties and responsibilities should *not* name or describe the talent but should only allude to those services to be performed. To do otherwise means personal holding company problems.

[4]   The compensation charged for services is paramount in an independent contractor agreement. All the tax planning can be perfect, but if there is a dispute over payment, the tax problems mean nothing. You must have income to save income tax.

Be as detailed as is possible when setting forth your compensation. If there is any doubt at all, put in a provision which is similar to Section 2.4. This cover-all language can help alleviate problems in the future. Also remember to refer back to your contract from time to time; you might learn that you are doing too much for too little or doing too little for too much.

[5]   The length of the service agreement is of some importance. Of more import is how the agreement is terminated. Personal service is, by its very nature, subjective. Good, bad, or indifferent is often determined by personality, not performance. A relationship can start smoothly but quickly turn sour. Always leave "out" clauses for your sake and for the sake of the master corporation.

One of the most important of these "out" clauses for the master corporation is set forth in Section 3.5. Master corporations always want to utilize a particular talent; the master corporation wants assurances that you are the person who is going to do most, if not all, of the work. This provision is designed to assure the master corporation that if you in particular do not perform the services, the contract will terminate immediately. It does not describe or name you; it only gives the master corporation cause if the expertise (yours) is not of the quality expected. This gives an almost surefire assurance that the talent who was expected to perform does perform.

[6] Who pays what expenses is important from a practical and tax point of view. Practically speaking, both sides of the agreement should know who is responsible for the various expenses incurred in the performance of the services. Equally important is that the IRS is shown that there is a reason that the master corporation picks up some expenses. This provision separates expenses in such a way as to demonstrate a separate and distinct relationship.

[7] Article V is the most important tax provision in the independent contractor agreement. It sets forth the independent contractor relationship in great detail. It is here that the master corporation agrees not to be involved in controlling how work is done. The master corporation is interested in results, not in the details of performance. This is the essence of the independent contractor relationship.

This article also provides for the payment of FICA, FUTA, and withholding. The master corporation is going to insist upon this type of language to ensure that it will not eventually have to pay these taxes on behalf the independent contractor. All in all, it is this provision which most aptly describes the independent contractor arrangement.

[8] Nondisclosure may or may not be a factor in an independent contractor agreement. We include it because we find that it is a common provision. While an agreement that you are involved in may not contain this type of arrangement, it is something that does arise.

[9] As was discussed in the context of the employment agreement, general matters cover a multitude of provisions that do not fit elsewhere. This is where countless arguments arise among lawyers as to fine legal points. You only need remember to read this part when you are reviewing a contract for your signature. It is surprising how many times provisions which were not thought to be in an agreement show up in this section.

Appendix

C

Health and Accident Plan

A health and accident plan is currently one of the most substantial nonretirement benefits afforded a regular corporation. While unincorporated Americans are severely limited as to the amount and type of medical payments that can be itemized on their personal income tax returns, a corporation can adopt a health and accident plan which not only pays the medical expenses of its employees, but the amounts so paid are fully deductible to the corporation and not income taxable to the employee. The effect is the use of tax-free dollars for the payment of medical expenses.

There was a time when these plans were not particularly complicated. With Congress's trend toward equalization of benefits for all employees, however, that has changed. Now, these plans are subject to many of the rules that are used to make sure all eligible employees are covered by qualified retirement plans.

The health and accident plan reproduced in this appendix is designed for the talent corporation that has more than one employee and wishes to eliminate non-shareholder-employees from coverage for as long as possible. Therefore, the plan is complex. The annotations will explain why some of the more complex provisions are included. For the pure one-person corporation the plan can be much more simple. That is one of the reasons why small is beautiful when it comes to incorporated talent.

HEALTH AND ACCIDENT PLAN FOR THE EMPLOYEES OF PERSONAL SERVICE CORPORATION

ARTICLE I
REIMBURSEMENT FOR MEDICAL CARE

[1]

Section 1.1 Eligibility.   The Corporation may reimburse any Eligible Employee of the Corporation for all expenses incurred by such Eligible Employee for medical care, as defined in Section 213(e) of the Internal Revenue Code of 1954 ("Code") as amended, or the Eligible Employee's spouse and dependents.

Section 1.2 Eligible Employee Defined.   All Employees of the Corporation shall be Eligible Employees for purposes of this Plan, except those who fall in any one or more of the following categories:

A.   Employees who have not attained age 25;

B.   Part-time or seasonal employees;

C.   Employees included in a unit of employees covered by a collective-bargaining agreement between employee representatives and one or more employers if accident and health benefits were the subject of good faith bargaining between such employee representatives and such employer or employers; or

D.   Employees who are nonresident aliens who receive no earned income (within the meaning of Section 911(b) of the Code) from the Corporation which constitutes income from sources within the United States (within the meaning of Section 861(a)(3) of the Code).

Section 1.3 Full-Time and Part-Time Basis Defined.   An Employee shall be considered as employed on a full-time basis for the purposes of this Plan if the Employee's customary weekly employment is for at least thirty-five hours. An Employee shall be considered as employed on a part-time basis if the Employee's customary weekly employment is for less than twenty-five hours.

Section 1.4 Seasonal Employee Defined. An Employee shall be considered to be a seasonal Employee for the purposes of this Plan if the Employee customarily works less than seven months in any twelve-month period.

[2]

Section 1.5 Reimbursable Expenses. Medical care expenses that may be reimbursed by the Corporation are those which are defined in Section 213(e) of the Code. These include all amounts paid for hospital bills, doctor and dental bills, drugs, glasses, any item related to the preservation of health or the prevention of disease, and premiums on accident or health insurance, including hospitalization, surgical, medical, and disability insurance.

[3]

Section 1.6 Dependents Defined. The dependents of an Employee shall be any of the following individuals over half of whose support of the calendar year was received from the Employee:

A. A son or daughter of the Employee, or a descendant of either,

B. A stepson or stepdaughter of the Employee,

C. A brother, sister, stepbrother, or stepsister of the Employee,

D. The father or mother of the Employee, or an ancestor of either,

E. A stepfather or stepmother of the Employee,

F. A son or daughter of a brother or sister of the Employee,

G. A brother or sister of the father or mother of the Employee,

H. A son-in-law, daughter-in-law, father-in-law, mother-in-law, brother-in-law, or sister-in-law of the Employee, or

I. An individual who has as principal place of abode the home of the Employee and who is a member of the Employee's household.

The dependents of an Employee shall also include any person over half of whose support is treated as having been received from the Employee under Section 1.7, relating to children of divorced or legally separated Employees, or Section 1.9, relating to multiple support agreements.

Section 1.7 Children of Divorced or Legally Separated Employee. A child of a divorced or legally separated Employee shall be treated as having received over half of his or her support from the Employee if:

A.   The decree of divorce or legal separation, **or** a written separation agreement, provides that the Employee shall be entitled to a dependency exemption for the child and the Employee provides at least $600 for the support of the child during the calendar year (unless the Employee has custody of the child; the noncustodial parent provides at least $1200 for the support of the child during the calendar year; and the Employee does not clearly establish that he or she provided more for the support of the child during the calendar year than the noncustodial parent), or

B.   The Employee does not have custody of the child, provides $1200 per year or more for the support of the child during the calendar year, and the custodial parent does not clearly establish that he or she provided more for the support of the child during the calendar year than the Employee, or

C.   The Employee has custody of the child and neither Subsection A nor Subsection B above apply to the noncustodial parent.

Section 1.8 Custody.   "Custody," for purposes of this Plan, shall be determined by the terms of the most recent decree of divorce or legal separation or written separation agreement. In the event of split custody, or if neither a decree nor agreement establishes who has custody, or if the continuing effect of a decree or agreement is uncertain by reason of proceedings pending on the last day of the calendar year, custody will be deemed to be with the parent who has physical custody of the child for the greater portion of the calendar year. If the parents have been divorced or legally separated for only a portion of the calendar year after having had joint custody of the child for the prior portion of the year, the parent having custody for the greater portion of the remainder of the year after divorce or legal separation shall be treated as having custody for a greater portion of the calendar year.

Section 1.9 Multiple Support Agreements.   Over half the support of an individual described in Section 1.6 for the calendar year shall be treated as received from the Employee if:

A.   No one person contributed over half of such support;

B.   Over half of such support was received from persons each of whom would have been entitled to claim such individual as a dependent had they contributed over half of such support;

C. The Employee contributed over 10 percent of such support; and

D. Each person described in Subsection B who contributed over 10 percent of such support, other than the Employee, agrees in writing not to claim such individual as a dependent for any taxable year beginning in such calendar year.

[4]

Section 1.10 Payments.

A. Reimbursement Procedures. Any Eligible Employee applying for reimbursement under this Plan shall submit to the Corporation all hospitalization, doctor, dental, or other medical bills, including premium notices of accident or health insurance, for verification by the Corporation prior to payment. A failure to comply herewith may, at the discretion of the Corporation, terminate such Employee's right to said reimbursement. The Corporation shall pay such amounts as are properly reimbursable under this Plan within thirty days of receipt of such evidence by the Corporation.

B. Direct Payment Procedures. The Corporation may, in its discretion, pay directly any or all of the reimbursable expenses in lieu of making reimbursement therefor. In such event, the Corporation shall be relieved of all further responsibility with respect to that particular medical expense.

C. Limit on Reimbursements. The reimbursements to, or the payments on behalf of, any one Eligible Employee, including the Eligible Employee's spouse and dependents, shall not exceed the total amount of $____ for medical care expenses incurred in any one calendar year. The Corporation may make payments exceeding $____ in any one year if they are for expenses incurred in a prior year, this Plan was in effect during such prior year, and the total medical care expenses incurred in such prior year and reimbursed by the Corporation do not exceed $____ .

ARTICLE II
WAGE CONTINUATION PLAN

[5]

The Corporation may, at its option, continue the wages of any Eligible Employee during any period in which the Employee is absent from work as the result of personal injury or sickness.

ARTICLE III
INSURANCE

[6]

Section 3.1 Insurance Coverage.   Reimbursement or payment provided under this Plan shall be made by the Corporation only in the event and to the extent that such reimbursement or payment is not provided for under an insurance policy or policies, whether owned by the Corporation or the Nonexcluded Employees, under any other health and accident or wage continuation plan, or under Medicare or other federal or state law.

Section 3.2 Reimbursement to the Corporation.   If the Eligible Employee is reimbursed under this Plan for any expense and if such reimbursement is duplicated by any other plan, insurance policy, or policies, Medicare or otherwise, then the Employee shall immediately remit such duplicated amounts to the Corporation.

ARTICLE IV
GENERAL MATTERS

[7]

Section 4.1 Exclusion from Income.   Benefits payable under this Plan are eligible for exclusion from the gross income of the Employees covered by this Plan, as provided in Section 105 of the Code.

Section 4.2 Copy to Eligible Employees.   A copy of this Plan shall be given to all Eligible Employees of the Corporation.

Section 4.3 Termination.   This Plan or any part thereof shall be subject to termination at any time by affirmative vote of the Board of Directors of the Corporation; however, such termination shall not affect any right to claim reimbursement for medical expenses under this Plan arising prior to the termination.

Section 4.4 Effective Date. This Plan shall be effective as of _____, 19__.

Professional Service Corporation

By: _____
               President

Attest: _____
               Secretary

[1]   Under this plan, an employee must be at least 25 years of age and a full-time employee. TEFRA rules may eliminate the age requirement, but as of the writing of this book, this is unclear. It is clear that you can determine your own rules much like you can in a retirement plan. Keep that in mind as you ask your professionals what the exact requirements are in your case.

[2]   The types of expenses that are allowed are much broader than those allowed when itemizing medical expenses on a personal income tax return. As long as the expense is related to the prevention of disease or the preservation of health, the expense is generally allowable. We have seen cases where some of the costs of a swimming pool have been allowed under a plan where a doctor prescribed the pool for health reasons. This is an area where you can truly be assured that medical expenses will be all-encompassing.

[3]   Not only can an employee be covered under a health and accident plan, but so can that employee's dependents. Thus the medical expenses of a whole household can be paid for by one's corporation. The Internal Revenue Code has a comprehensive definition of dependents. This section sets forth that definition.

[4]   The corporation can either reimburse the employee for medical expenses paid by the employee or pay them directly. This plan allows both methods in order to facilitate the convenience of a shareholder-employee who may prefer to use a corporate check.

A monetary limit is necessary whether or not non-shareholder-employees are covered in the plan, because the IRS requires certain ascertainable standards for health and accident plans. The same limit must apply to all employees. This means that an employee who is eligible for the plan and who earns a salary of $10,000 a year will have the same benefit as a shareholder-employee who earns $100,000 a year. Covering all employees, as the Internal Revenue Code requires, can become quite expensive if several employees are covered by the plan.

[5]   This short section allows the continuation of wages upon the illness of an employee. It is used in two ways. The first is to give more credence to the wage continuation plan found in the employment contract. Repetition, at least for tax purposes, is good practice because it strengthens the tax position. The second reason is to bolster the fact that when an employee is ill or hurt, wages can be continued as part of a plan. This could spell the difference between the ability to deduct salaries paid during sickness or injury and having them characterized as dividends (at least as to shareholder-employees).

[6]   In our experience, many people believe that they can double-dip in their plans; that is, they can have the corporation pay for the expense and then additionally collect from the insurance company. This is not so. If there is double reimbursement, the employee must pay the corporation back. Otherwise, all amounts that are taken will be taxable to the employee and may not be deductible to the corporation.

[7]   General matters pop up once again. We highlight it here to point out that the plan can be terminated by action of the board of directors of the corporation. Unlike a retirement plan, which should be terminated with IRS approval, a health and accident plan can be dropped at the will of the corporation. This flexibility makes these plans even more attractive.

Index

About the Authors

Robert A. Esperti and **Renno L. Peterson** are tax attorneys and consultants. They have lately shared their expertise with many readers in their highly successful *Handbook of Estate Planning*, also published by McGraw-Hill. Now, in this new treatment of personal incorporation, they have combined their talents to present an informative, practical, and clearly written look at another area abounding in tax implications for the individual who is incorporated or is thinking of incorporating. In addition to their writings on important legal subjects for laypeople and professionals, Mr. Esperti and Mr. Peterson consult and lecture extensively across the country on financial and tax matters. Their clientele includes some of the most talented people in the United States. Their audiences include top-management personnel in Fortune 500 companies as well as various professional and trade associations.